AMERICA DREAMING

AMERICA DREAMING

A ROMAN À CLEF

BY

TONYO MELÉNDEZ

Copyright © 2023 Tonyo Meléndez.

All rights reserved. No part of this book may be reproduced, stored, or transmitted by any means—whether auditory, graphic, mechanical, or electronic—without written permission of both publisher and author, except in the case of brief excerpts used in critical articles and reviews. Unauthorized reproduction of any part of this work is illegal and is punishable by law.

ISBN: 979-8-89031-537-3 (sc)
ISBN: 979-8-89031-538-0 (hc)
ISBN: 979-8-89031-539-7 (e)

Library of Congress Control Number: 2011914180

Because of the dynamic nature of the Internet, any web addresses or links contained in this book may have changed since publication and may no longer be valid. The views expressed in this work are solely those of the author and do not necessarily reflect the views of the publisher, and the publisher hereby disclaims any responsibility for them.

One Galleria Blvd., Suite 1900, Metairie, LA 70001
(504) 702-6708
1-888-421-2397

With love

to:

My wife Darlene

and

My children

Tanya and Triana

FATHER HOPES

Any minute now, Memo's father was going to walk in! It was 1956, and the 14 year old boy sat nervously in the living room of his godfather Ted. Seeing his godson in such state, Ted offered to give Memo something to calm him down. Memo refused, insisting he was alright and needed nothing. *I'm a man. Girls need those things*, Memo thought. It had been only ten minutes since Ted, hanging up the telephone, said: "Your father is on his way." Though Memo had traveled all the way from El Salvador to meet his father, now that it seemed it was about to happen, Memo wasn't sure it was such a great idea.

Memo had been walking out of one of the movie theaters his Tío Lalo managed, when his uncle ran into him. Tío Lalo asked what Memo was doing for the summer. Memo had no specific plans but did not want to be seen as lazy, so he said, "I'm not sure, uncle."

"Why don't you come with me to Nicaragua? I'm going there with my company. We'll tour around Nicaragua for ten weeks."

"That sounds great, I'll ask my mother."

"It's not for free," his uncle said. "You'll work as stagehand and also as the company's prompter. I'll take care of your room and board."

Within a week, Memo was on his way to Nicaragua. Traveling by land, the three trucks meandered up and down the mountainous Central American terrain. The narrow, unpaved roads reminded Memo of a French movie he had seen not too long ago: *The Wages of Fear*. In it, all the travelers including the hero, played by Ives Montand, died on a similar road as the one he was on. *Was this an omen?* The road was flanked on one side by the mountains and on the other by bottomless abysses. The dusty, rough roads were so narrow that whenever a vehicle encountered oncoming traffic a decision would have to be made as to who was to back up until a bit of shoulder could be found where one of the vehicles would pull in to allow the other one to pass. Going forward was dangerous enough, backing up was even more so. The drivers, aware of this, obeyed some unwritten code and kept the famous Latin temper under control.

All the men in the company traveled in the back of the trucks, while the ladies and Tío Lalo rode in the cabins. Memo had the misfortune to be on the third truck and for three days and two nights a steady cloud of dust enveloped him and the men. The first day, when they stopped to eat by some roadside comedor, their dust-caked faces and gray hair were the cause of great merriment. Tío Lalo and the women were laughing so hard they were barely able to eat. By the second day, no one, except Tío Lalo, found it funny. But even Tío Lalo, not known for his tact, did not dare laugh by the third day. The men were very grumpy that interminable day. The men's sense of humor returned when they arrived in Managua, the capital of Nicaragua, and they were able to take long, long showers.

Those three days not withstanding, Memo was having a wonderful time. His mother had mentioned many times how much she enjoyed traveling, which she had done for almost two decades. In fact, Tío Lalo had started it all when he had married Memo's aunt, Dahlia, many years ago. That was how the family had entered show business. Years of listening to his mother's travel adventures had planted a seed of desire in Memo to do the same. Even though, he gathered from his mother, the life of an artist had been hard; the good times outweighed the bad. Besides, his yen to travel and, more importantly, his wish to meet his father, was the reason he accepted his uncle's invitation. When he asked his mother, she seemed reluctant to grant her permission but, perhaps feeling that she owed her son that much, somewhat unhappily she let him go.

Due to the dust, Gil, the lead tenor, was sick and the company had to wait until he could perform. In the meantime, they all were free to do as they pleased. This was fine with everyone, except Tío Lalo, who was known as a tightwad. Having to wait was killing him. Memo had never felt so alive. Traveling was intoxicating and he was drinking it in great gulps. He seemed to be in tune with color, light and sound. Everywhere he looked, something new assaulted his senses. This feeling was to repeat itself each day. Memo promised himself he would seize every opportunity to visit foreign lands.

This morning, when he finally reached his godfather Ted on the phone and asked him if he could help him find his father, Memo's heart almost burst when Ted unhesitatingly said, "Yes!" Not only that he could, but that he would do it that very day.

"Where are you? I'll come pick you up right away," his godfather had said.

Ted was a tornado. His motto seemed to be: Never leave anything for the next hour that you can do this minute, never sit if you can stand, never walk if you can run; which is exactly how he entered the cheap pension where Tío Lalo had the company stay. "Where's my godson, Guillermo Antonio!" He roared, giving Memo a bear hug. Guillermo Antonio was his given name. His mother liked to call him Memo, but to his Nicaraguan relatives he was known as Guillermo Antonio. "Let's get something to eat and then I'll take you home to meet my family and call your father." This is how Memo had hoped he would be received by his family. This bode well.

Memo longed to be accepted by his Nicaraguan family. His mother had told him that Ted, who was then only a teenager, had insisted on being Memo's godfather. His family owned a ranch and to show

Memo's mother that he would take his duties as godfather seriously, he had a young cow selected to be used exclusively for Memo's milk. And so it had been, until Memo's mom took that decision which completely changed the course of Memo's life for the worse.

After lunch, and just as he had promised, Ted took Memo home to meet his family and immediately after that, he picked up the phone and made several calls until he found Elías. "He'll be here in a few minutes," Ted said, hanging up the phone. Everything was going well. It had been a perfect day. But, why was Memo suddenly filled with fear?

He could not understand it! He had wanted to meet his father ever since he could remember and now he felt like running out of his godfather's house, out of Managua, and into his mother's arms. She had asked him if he was sure he wanted to take the chance. Maybe his father would not want to see him. Was Memo sure he could handle the rejection? Why wouldn't he? Memo had replied. What father would not want to meet his son? His mother had told him that he was the spit and image of his father and that Memo had inherited from him, not only his good looks, but his intelligence. His mother had always praised Memo on both, never failing to say, "You get those from your father." Memo was proud of that.

"My father will take a look at me, realize what a great kid I am, and accept me."

"Are you *sure*?" his mother asked in a tone that made Memo give her a second glance.

"Of course I'm sure," Memo said with the confidence only a teenager can have. At least, on the outside. On the inside he had not been so sure.

And now, a few minutes from that long awaited meeting, he was sure he was not sure. He could hear La Cheli's voice saying, "El tísico, (meaning he was tuberculous), skinny as a rail, I hope he dies from it." She never had much to say about Memo's father, but what she had to say was always bad. But La Cheli had nothing good to say about anybody. It seemed to Memo that his grandmother's philosophy was: If you don't have anything bad to say about somebody, don't say anything at all; which was why Memo chose not to listen to her rantings against his father. But repetition is powerful and now, as he awaited his father's arrival, all he could hear was La Cheli's angry voice. Reluctantly, he asked Ted for the pills he had turned down a few moments ago. He swallowed them quickly, hoping they would do whatever it was they were supposed to do. So far, they had not. It was summer and Managua was very hot. Managua is always hot and so all the doors are left open to allow the air to circulate freely, including the front door. Another jeep went by and Ted sprung to his feet, saying, "that's your father's jeep." Memo did not know how Ted knew that because it seemed to him almost every vehicle in Nicaragua was a jeep. Ted stuck his head out the door and said: "Yeah, it is Elías." Memo's heart sank. This was not how he had hoped to feel when *The Moment* arrived. He would have run away if his legs would have obeyed him, instead he sat there frozen. "Elías, how are you, man? I never see you anymore." "Busy," the voice said, "always busy."

Memo thought the occasion demanded he be standing when his father entered and somehow he managed it just before his father's figure filled the door's frame. He was bigger than he had expected, both in height and girth. And he was not skinny; not at all. He was not fat but rather powerful looking. His hairline was receding, which made Memo worry his hairline would start receding too. Memo searched for himself in his father. *The eyes! I have his eyes!* He had suffered some ribbing from his friends because of his large eyes. Tecolote, his friends had nicknamed him. His father had owl eyes too. He was an impressive man and, without knowing why, Memo felt fear. He had felt this peculiar fear once before. A few years back, his aunt's lover had chased him around the beach one summer. The man was having fun watching Memo beg him to stop. The more he begged, the more the man laughed and chased him. Memo understood the source of his fear, it was the primal fear all male animals feel for the leader of the pack. It seems to say: "I'm stronger than you, don't challenge me for I can kill you if I wish." He was feeling it again, and he did not like it. It made him feel inferior, which is probably why he did what he did.

His father was looking at him, or rather, inspecting him. Much like a sergeant inspects a private; trying to find fault. Protocol for these occasions does not exist. Memo did not know whether to embrace the man, or shake his hand. His father made no attempt to do either. Maybe he, too, did not know. But, at that moment, Memo thought that whatever was wrong had to be his fault, and felt he was lacking something, though he didn't know what. His father sat on a white wicker armchair on the other side of the living room. Ted also took a seat, leaving Memo standing there waiting for something that never came. Self-conscious, Memo hastily sat down, and waited. No one said anything.

Finally, his father spoke. "So, how's your mother?" For some reason, this was not the first thing Memo thought his father would say to him. Memo felt disappointed. He had expected his father to say something memorable. His father's question sounded like the continuation of a conversation that never had happened. It seemed banal. It should have been something dramatic, like in the movies. Before Memo could answer, his father said: "Does she look as good as me?" Memo did not know what to make of that either. His mind raced for an answer. He sensed the question carried hidden meanings.

The marriage had ended quickly. He did not know the whole story, for his mother was not one to share intimate details about her past. She had told him, however, that the last time Memo had seen his father, or, rather, the last time his father had seen Memo, they were in the hospital where he was born and Memo was a few days old. His father had asked his mother what she intended to do with her acting career, but, before she could answer (apparently his father did not wait for answers even then), he had said: "Surely you're not going to continue acting?" Before she could respond, he had said: "You're my wife now. No wife of mine is going to bounce from town to town and theater to theater. What is it going to be?" And again, before she could answer, he had said the words that would change the course of Memo's life forever: "Me, or the theater?"

Memo's mother chose the theater. You have to understand that Memo's mother had been a professional actress for ten years by then, and had achieved an independence few women of her time had. She was what years later would be called, "a liberated woman" and, married or not, she intended to keep her independence. So, mother kept her career and Memo lost his father. Just like that the destinies of children are decided.

"Does she look better than me?" his father asked. Memo was still trying to figure out what his father meant by "good", now he had to decide what he meant by "better?" *How am I to know that?* La Cheli's voice rang in his head: "Vain, vain, vain. He thinks he's God's gift to the world; always dressed in white." *He was dressed all in white!* For the first time in his life, Memo began to consider the possibility that she might be right. Choosing the lesser of two evils, Memo said: "She looks good." His father seemed disappointed. "She's older than I am, you know?" said his father. Memo did not know that, and it shook him up. He had struggled, spite evidence to the contrary, to see his life as normal.

The phrase "dysfunctional family" had not yet been invented. *I didn't have a father to bring me up, but everything else is okay.* But this bit of news was not okay. The father must be older than the mother! That was the accepted norm.

Why was his father telling him this? Why had his mother not told him? Somebody was guilty of something. *What else had his mother not told him?* Ah yes, his mother had not told him about sex.

Memo was still reeling from what a kid had told him a year or so ago about how babies were made. He was playing in the nearby park with a boy about his own age, and the conversation had turned, as it usually does with boys, to sex. The kid had asked if Memo knew how babies were made. Memo knew it was God who made them. He also knew that if he said that, the kid would laugh at him. Memo had questions about things that had been said to him about God that made sense once, but no longer did. This was one of them. He had not had the courage to ask his mother about them, afraid this might arouse suspicions in her mind as to what he was doing when she was not home, which was most of the time. He adored his mother and her approval was the most important thing in his life. Whom to ask? This was a time when having a father would have helped. An older brother would have done. No such luck.

Memo knew more about sex than his family thought he knew. He had gathered bits and pieces from the kids in school, but mostly from the neighborhood kids. A lot of them were sons of whores, literally. Memo's family was middle class. Lower middle class perhaps, but middle class nevertheless. He was one of the few kids whose family owned a home. Half a block from his house was a large meson. A meson, in its original meaning, is an inn, a public house. In his neighborhood it was public housing of the poorest kind.

The meson was a series of one or two room wooden shacks, with dirt floors and no hygienic facilities whatsoever. The tenants had to go to a common restroom, half lit by whatever light filtered through the boards that made its walls. Anybody could peek in if they wanted to, but only kids found it entertaining. Adults had long grown weary of that show. There were several deep holes in the ground over which the tenants squatted to relieve themselves. The stench was staggering. The tenants had to take a deep breath before entering and hope they could do what they had to do, before they had to breathe again. If they washed their hands, and most of them did not, they had to go find the public faucet where people gathered, much like people do around the water cooler in office buildings, and wait their turn to fill their pots and buckets which they hauled to their shacks to wash themselves and cook their meals. The only good thing about the faucet was that the tenants, mostly women, made the best out of a bad situation and used the waiting time to gossip. All liquids traveled in trenches that meandered through the shacks, reeking of the combined refuse, and emptied into the gutter and eventually reached the sewer system. That the meson owners charged rent for these shacks was a crime. The kid from whom Memo was about to get his sexual education lived in the meson.

Most of the meson kids were whore's sons because that was the only way the women could take care of their children. By day they would sell fruit, tortillas, or cigarettes. They would open a pack of cigarettes and make little bundles of five cigarettes each which they would sell for ten cents, turning a small profit that way. At night, when their kids went to bed, they would sell themselves to the males in the neighborhood for fifty cents a pop. Not all the mothers did this, and those who did were seen as survivors more than sinners. The kid had seen and heard a lot more about sex than Memo.

It was from kids like him that Memo had heard about pussies, pricks, and fucking. This language was never used in his house, but on the street it was daily fare. Once Memo, while reading a comic book, had exclaimed "Son of a bitch!" and his mother upon hearing this, let him know in no uncertain terms that he was not to use such language and, if she heard him use that language again, there would be dire consequences. Memo's mother hardly ever got angry, which made her warning even more meaningful. Never again did he swear in front of his mother. It was clear to Memo that those words, and the activities they described, were for prostitutes and pimps, not decent people.

The kid, seeing Memo demurring, decided to tell all. Using his extensive street vocabulary, he launched into a lurid description of the sexual act that left Memo aghast. When the kid was done, Memo, enraged and ashamed of not knowing what every boy in the street seemed to know so well, yelled:

"That may be how whores do it, but my mother has never done that!"

"Yeah?" said the kid, "then how do you think your mother did it. They all have to spread their legs like this," the kid demonstrated, "and the man puts his prick here" and so he went on explaining some more.

Memo had ceased to listen; he could not believe his mother would have done that, worse still, that she would have lied to him about it. The kid laughed at Memo's embarrassment, further deepening his shame. Memo yelled something to defend his mother, and ran away, crying.

Memo was sure the kid would be having a great time telling every boy in the neighborhood about Memo's ignorance. He would be the butt of all the jokes for who knows how long. The price he was going to have to pay for not having been told the truth. As crudely as the boy had told Memo about sex, somehow he knew the kid was right. That made his mother wrong. His mother fell from the pedestal that day. In some deeply fundamental way, his relationship with his mother changed. *What else had my mother not told me?* And here was his father giving him information he thought his mother should have given him. *Why didn't she?* It was not a big deal, but her not telling him made it so.

Memo looked at his godfather for help, but Ted had decided to stay out of it. Maybe it was news to him too. That's when Memo did what he did and made his first mistake. Trying to seem more sophisticated than he was, Memo pulled a pack of cigarettes out of his shirt's breast pocket, got up and offered one to his father. "I don't smoke," his father said in an accusatory tone. Years later, Memo found out his father did smoke, but it was too late. Memo knew he should have put away the cigarettes, but instead, he sat down and lit up. He knew he was making a mistake, but his pride, his manhood—his youthhood, if there is such a term—felt threatened, and he went ahead, recklessly. He could tell his father was not pleased. He was ruining his chances that his father would accept him. Memo had been smoking for all of one week, but as far as his father was concerned, he might have been smoking for years. His father did not know, and Memo was not about to explain. Later on, Memo wished he had. It might have made a difference. But on this day he would not; he could not.

The truth was that Memo had smoked off and on for a few months. Once in a while, he would buy those five cigarette bundles and shared them with his friends. All his friends were doing it, so he did it too. He was afraid that if he bought a whole pack his mother would find it and all hell would break loose. This way, he would smoke a couple and be done with it. It was only when his Tío Lalo invited him to come with him to Nicaragua that, free from his mother's eye, Memo bought his first pack. His uncle did not seem to mind. Memo sensed his uncle would not tell on him.

"Are you in school?" his father asked, thus reminding him he was just a boy.

"Yes. I'm starting the ninth grade this year." he said. Memo felt he was being grilled and decided to turn the tables. That's when he made his second mistake.

"Are you married?" He asked, using the familiar "tu" form. He had considered using the formal "usted" but he addressed his mother in the familiar and felt he would compromise his integrity by treating his father any differently than he did his mother. And anyway, "usted" is used to show respect, and of his two parents his mother deserved more respect from Memo than his father. *What has he done for me to have earned my respect?*

"I have a wife and three children," his father said in a way that excluded Memo. *He could have said three 'other' children* Memo thought, suddenly realizing that being a part of his father's life was not going to be easy. The door he had come here to open was closing with every moment that passed.

"What are you doing here?"

"I came to meet you," Memo said hoping that would impress his father.

"You came alone?" his father said in a tone of voice that sounded somewhat approving. And then Memo made his third mistake.

"No, I came here with my Tío Lalo."

"Is that the same Lalo who had the acting company your mother used to travel with?"

"Yes, as a matter of fact I'm working for him to pay my way." Memo hoped that too will meet with approval.

"So, you're in show business?"

"No, I'm doing it only for the summer."

"You *are* in show business," his father said with a sense of finality.

No one said anything for a few moments. Then, his father got up and said,

"Well. Ted, I got to go."

"So soon?" asked Ted.

"Busy, very busy."

And with that, he headed toward the door without saying goodbye to his son. Memo was flabbergasted. He stumbled out of his chair and ran to the doorway. His father was already by his jeep.

"What about *him?*" Ted reminded Elías.

"Oh, yes, I'll pick you up Sunday and take you to lunch or something."

And he was gone.

Memo watched until the jeep disappeared. He looked at his godfather who, sensing memo's pain, said, "He'll be here Sunday, and you'll have a great time, you'll see." But it sounded hollow, even to Ted. Memo felt like a batter who, with the game on the line, had just struck out.

The next three days lasted a week. He went through his fifteen minute meeting with his father over and over again. He blamed himself for the failure that it had been. He promised himself to do better. *I won't mess up this time around.*

Early Sunday morning he left the little pension where the company was staying. He told his uncle he was having breakfast with his godfather and spending the rest of the day with his father. Though he had not told his uncle the fiasco of the first meeting, his uncle did not seem optimistic about today's encounter. Tío Lalo sensed something had gone wrong, but took no sides. If he knew something about Memo's father, he was not saying. Tío Lalo had not been a great father himself, so he was not about to judge Elías. "Tell me all about it," he said halfheartedly.

Memo walked the deserted narrow streets of Managua. He was struck by how straight the streets were. It was easy to orient oneself in the city. The streets were either parallel to Lake Managua, or perpendicular to it. Managua's lake lies below sea level, so if you're walking toward it, you are going downhill, if away from it, you are going uphill, toward the mountains. Memo was walking uphill. It was already hot, but Memo prided himself in never sweating much. He was happy about that this morning because he wanted to look fresh when his father saw him. *My life is going to change for the better today, if my father likes me. And he will!*

He had a wonderful time at breakfast with Ted, his wife Penny, and their two children. Memo enjoyed being the older child in the house. His godfather's kids treated him with deference. No one had ever looked up to Memo. He liked the feeling. His godfather was a rich man and so was Memo's father, Ted had told him. They belonged to private clubs and such. Memo could be happy in Managua. In El Salvador his social status was lower middle class at best. In Nicaragua he could belong to the upper class. He envisioned the good life he could enjoy if his father accepted him; private school, beautiful house, private club. No prostitutes, no lowlifes, no more financial struggle. Memo had left his cigarettes in his room; he wanted to show his father his best side. *I'll do better today. My father will like me.* He could not wait for noon to arrive.

Noon arrived, but not his father.

"I'll call him again," said his godfather, "maybe now he's there."

Though Memo wanted him to call again he also didn't want him to call anymore. It was now almost two in the afternoon. It was clear to Memo that his father did not want him. Ted tried to convince him that his father was a busy man, or perhaps that some emergency had happened that precluded him.

"He hasn't forgotten, he will come," Ted said.

The more Ted tried to lessen Memo's pain, the worse he felt. He wanted to leave so he could find a secluded place where he could release the tears he was holding back. He edged toward the front door. He would not let his godfather see him cry.

"I have to get back early. We are living for Masaya today," Memo said half lying. They *were* leaving that afternoon. The lead tenor was feeling better and Tío Lalo had decided that Gil was feeling good enough to sing for the less demanding audiences of the provinces. Each day the company did not perform cost Tío Lalo money, and, even though the company was staying in less than stellar accommodations, it was more money than his uncle was willing to waste. With the strength the half truth gave him, he was able to tear himself away from Ted.

"Write me," his godfather called. Memo walked quickly away.

"I will", he yelled over his shoulder as the tears began to wash his cheeks.

Memo was a happy kid, with an optimistic heart. His mother had seen to that. Although a dark cloud often hovered over his mother's head, she always had a smile for her Memo. He sensed, and years later came to understand, her struggles. Like Sisyphus, she was doomed to forever push the rock of life uphill only to have it roll back down again. That was her lot, but it was not going to be Memo's.

María was a good woman who hardly had finished elementary school and might not have amounted to much had it not been for, of all people, Tío Lalo. Lalo was already a well traveled, sophisticated and skilled actor/impresario when he heard Dahlia sing. He was the successful director of his own theater company; the famous Compañia Encanto. He was 40 years old, Dahlia was16. María was Dahlia's younger sister and though they were only two years apart in age, they were light years apart in appearance. They shared the same parents and yet María had the dark skin of an Indian, Dahlia had the light skin of a Spaniard. Dahlia was beautiful, María, common, Dahlia, charming, María, charmless. Dahlia was a queen, María a peasant. When the girls' mother died, La Cheli, their spinster aunt, brought them up as her own. Being Indian in El Salvador is not good; almost all peasants are Indians. If you want to insult someone, call him Indio. Though La Cheli was of pure peasant stock and should have identified with María, she preferred Dahlia, and treated the girls accordingly.

Lalo was enthralled. As he stood at the back of the school hall, he could not believe his luck. There, singing like a bird, was this lovely teenage girl. "What's her name?" he asked someone next to him. "Dahlia." *Dahlia,* Lalo thought, *was money in the bank.* Right then and there he decided he would get her to be part of his company. Even if he had to marry her. Dahlia was worth the sacrifice. But, first, he had to get past La Cheli. In order to do this, he quickly understood, he had to charm the cantankerous spinster. He set out to do this. Dahlia was worth the sacrifice. In a relentless campaign that lasted almost two years, Lalo promised to make Dahlia the queen of the Salvadorian— nay, the Central American—theater world. "I will have to come along," demanded La Cheli. "Fine!" said, Lalo. "How about María?" "Done!" said, Lalo. Dahlia was worth the sacrifice. La Cheli allowed the marriage and around and around they went for ten years hopping from country to country, town to town, theater to theater. María knew she was just an appendix to Dahlia but, what else was new?

Right away, Lalo made it clear that the appendix had to earn her keep. To everyone's surprise, the appendix had a lot of talent and, though she was never the star that Dahlia was, María took all the character parts, playing all the second leads from sixteen to sixty. In addition, she was equally adept at comedy as she was at drama. And though, she had a small voice, she had an excellent ear and could carry a tune well. Further, with her innate musicality to go along with a lovely pair of legs, she became an exceptional dancer. *Two for one,* Lalo congratulated himself, *money in the bank!* Until María met Elías.

In order to overcome the family's low expectations, María had to work hard, but she had perseverance and desire. Slowly but surely, after years of travel, years of treading the boards, years of dedication, María became a skilled entertainer and a sophisticated young woman; the second lead in the best theater company in Central America. She was admired by many. One of them was a handsome, light-skinned, green-eyed man named Elías Granda. Over those ten years, many men had shown interest in María, but La Cheli, Dahlia, and/or Lalo had dissuaded her. Not this time. María had waited enough. The young man dressed all in white was it. La Cheli gave her an ultimatum: "If you marry this man you are no longer a member of this family." María married Elías.

Their marriage changed the dynamics of the whole family. La Cheli lost her companion, Dahlia her second fiddle, and Lalo his most versatile performer. None of them forgave María for what they saw as her betrayal. María's choice of the theater over a life as Elías' wife was also seen by him as a betrayal. Something inside María broke. The years of struggle had begun. Eight years would go by before La Cheli would forgive her and allow her to return home. Elías never did.

Memo, the bundle of joy, became María's Sisyphus stone. The dark cloud began to hover over her head. That was her lot, she repeated to herself, but it was not going to be Memo's. But of course it was. Though she did not know it yet, her best years were behind her. The life of an artist always difficult was, for a single woman with a child, more so. Try as she might, she was always catching up. As she got older it was increasingly difficult for her to take care of herself and her son. Memo became the one person she could confide in, and in doing so she had shown him her cloud. She had no choice. She regretted that her decision might have taken away his possibilities and she went out of her way to praise him, to make him feel special. She fought her pessimism and tried to foster in him an optimistic heart. And she had succeeded. He placed all his trust in her. He idolized his mother and if she said he was special, he was. Whatever confidence and sense of self he had came from his mother.

Within a few days of leaving Managua, Memo had recovered his smile. His pain got mixed in with the barrage of new experiences he was having. He did not enjoy the labor that it took to unload the trucks, set up for the performances, strike the set, reload the trucks and repeat the process again and again. He noticed that Tío Lalo required this from everybody, including the lead tenor, so who was Memo to complain. He did enjoy his job as prompter. He would slide down into the hole at the foot at the stage, follow the script, and cue the actors if they forgot a line. He liked the responsibility. He thought he was blazing trails but he was only following in his mother's footsteps.

Not quite. This La Compañia Encanto Memo had joined paled in comparison to the one his mother had joined. That one had forty of the best artists not only from Central America but from Europe.

This company was comprised of fifteen third-rate artists that Tío Lalo had been able to scrape up. He was capitalizing on the company's past glories. Even Memo realized that, but the chance to come meet his father, Memo could not let pass. Memo had been a victim of the social discrimination the poor suffer in El Salvador and subconsciously he hoped to change all that. Just like in the American movies. And just like in the movies, it all was going to turn up well! His father had the power to do that. Memo did not know that his father had a score to settle.

After six weeks of touring, the company returned to Managua for its last stand before returning to El Salvador. In that time, Memo had healed enough to think he could get his happy ending. He had played and replayed the scene in his mind; *I'll get his address from my godfather and I'll knock on my father's door and when he answers I'll convince him that I'm a good boy. He will ask me to stay and live with him.* He did not think about how much this would hurt his mother; he wanted so desperately not to be poor.

"I'll drive you to his house," Ted offered. "No," Memo said, feeling heroic, "I have to do this alone." He probably was borrowing the line from some movie. Up the hill he went. He stayed on the left side of the street to avoid the scorching Nicaraguan sun. He finally reached the block where his father lived. Just as Memo had hoped, it was a very nice neighborhood. *It would be a dream come true to live here!* Memo began looking for the number and at the same time imagining what it would be like to live in such a nice area. *There is my father's house, across the street! And there is my father's jeep right outside!*

He started to cross the street. The closer he got to the house, the faster his heart beat. He stared at the door for a long time. The heroic feeling was gone. The fear he had felt just before he had met his father returned. *He doesn't know I am here so if I go without knocking no one will ever know it. I can always say that he wasn't in.* But he could not go. He raised his hand and . . . knocked.

A long paused ensued, then the door opened. It was the maid. Memo asked for his father. The maid said that he was out. Memo asked if she knew when he would be back. She said, "Later," and closed the door. Memo sensed contempt in her voice. He had not counted on his father not being in. He stood frozen in front of the closed door for several minutes until the heat of the sun burning his neck brought him back to reality. He crossed the street to seek refuge in the shade. After several moments of struggle he decided he would wait for as long as it took for his father to return! That's how the hero did it in the movies.

He stood there for over two hours. Somehow he felt he was being watched, but each time he peered at the window he could see nothing. The glare bouncing off the window's glass made it difficult for Memo to see inside. His courage wavered, his pride hurt. The longer he waited, the more foolish he felt. He knew his father was inside. He just knew it.

He crossed the street and knocked on the door again. No one answered. He knocked again—nothing. Not even the maid. He waited in the sun. His courage gave way to shame. It was obvious he was being shunned. He was not wanted. He looked down toward the lake; the street was deserted. He looked up toward the mountain; the street was empty, except for a dog sleeping in the middle of the road. Memo stared at the dog. A fly buzzing around the dog's ear woke him up. The dog snapped at the fly, missing it by a mile. The fly meandered away. The dog licked himself for a moment, then rolled over and went back to sleep. Memo was relieved that no one was witnessing his rebuke. He waited. The heat was oppressing. Like in a Thomas Mann novel, the weather was a character adding its two miserable cents, making Memo feel more rejected. He was angry, he was beaten. The future he had envisioned was not going to happen. Memo walked slowly away, down toward the lake, toward his past.

Memo avoided going by his godfather's house. He had promised Ted that he would tell him what happened, but he couldn't do it. Not today. He went instead to the theater where the company would be performing that night. He had to pay Tío Lalo for his trip. The next day his godfather called. Memo needed a sympathetic ear so he told all.

Ted said softly, "That Elías. Don't move. I'll be right there." Minutes later, Ted stormed in.

"Let's go eat and let's go shopping."

"Shopping?" said Memo. "Yes! I'll buy you a pair of shoes just like mine."

Memo had admired a pair of brown shoes he had seen Ted wear. They looked well made and expensive. Memo hated cheap shoes, especially cheap black shoes. Poor people always buy black shoes because they go with everything. He had concluded that a man's station could be discerned by the shoes he wore. Once a year, before school started, his mother would buy him a pair of black boots. They came up just above his ankle and had a strap that ran from the inside of his foot, across the top and buckled near the outside bone of the ankle. They were called Napoleonic boots. The story went that Napoleon had made the style popular. María liked them because they looked durable and were cheap. She would admonish Memo that they had to last him the whole year for she did not have money to buy more. Actually, they did not look bad but they were badly made. The things were nailed together rather than sewn, and at some point the nails would come up into the edge of his feet's soles. Sometimes the inside edge, sometimes the outside one. He did not complain because he knew she was doing the best she could, so he would adjust his walk to avoid the nails. He began to observe shoes and concluded that the richer the person, the nicer the shoes. Conversely, he figured, the nicer the shoes, the richer the person. He made himself a promise that when he grew up he would always buy expensive brown shoes.

"Nicaragua makes the best shoes in Central America," his godfather said while Memo was tying the beautiful, elegant brown shoes.

"How come?" he asked Ted. Memo wanted to be able to tell his friends why his shoes were superior to anything they had.

"Because," said Ted, "we have the biggest and best cattle ranches. We have the best leathers."

Ted should know, Memo thought, *he is a rancher. So is my father, a rancher!* He suddenly felt sad. He was never going to be a rancher's son.

"How do you like them?" Ted asked bringing Memo back to the present.

Memo had finished tying the laces. He stood up. He noticed how the shoes hugged his feet. He never had had shoes that felt like that. *The hug of the expensive shoe!* He now had a rule by which to judge good shoes. He walked about the store. Then Memo noticed something even more remarkable. The shoes did not hurt his feet. All the new shoes he had ever had, hurt his feet. His mother had told him this was normal. "After you break them in they won't hurt." True enough. A week or so later, the shoes did not hurt. But these did not hurt already! He now had two rules by which to judge good shoes. *This is how rich kids' feet feel. Amazing!*

For a brief moment Memo considered asking Ted to adopt him, but even Memo knew things like that only happen in the movies. *At least*, he thought, *I'm going back to El Salvador with my beautiful, brown, expensive, Nicaraguan shoes!* He looked at Ted, smiling broadly. Ted was smiling too.

"How much longer will you be in Managua, Guillermo Antonio?"

"One more week," said Memo.

"Good! Then you can come this Sunday afternoon to a fiesta rosa we've been invited to attend. Would you like that?"

He had heard of fiestas rosa. The rich gave them to celebrate their daughters' fifteenth birthdays.

"Great!" Memo said.

As they got into his godfather's jeep, Memo felt that, all things considered, life was good. The power of a pair of good shoes!

Everyone in the company admired his shoes. He wanted to wear them every day, but realized he would scrape them up if he did, so he decided he would wear them only for special occasions, like this Sunday's party. The kids at the party would know he belonged with them when they saw his shoes. He could not wait for Sunday!

At four o'clock Ted arrived. Tío Lalo told Memo to be sure to get back by seven-thirty for the last performance. The company would strike that very night and leave for El Salvador Monday morning. Ted promised to get him back in time. Ted's wife Penny and their kids were already at the party. What a wonderful way to end the trip! Three hours of joy rubbing elbows with the rich!

Memo kept admiring his beautiful shoes. They *were* beautiful, that was the problem. They made everything else he was wearing look inferior. Although he was wearing his best, it just was not good enough. The kids did not hide their feelings. They took a look and stayed away from him. Memo got the message loud and clear. *They know I'm not one of them.* Though Penny and Ted tried to soften the blow, Memo felt the full force of the rich kids' prejudice. He had met it first in Mexico, then in El Salvador, and now here in this party in Nicaragua—but never so blatantly, so publicly. *It's not my fault that I'm poor. I hate it!* He did not blame the kids. He understood that it was the way of the world. If he had been Penny's son he would have been accepted. He happened to be born of the wrong woman. It was not him, and it was not his father. It was his mother. Who else was there to blame?

He could not wait for the ritual to be over: The piñata breaking, the happy birthday singing, the cake cutting, the presents' opening. It all took too long; especially the presents. He had never seen so many presents for just one child. Memo had never had a birthday party. For his birthday, he usually got underwear or socks—maybe a book. The three hours of joy became three hours of annoyance, his discomfort palpable enough that even Ted could not wait to take him back. The ride to the theater was done in silence. There was nothing to say. He thanked his godfather as he hugged him good bye. Memo promised to write. He never did.

It was a turbulent return full of contradictory emotions, full of questions. He knew he could not ask his mother, and if he could not ask his mother he could not ask anyone. Could Memo tell her what happened in the trip? How much could he tell? he remembered the way his mother had asked if Memo was *sure* he wanted to meet his father. Her tone of voice had more meaning now. There was much he did not know, much his mother had not told. What was it, and why? He knew what a private person she was and, even though they were close, there was a line he never could cross. She had kept information away from him. He had a right to it. Did she have a greater right? He needed to feel wanted. He did not want to antagonize the one person in the world he knew was totally supportive of him. And yet, she was the one who had the answers—some of them anyway. How to ask her and not hurt her? He resented her for something she had done. What had she done? She would not tell him anyhow. Since she had not before, there was every reason to believe she would not tell him now. Why did she not want to tell him? What had happened? Who was at fault? Did Memo have anything to do with it?

"How was your trip?" his mother asked.

Memo knew she meant to say if he had met his father. He decided to give her the good news first. He opened the suitcase his mother had bought for him at the market just before he left, and which now had the proud scuffs of the traveled. Memo brought out his new shoes. María turned the shoes in her hands, inspecting them. He could tell she was impressed.

"Beautiful," she said, "beautiful. Your father bought . . . ?"

Memo considered saying yes but decided against it.

"No, my godfather gave them to me."

"Ah, I see. Well, we won't buy you shoes for school this year now that you have these."

"No mamá, these are for special occasions only, I want them to last a long time."

"I understand," she said. "Well, tell me everything."

"Here, I brought you some pinolillo, I know you like it."

His mother had told him about the Nicaraguan native drink.

"Yes, I'll make it while you tell me everything."

Memo told her everything. Well, not everything. He told her about the dusty three days trip (they laughed at that), the cheap accommodations (they laughed at that too), the towns, the theaters (she remembered having been there), the bad shows (she was sorry, but then, that was Lalo), his wonderful times with his godfather (she expected no less), and finally his not so wonderful time with his father (she expected no less). She did not ask anything more about his father. Although Memo wanted to, he, too, did not ask her.

"All told," she said sounding relieved, "not a bad trip."

"No," Memo said, "not a bad trip."

If she only knew.

He had skipped the waiting outside of his father's house, the shunning by the kids at the fiesta rosa, the smoking, and the drinking. Oh yes, Memo had gotten drunk for the first time in his life. It happened early in the trip, while the company was waiting for the lead tenor to feel better. One afternoon, three of the men invited Memo to a cerveceria to have a few cold ones they said, and Memo, flattered the men wanted him with them, happily said yes. Looking back on it, it was a prank played on Memo, but he did not know it at the time.

The almost empty cerveceria had tables set up outdoors and the men chose a table under the shade of a large avocado tree. It was a hot day and the idea of a cool drink appealed to Memo. The waiter came and the men ordered four steins of draft beer. Memo wanted to tell them he did not drink, but, afraid they would make fun of him, he said nothing. Soon enough the waiter returned with the four steins and placed one in front of Memo. Each man grabbed one. Memo followed suit. "Salud!" one of the men said, and with one big swig they drank about half of it. Memo was still holding his stein deciding whether or not to drink. The men slammed their steins down and let out a communal sigh of satisfaction. They started an animated conversation. No one looked at Memo, yet he knew he had better do something. He had hoped for the day when he was old enough to do this, but the day had come sooner than expected. He smelled its powerful aroma and, gathering his courage, he took a sip of the cold beer. *It's awful! It tastes bitter! Why would anybody like to drink stuff like this?!*

The men picked up their steins again. Just then, the waiter returned with several dishes full of delicious looking snacks. Memo was hungry but felt he had not earned the right to eat if he had not drunk. "Don't go," said one of them, and they drank the rest of their beers. "Bring four more." The waiter took the three empty steins and left. Memo forced himself to drink as long a swig as he could before putting his stein down. To his dismay, he had more than two thirds of it left. The men started on the snacks. Judging by the way they were eating them, it seemed to Memo the beer had made them ravenous. Afraid they would eat them all; he reached for a snack to get rid of the bitter taste. He felt the pressure coming from his three-quarters-filled stein. He picked it up and took another big swig of the bitter brew. He was barely putting his stein down, when the waiter brought the second round. Memo's stein was still half full.

The men, seemingly oblivious to Memo's predicament, raised their new steins and gulped half their beer down. Memo was one full stein behind! The men, conversing casually, polished off the rest of the snacks. Memo was desolate. *How am I going to drink this awful stuff without anything to erase the taste?* Fortunately, the waiter returned with another batch of snacks. The men assaulted them. This time Memo took two; one he ate immediately, the other one he kept near him as reserve.

To his horror, one of the men asked; "Another round?" "Yeah!" said the other two gleefully. The men emptied their glasses. Their enthusiasm was augmenting as fast as his was diminishing. One of them let out a huge burp. They all roared in appreciation. A burping competition ensued. Each burp celebrated in direct proportion to its size and sound. Their mouths full with food, the waiter had left before they could order. Memo was relieved. *They would have to call the waiter, he will have to walk over, they would give him the order, he would return all the way to the bar, relay the order to the bartender who would fill it, the waiter would bring it.* Memo figured he had time. Suddenly, the men started to beat their glasses with their forks. This he knew was an accepted way for costumers to get the attention of a waiter. Soon he appeared by the bar. One of the men raised his hand signaling four more. Memo's heart sank. He looked at the table. There were five steins on it and two belonged to him. In the distance he could see the waiter beginning to load up his tray. This was more than Memo's pride could suffer. He was not going to be behind by two and a half steins. The waiter began to walk toward them. Memo picked up the stein with one hand and the snack with the other. The waiter's arrival was imminent! Memo took a deep breath and drank, drank, drank. The waiter plunked down the four steins just as Memo emptied his. As he ate his snack Memo felt he had won some kind of a victory. Proudly, he handed his glass to the waiter, hoping the men had noticed. They had not.

His head began to spin. He looked at the men and wondered if they could see he was getting dizzy. They didn't seem to be too interested in him. He stared at the two full steins in front of him. Memo was hoping the men would slow down and give him a chance to gather himself but instead the men picked up their glasses and toasted to Memo! They waited politely for him to pick up his glass. Reluctantly, he did so. One of the men said; "Hasta ver a Dios!" Memo knew what that meant. They had to drink until they could see God through the bottom of their empty glasses. Their confidence in him overwhelmed him. They all drank. Memo held the glass to his lips as long as they did and pretended to drink as much. The men did not stop until they saw God. Memo was glad not to be as religious as they were. Slowly, they set down their empty glasses admiring their handy work. One of them counted: One, two, three! As if they had rehearsed it, they let out a humongous collective burp; their timing sublime. Memo could not help but admire them. *These men are artists,* Memo thought. The waiter arrived in time to hear the amazing burp. He put down the snacks and applauded them. Like a Greek chorus all three got up and bowed. Memo took advantage of the moment and poured half of his glass unto the stone floor.

"Gentlemen," the waiter said, "that deserves another round. "On the house!" The men applauded the waiter, who bowed in return, then left. The men sat down and attacked the snacks. *Nicaraguan drunks must be the best fed men in all Latin America,* Memo thought. He felt he had earned his snacks and dove in with the men. They were congratulating each other, describing the salient qualities of their magnificent burp. Even Memo laughed. He was in mid laughter when he felt it! Some horribly tasting liquid was coming back up his throat! It tasted like beer, only worse. He got up quickly and tried to excuse himself. An eruption was about to happen before he could get to a bathroom! He ran behind the nearest tree and vomited. It would be years before he could stomach the smell of beer, let alone drink it.

The men were kind. They told no one in the company, or if they did, no one in the company ever mentioned it to Memo. He felt his secret was safe and thus he kept it from his mother. She had her secrets, and he had his. Sometimes it is better not to know, he had learned. Maybe his mother was right; all told, not a bad trip.

But the trip was not over. It seemed to be, but it had a long way to go.

CORE OF DESIRE

His father's remark turned out to be prophetic.
"You *are* in show business," he had said.
"Only for the summer," Memo had said.
In fact, it took the summer of Memo's life. It was not so much that Memo wanted to be in show business, but rather that show business wanted Memo.

Memo knew, before he went to Nicaragua, how important money was. He knew that those who had money were powerful, those who did not, were weak. He understood it more clearly now after his experience in Nicaragua and it had affected his world view. *Trapped! I am trapped!*

There was only one way out of the trap: Power. He asked himself: *Who are the powerful in this country? Those with the right family name, those with the right education, those in the military, those in the government, those who have businesses, those who have land. You need at least one of those things to get out of the trap.* Memo had none of them.

Well, maybe he had half of one. El Salvador is divided into 14 provinces called departamentos. There are 14 prominent families in the country and the story goes, probably apocryphal, that each one of these departamentos is owned by each of the 14 families. They are the royalty of the country. They control most of the land, the businesses, the military, and the government. They have the education, and of course, they have *the* names. The right family name can make a big difference in El Salvador. Out of loyalty to his mother, Memo used her maiden name instead of his father's. Memo's family name was the same as one of the 14 families. Now, if you are related to this family all doors open for you, but you have to belong to the right branch of the family. Memo had learned this the hard way. Too many times Memo had been asked, upon meeting someone, if he belonged to *the* family and he had gone as far as saying that he did. The next question would be: "Then, you must know so and so?" If Memo did not know so and so, the conversation was over. He had failed the test. It was automatically assumed he did not belong to the right side of the famous family. If Memo said he did know so and so, the next question was, "Really? Then, you live in such and such neighborhood?" Or, 'You must belong to such and such club?" Or, 'You must attend such and such private school?" A no answer to any of these questions would expose him not only as a fraud but also as a pretentious liar. Contempt would then be added to condescension. He tried an oblique approach. "Remotely," he began to answer to see if that would keep the door from closing, but his answer implied that he did not. Soon he began to answer truthfully, wincing inside as he said no, for he knew the patronizing reaction that was coming. It was a form of mercy killing, but at least it was over quickly.

One way of avoiding the whole thing, or at least delaying it, was to not give his last name. This gave Memo time to show his breeding, in hopes that would qualify him. Sometimes this worked, but only until the inevitable questions came. Then the house of cards would fall apart; his 'new friends' would recoil from him as from a leper. Maybe it was not that brutal, but years of rejection had made him extremely sensitive to their reaction. The pain became intolerable. *Why do I need their approval so much?* The answer came: *Because I feel inferior! Why do I feel inferior? Do I feel inferior because of the way La Cheli treats my mother and me?* Yes! *Because she favors Tía Dahlia and her children?* Yes!

Because Tía Dahlia is light skinned and my mother isn't? Yes! *But I'm light skinned, like my father!*

In fact, his light skin once got his mother arrested. He was born with blue eyes which after a year turned green like his father's. One day, in Costa Rica, when he was seven months old, his mother was sitting on a park bench holding him in her arms. A policeman walked by and saw them. When he got to the corner he stopped and looked back at them. He retraced his steps and asked Memo's mother whose child was he. She said it was hers. He did not believe her and arrested her. She had to show documents to prove she was Memo's mother. Apparently, since the kidnapping of Charles Lindbergh's child, a rash of kidnappings had taken place and the policeman thought he had found some important person's kid.

Life being life, in an ironic genetic reversal, Dahlia's children were as dark as La Cheli. Now that he had seen his father, it occurred to Memo that perhaps his mother had chosen his father *because* he was European looking. She might have hoped to win approval from La Cheli by having a light skinned child. But spite Memo's light skin, and in another reversal, La Cheli loved Dahlia's children the more maybe because they were dark like she was. Memo's mother's strategy, if there had been one, had backfired! It was like a bad movie, one of those movie melodramas, like *Imitation to Life,* that show the ambivalence that has been bred into the conquered by the European conqueror. This pattern—Memo would observe years later when he got to the United States—would repeat itself again and again; the self-hatred which metamorphoses into a desire to be accepted by the dominant culture, to be liked by the very people who demean you. Though she was unaware of this, La Cheli was a victim of it. Memo was having trouble with this. He seemed to be on the same quest as his mother had been. He, too, wanted to be accepted by La Cheli, but she did not want him. This rejection by his mother's side of the family baffled him. He had hoped to end it by gaining acceptance by his father's side, but that, too, had failed. If, as it seemed to him, Salvadorian society at large shunned him, where did he belong? Who would accept him unconditionally?

He began to formulate a theory: *It is clear to me, as one of the have-nots, that things are what they are and are never going to change. It is also clear that this pattern isn't going to change because the powers-that-be like it that way. This situation exists by design! It is to the advantage of the ruling class to keep it that way. And it has worked so well that it is now deeply rooted in the psyche of the poor as the natural order; a caste system that isn't questioned anymore. It is accepted as a divine right. That's why I feel trapped; I cannot fight the caste system. Therefore, I have to go to a country where I have the chance to be accepted for my merits. I have to get out!*

That became the core of his desire to go to the United States. There, he could see clearly from the many motion pictures he had seen, one *could* move out of the poor class and up as far as one wanted to go. Which is why Memo loved the movies; they held within them an implicit promise.

Memo had seen a *lot* of movies. He owed this to Tío Lalo. Television had yet to come to El Salvador and Memo could afford to see only one movie a week. On Sunday mornings his mother would give him one Colón, which was equivalent to forty U.S. cents. With his colón, Memo could see a movie and have enough left to buy a bit of candy. So, every Sunday Memo would walk eight blocks to the Apolo Theater and see the first show of the day. He loved the 9:00 a.m. movie because they always showed three cartoons before the main feature. Memo loved cartoons! There was nothing more American than cartoons! In El Salvador, the theaters played six different movies on Sunday and Memo hated to have to leave after the first one. *If only I were rich, I could watch all six pictures. If only, if only.* Then a miracle happened!

A couple of years before his trip to Nicaragua, Tío Lalo was named general manager of the government owned theater chain. From then on, Memo spent all his free time in a movie theater. At first, all he had to say was that he was Lalo's nephew and in he was. But after a while the personnel from all the theaters knew him and Memo would just march in. He loved it! He loved it so much that he betrayed his other love: Basketball.

Up to that point Memo's passion had been basketball, even though it was considered by most kids a sissy's game. Soccer was the national game, with baseball a distant second. Anyone could play soccer. All you needed was a ball and an empty lot. If there was grass, fine, but if there was not, one could play it on dirt, cement, pavement, anywhere. Baseball required balls, bats, gloves, etc. Basketball required a court and boards and hoops, and most expensive of all; basketball shoes. Tennis, which Memo wished to learn, was played only in country clubs by the rich. Basketball Memo enjoyed it, not only for its own sake, but because it was a game which had originated in the U.S. In some way he felt closer to the American culture by playing it. However, the movies made Memo feel he was *in* the U.S. and so he gave up basketball for the movies.

Memo would spend every moment he was not in school in the movie theaters. He would arrive early so he could experience the whole ritual. Finding the right seat was important. He did not like having anyone sitting in front of him so he would wait until the audience would settle in and then he would find his place. He would wait with great anticipation for the house lights to darken until the theater was illuminated by the light coming from the silver screen. He loved Technicolor movies, and in Cinemascope even more so. Only American movies were in Cinemascope and Memo equated the wide convex screen with the richness, power, and abundance of the U.S. But he was not choosey, any movie would do. In Spanish he saw Argentinean, Spanish, and Mexican movies. With subtitles he saw French, Italian, German, and British films. But mostly, he loved American movies.

Tan ta ta ta, ta ta ta ta ta ta ta ta ta, ta ti ta ta, ta ti ta taaa, ta ti ta taaaaaaaaaa, sounded the music as the 20th Century Fox logo came on the movie screen. The excitement built in Memo's young heart because the musical theme signaled the beginning of another adventure. The banner above the roaring MGM lion's head that read: Ars Gratía Artis elicited the same reaction. Oh, the anticipation of the trip he was about to take was almost unbearable. Great American stars like Cooper, Gable, Tracy, Flynn, Power were about to take him into the land of dreams. Or the new crop: Tony Curtis, James Dean, and Troy Donahue. Troy Donahue, you ask? Yes! Troy, in *Peyton Place* and *Parrish*. Curtis, in *Mr. Cory*, and Dean in *East of Eden* and *Rebel Without a Cause*. Memo identified with these young men who fought to be accepted by society's many authority figures. *Someday, I will live in the United States of America and I will strive to better myself as they do, and I, too, will succeed!*

But how will he get there? There was one possibility. Tía Dahlia's oldest child Violeta had graduated high school and had been sent to the United States. It was the thing to do; you went away to the United States for a few years and came back having learned English and having earned a diploma of some kind. That was one way to fulfill one of the requirements for inclusion, if not into the upper class, at least the small but also exclusive upper middle class. Tía Dahlia knew her children belonged to a better class than the one they had been born into and she was determined to get them there. Violeta would be coming back to visit for Christmas that year and Memo harbored hopes she might help him get to the land where everything is possible.

Even though Violeta had been brought up by La Cheli and her prejudices have been instilled in her, Violeta liked Memo and had been kind to him in many occasions. Once in a while he would write to her and Memo would always ask her how it was living in the great country. Memo would make his hopes known to her. Then he began to ask if she would help him come. "Maybe someday," she had said. Perhaps she had said it to stop Memo from asking her anymore but he construed her answer into a promise. He clung to that hope as a drowning man does the rope thrown to him by a lifeguard. Memo wanted it so much he convinced himself it would happen.

Unexpectedly, another possibility arose. One day, María told Memo about an American gentleman she had met. He was in El Salvador on business.

"He has asked me out. Should I accept?"

It was frowned upon by Salvadorian society for single women with children, to date. Innocent as it might have been, Salvadorian society did not approve of such goings on. It was very difficult for a woman to marry for a second time under this strict unwritten code. The men were free to do as they pleased but not the women. Violeta's mother had faced the same restrictions since she divorced Tío Lalo. Tía Dahlia was still an attractive woman and many a man had courted her. It was a risky thing to do but Tía Dahlia was a willful woman who was not about to let Salvadorian society tell her what to do, so she dated whomever she pleased, even if La Cheli didn't like it. Memo's mother was in a different situation. She had just been allowed to return to the fold after eight years exile and María knew La Cheli was keeping a wary eye on her. Even though she had been back for several years by now, she was on a kind of probation. La Cheli could be caustic and her criticism unsparing if she felt Dahlia and/or María were soiling the family name. Still, she had her double standard and she allowed Dahlia a leeway she did not allow María. She had to be careful or she might get banished again. La Cheli allowed her and her son to live in one room without charging her rent. María was barely making ends meet as it was. She could not afford to antagonize the old lady. Still, it was more important to her to obtain Memo's approval before she tackled La Cheli's.

Memo was María's man in her life. The news that she was about to date someone did not sit well with him. It was a combination of two things; jealousy that her mother would have someone to take his place in her heart, and fear of the stigma attached to being the son of a woman of loose morals, which was how Salvadorian society would view it. He had heard the cruel comments made about women whose behavior was perceived as outside accepted mores. On the other hand, he knew her mother's struggle to keep her head above water. Every hard earned penny was already spent by the time she received it. She could be spared this exhausting existence if he let her have a chance at seeing someone who could change it all. The fact he was an American was a plus, not because Memo wanted to go to the U.S.–though subliminally that might have played a part—but because Americans were viewed as square, straight shooting guys who were more morally upright than Salvadorians. His mother awaited his answer. "Yes," Memo said, "Why not?" And so she did.

After the first date, Memo asked how the date had gone.

"Fine," his mother said laconically.

Memo knew how private she was about everything, so he let it go at that. A few weeks went by and Memo did not ask nor María tell if she was still seeing the gentleman from Texas. One day María told Memo she needed to discuss something important with him. He could tell by the tone of her voice that it was serious. They sat on his bed, in the one room they both shared.

"He has asked me to marry him," she said. Memo knew who 'him' was.

"He wants to take us to Texas, and he wants to adopt you."

Memo's heart leapt! He was in a movie! In an American movie at that! He was about to go live in Texas, U.S.A. American schools, American friends, American everything!

"Should I say yes?"

Memo looked into his mother's eyes; into his mother's soul. There, he saw the answer to the question he knew he had to ask.

"Do you love him?"

His mother's eyes locked with his, she paused then sighing sadly said, "No."

He understood. His mother wanted to love the American because she knew it would improve their lives immeasurably. She also knew Memo's dreams.

"If you want me to, I'll marry him," she said, and waited for his answer.

"No," Memo said, "Not if you don't love him." They knew the cost of the decision. They embraced, for a long time. Neither one ever mentioned it again. *I'll get there . . . someday, somehow,* Memo promised himself. *All I need is money! I will get the money! But how? How? I'm not qualified to do anything. How am I going to earn money? I have to stay in school three more years and graduate.* However, as his desire for money grew his interest in education lessened.

The Instituto Nacional General Francisco Menéndez was the only public high school in all of San Salvador, El Salvador's capital. There were other high schools called Colegios, but they were all private. María had told Memo his only chance to continue his education was to make it into the Instituto Nacional; otherwise he had better start looking for a job. Memo would have to compete with all the other students from all the primary schools by passing a rigorous test. Only one hundred students were admitted. The odds were ninety-nine to one that Memo would not make it. The twelve year old had to make it.

Memo was an excellent student only during the month of May. His mother always asked that as her Mother's Day gift, Memo present her with a straight A's report card. Memo managed to do this every May. The rest of the year he would get mostly C's with a few B's thrown in. Memo had a horror of work. At least the kind of work he knew he would get with only a sixth grade education, so spurred by this, he studied hard, took the test, and won one of the one hundred scholarships offered. It was a mixed blessing. The fact that a boy made it into the Instituto Nacional meant he was somewhat smart. It also meant he was poor; otherwise he would attend a private Colegio. The Instituto required that the boys wear a military uniform. No other school required this, so everybody knew where he studied. It was at once a badge of honor and of shame.

Unbeknownst to Memo, he had scored a minor victory. La Cheli had not expected him to make it to the Instituto Nacional. Dahlia's son, Marcelo, had made it but then again, he was Dahlia's son. Still, Memo thought he spied an approving glance when he announced to her he had made it to the Instituto.

Upon his return from Nicaragua, his mother did what she did every January, at the beginning of the school year; his mother got him his black boots. She sewed a third black star to the flap of his uniform's left breast pocket, and off she sent him to the Instituto Nacional. The third star meant he was now in the ninth grade.

At the end of that year Memo would have finished the Plan Básico. At that point a decision had to be made. If the student was not considered college material it was recommended that he leave school and pick up a trade like a mechanic or a carpenter. Memo was not thrilled about going that route. If a student's grades were good enough, he was allowed to continue and graduate as a Bachiller, the equivalent of a High School diploma in the U.S. As a Bachiller he had more opportunities. He could join the bureaucracy and aspire to some middle management position twenty years down the road, or he could go to college. La Cheli did not think Memo would go that far. She told María he should finish the Plan Básico and find a trade.

Memo wanted to get his Bachillerato but then what? There were two options: One was to be sent to study abroad, which he knew his mother could not afford to do. The second was to study in El Salvador. There were two universities:

One private —out of the question, and the other one was the Universidad Nacional de El Salvador. To be accepted to the National University one had to pass another even more rigorous examination, in which all the students from the whole nation competed. Could Memo handle that? He was not sure. If he did not, he was doomed to a life of servitude; a boring bureaucratic job behind a desk. He shuddered at the thought. Could he handle that? He was sure he could not.

Not the way Memo was feeling about his chances in El Salvador. He sought refuge in his desire to go to the U.S. *I have to get out of this country. I have to go to a country where there's a chance to make something of myself. I have to go to the United States! I need money!* His interest in education fell further. Money was the only answer. But how was he going to get money? That's when show business called Memo for the second time.

THE SECOND CALL

The first call had been when Memo was a baby. Whenever the company needed a baby, Memo would be the one. His mother had told him that he had played baby Jesus in Passion plays and the stolen son in a melodrama in which Memo had had to exclaim, "Marre, marre!" as he was being taken away from his mother, played by María. She was fond of telling the story because Memo was so young he mispronounced the word madre. She thought it was cute. Memo no longer thought so. When Memo was a little older, he had played the Pontius Pilate's attendant who brought a pail of water and a towel for Pilate to wash his hands before pronouncing sentence upon Jesus the Nazarene. That had been the extent of his acting experience. His mother had made that decision for him. Then, show business came a-knocking again.

After her return from Mexico, María had found it difficult to get acting jobs because there were just a couple of theater companies and, even when she got one, the pay was pitiable. She had gotten a few dancing jobs in night clubs but even though she still had a good figure and was an excellent dancer, she couldn't compete with younger women whom the drinking patrons preferred. It would infuriate his mother that young women, who could not dance, would beat her out of a job. The night club patrons were not interested in an artist with years of professional dancing experience who had appeared in the best theaters in seven countries. They were interested in a lovely young body they could buy drinks for, and hopefully take to bed. For this reason, dancing in night clubs was several notches below dancing on a theater stage. The opprobrium that this brought upon her made it increasingly difficult to continue dancing in night clubs. La Cheli vociferously disapproved and started to make threats. Her threats made Memo aware of the stigma night club work could bring upon the family. María's only hope was to turn to radio.

She had never done radio but she had fine credentials: Two decades of acting experience and an international reputation as an artist who had succeeded abroad. Ironically, this worked against her. The radio artists she was now working with admired her but also resented her. If anything, her credentials were too good. She was coming down to radio and they knew it. A theater actress is much more accomplished that a radio one. In the theater, actors have to be graceful, their bodies expressive, their voices powerful. Beauty is often required. In radio only the voice is important. In the theater you have to memorize your lines and if you forget them during performance you have to improvise your way out of the error. In radio you read the lines and if a mistake is made, the taping is stopped. The tape is rewound and the actor gets another chance at doing it right. A theater actress could do radio rather easily, while a radio actress would have difficulty doing theater.

The radio station chain had a standing group of actors who taped nine soap operas daily. The actors had to be good at what they did because the shows taped today were broadcast the next day. There was little room for mistakes. The shows were rehearsed between 8:30 and 10:30 a.m. By 11:00 a.m. taping started in studio A. All nine soaps had to be done by 3:00 p.m. The pressure was immense, the competition fierce. When María started working with them, most of the actors took a 'show me how good you are' attitude, which only increased the pressure. Fortunately, her years of theater experience served her well and little by little she was accepted—after a fashion.

Memo would visit her at the station and had become known as María's son. It wasn't long before he noticed the actors had a vitriolic nature. As soon as an actor would leave the room, someone would make a rancorous remark about him or her. It took courage to leave the room, however briefly, for the actor knew he would be the recipient of spiteful barbs. Upon returning, if the cast was laughing, he would assume they were laughing at him—even if they were not. Sometimes, a courageous fool would ask upon entering "All right, what you said about me?" Most of the time they would deny that anyone had said anything, and that would bring on a knowing grin to all. Sometimes, they would actually tell him! And everybody would laugh; the more hurtful the remark, the louder the laughter. It was acceptance, at a price.

Memo got the impression all actors were mean and petty. He hated the backstabbing and saw it as endemic to the profession. It was not. The actors were fighting for survival. It was a way of weeding you out. If you could not take it, you got out. The rapacity was rooted in the country's inability to provide opportunity for its artists. There were only two radio stations in the whole country that had a standing company of actors. Each company had about ten members. The competition to get and keep one of those jobs was fierce. They got a dollar for playing a part in each episode. The size of the part didn't matter; the lead and the one liner got one dollar. Of course, it was better to have the lead because it appeared more often, but if not, a bit part would do. Potentially, an actor could earn nine dollars in one day, fifty-four dollars for the six day week. That was a lot of money, by Salvadorian standards. This rarely occurred. If an actor made four or five dollars a day he was lucky.

"María," the director said, "Do you think your son could play this small part?"

"Sure!" María responded.

"Here, Memo," he said, handing Memo a script, "you are the Indian. It's only one line. We'll tape it in an hour."

Memo read the line to himself. In the recording studio, an hour later, Memo, more nervous than he had ever been in his life, leaned into the microphone to deliver his one line. He knew he had better get it right. He had seen them pounce, like a pack of hyenas, on an actor who flubbed a line. The ribbing was done in 'fun' but it was anything but that. The women sometimes cried while the men took it stoically. The hyenas were ravenous and Memo was fresh meat. His mother's experience helped her. Memo was a rookie. Memo was competition. Memo wanted that dollar. The cue came and Memo spoke the immortal line:
"This is a very heavy rock!" Thus, Memo started his professional acting career. Memo got his dollar!

Memo got another line a week later and another one a few days after that. Little by little the director gained confidence in Memo and gave him bigger and bigger parts. It was only a few dollars a week but it was more money than Memo had ever had, and he liked it. For the first time in his life he had money in his pocket. Money was an equalizer. He could get things now he could not before. Memo's interest in education sank a little lower.

He did well enough the next school year and finished the Plan Básico. His grades were good enough to stay on the university path. His mother sewed a fourth star to his breast pocket flap and he entered the quarto curso. One more and he would graduate. But his heart was not in it. He wanted to make more money and even though he was not sure he wanted to be an actor it seemed he had some talent for it. At sixteen years old, it seemed an eternity before he would graduate. And then, if he got lucky enough to be accepted to the Universidad Nacional, another five or six years to become a lawyer. *I'll be twenty three years old!* Memo could not see that far.

Memo was supposed to be the lawyer in the family, Violeta, the doctor, and Marcelo the architect. This was not a decision he had made. Violeta had made it for him. Memo was good at defending his point of view and Violeta was the one who had said in more than one occasion: "Memo will be a lawyer." He did not know if he wanted to be a lawyer but Violeta had shown a confidence in his intellect no one else in the family had, except his mother. Memo wanted to please Violeta. But she had left four years ago and his hope that she would help him go the United States dimmed with each year that passed. La Cheli did not expect much from him, Dahlia disdained him, and Marcelo was indifferent. María cared but was too busy eking out a living to see his disillusionment.

One day, his aunt announced Marcelo was leaving for the United States. Apparently, Marcelo too was losing interest in education. He was studying the architecture of women more than that of buildings. Besides, the Salvadorian culture encouraged men to drink and Marcelo was showing a talent for that activity, which worried his mother. Dahlia was going to the U.S. with him to make sure Marcelo learned English before entering an American university. This, Memo realized, further dimmed the possibility that he would be going to the U.S. any time soon. What infuriated Memo the most was that Marcelo was kicking and screaming about having to go; he was having too much fun in El Salvador. He was socially in demand not only because he was handsome, but because he played the guitar and sang with a trio he had formed. He was also very much in love with a beautiful and intelligent law student who returned his affections. Dahlia did not think he was ready for marriage, so the trip would also solve that problem. Memo was dying to go and Marcelo was dying to stay.

Their departure left a hole in the house no one could fill. La Cheli had lost her three favorites. She was an unhappy woman to begin with and now she was even more so. With an astonishing display of hubris and insensitivity, Dahlia forced La Cheli, who had been like a mother to her, to move from the best part of the house and into one of the small, lesser quality rooms vacated by one of the tenants. Just a few months earlier, Dahlia had extracted a will from La Cheli making Dahlia the owner of that part of the house. Dahlia closed and locked all the doors of her part of the house, let the maid go, and left for the U.S. King Lear would have understood. María was left to care for the disgruntled old lady. She would stay in her tiny room and not come out unless she wanted something, and when she did, it was a command that had to be obeyed immediately. The only time she would be happy was when she received a letter from the U.S. As time passed, the letters became more infrequent and La Cheli became more cantankerous. La Cheli's health began to decline.

Violeta never did go to medical school. Instead, she studied two years in a business college and had become a bilingual secretary. Marcelo was studying English and maybe he would become an architect. If the cream of the crop was not living up to expectations why would Memo think he could become a lawyer? Dahlia and Marcelo never wrote to him. Violeta would write to him about once a year. He would answer immediately and express in every letter his hope that someday he would join her. But his chances of ever going to the U.S. seemed more and more remote. It looked to Memo he was stuck in El Salvador.

Memo gave up school in his tenth year. In order to pacify his mother, he enrolled in night school and worked as a radio actor during the day. Ironically, while he was disappointing everyone at home, others saw more in Memo than he did himself. Somehow he was becoming a good actor and the radio station's new artistic director took notice of him. He requested the director of the acting group to give Memo three of the nine soap opera leads. This surprised everyone in the group, most of all, Memo. He was not even seventeen and he was leading three serials. The group was not happy about this and increased the pressure. If Memo made a mistake while taping they made him pay. Spite the pressure, he managed to do well and now was making star wages: twenty five dollars a week!

Shoes! With the money he was now making, Memo could afford good shoes. He would buy Italian or French made shoes. Better still, he had a cobbler, who lived half a block down the street, make him shoes that Memo himself designed. Maybe Memo had an innate sense of style or maybe he had borrowed it from the stars he had seen in movies, but no one had shoes like his. Either way, though he was not rich, he dressed as if he were. His shirts were Italian made, his suits American. He could now go to parties, be seen as a classy young man who was well received in most upper middle class homes. That was the good side.

The bad side was the stress he was under. The pressure the actors put on him because he was the youngest actor in the group turned an already serious boy into a serious young man. He had always been too serious for his age. His mother had no one to confide in and so she had turned to him. Since the age of eight, she would tell him the truth about their situation. The situation was that there was no money. She thought he should know how little money they had so he would understand why birthdays and Christmas days brought no toys. He would get a present from her but it was something he needed; such as socks or underwear. As the years went by, he lost any childish illusions about Santa Claus, El Niño Dios, or any other foolish celebrations. He dreaded the coming of those dates for invariably someone would ask him what toys he had received, and he had nothing to show. She treated him like a little adult by sharing her problems with him. She liked to say that she never hit him because she could reason with him. If he misbehaved, she would reason with him. Memo was flattered that she had such confidence in him and became a reasonable little boy. He was her "little man" who understood her, and he was proud to be given such responsibility.

Although the opportunity to lead three of the serials was a great compliment to his talent, it put more weight upon his young shoulders. He had to be good, even though he had no acting training of any kind. It was assumed he had inherited talent, since he came from an acting family. The truth be told, he was terrified every time he stepped up to the mike. The more parts he had, the more terrified he was. The group's relentless criticism was the source of his fear. He managed not to show it, for if they knew how tense he was they would have taken advantage. He had to act as if he was in total control, which meant he could not afford to make a mistake. But inevitably, make mistakes he would. Everyone did. And everyone paid the price. This was no consolation to him, so he worked hard at being letter perfect. After a mistake, the pressure rose even more because the group lay in ambush waiting for the next mistake with more hurtful remarks. Besides the fact that the group resented his being so young and leading one-third of the serials, they also did not like that he refused to participate in the ribbing of others. He had hoped that if he did not, they would spare him in return, but instead they thought he was trying to act superior to them and thus they would ride him harder whenever he gave them a chance. He would take it on the chin and laughed it off, but it hurt. All of this conspired to make him even more serious. At an age when most teenagers were having fun, he was shouldering the responsibilities of a professional actor. There will be a price to pay for this, later in life. Nevertheless, spite the tension, he was learning and improving and more work continued to come his way.

Other radio stations took notice and asked him to guest star in their shows. The Salvadorian National Repertory Company came a-calling and he joined them at a salary of forty dollars a month. All told, Memo was making about two hundred dollars a month! Now that he had money, Memo began to lose his sense of purpose, spending his money in frivolous things. He gave up school altogether. If his mother was unhappy, and she probably was, she never said so.

María was also doing better. A couple of years earlier, television had been brought to El Salvador by the rival station chain and María had been asked to star in its first comedy series. The money she made, she spent on herself. The money Memo made, he spent on himself. There was no acrimony on either side. Though she might have been disappointed that he had quit school, she also might have been relieved of the financial burden. She never asked him for money nor did she give him any. They came to this agreement tacitly. It didn't occur to them that they were, what is now called, a dysfunctional family.

To make matters worse, more opportunities came his way. The radio chain for which he worked also got a television channel and Memo was tapped to star in its first drama series. Just like that! One day, he was told, not asked, that he was going to be one of the stars, and that was that. He did not know anything about television but then, nobody else did. The powers had decided it was time for El Salvador to have television and part of that decision included creating national television stars. Those who were already jealous of him became more so. They hoped the show would fail. There were plenty of reasons why that should have happened. With the aplomb of the ignorant, all involved with the show plunged headlong into it.

The cast was handed a script and told the first rehearsal would take place the following Monday. At the appointed time, Memo reported to the TV studio. If there were apprehensions, no one showed them. Everybody in the cast was a member of the radio acting group with which he worked. They were borrowing their modus operandi from Mexican television which in turn had learned it from American television. The first day, the cast sat at a table to read the script for the first time. On Tuesday, the Artistic director blocked the show. On Wednesday, everybody had learned their lines and the Mexican Technical director the station had imported for the purpose took them through their first camera rehearsal.

Incredibly, on Thursday night, at eight p.m. the show went on the air. Live! Sink or swim. All of them, totally ignorant of the requirements, jumped in and did it! The show was an instant hit!

Though everybody who listened to the radio serials knew his name, few knew his face. Those who could afford T.V. sets were the affluent and, as he became familiar to them, their doors opened to him. His income wasn't high enough to buy a car but he now had friends who had and would take him to their parties. Some people took to calling him the Salvadorian James Dean. Life was good!

Not exactly. He had achieved much in a few short years: He was a radio and television star, he was a member of El Salvador's National Repertory company, and he was famous. And yet, his mother had never congratulated him for any of these accomplishments. His television series was the most popular show in the country. Not once did she comment on his performances. It was puzzling because his mother had more than two decades of experience in the field he was just starting.

She never gave him an ounce of criticism, nor of advice. Memo was fumbling his way to the top of El Salvador's artistic world. Maybe she thought he didn't need her advice. Maybe she was waiting for Memo to ask. He never did and she never offered. Although it did not surprise him, it hurt him. As they had done before with other private matters, they never mentioned it.

Maybe his mother was angry at him. He had seen his mother tormented by the favoritism La Cheli had shown for Dahlia and her children and maybe it irked María that, by dropping out of high school, Memo had proved La Cheli and Dahlia right; he was inferior to Violeta and Marcelo and thus, María was inferior to Dahlia. María didn't have to say it, for Memo felt the same way. It hurt him to admit it, and yet, what was Memo doing that his mother had not done? She had not finished school herself. Instead, she had gone into the acting profession. How could she tell him he was wrong without devaluing her own life? In condemning him she would be condemning herself.

Self-condemnation was bad enough. Memo knew he had fallen short. He felt it reflected on his intelligence. He knew, somewhere down the road, it would cost him. He already had to hide the fact he did not have his Bachillerato. He felt ashamed. The friends he could now afford to have were about to start their university studies. Some were going abroad, some were staying in El Salvador, but he could not join them. He could go to parties with them, he could go drinking with them, but some day they would graduate with some degree or another and become professionals. Memo would be . . . an actor.

Actors in El Salvador are not accorded much respect. It might be good to have them over for a good time but don't marry one. Memo knew this was the fate that awaited him because he worked with older actors and all were unhappy about how society treated them. In fact, all artists in El Salvador are subjected to this treatment. He knew there was a stigma attached to what he was. He decided he could not live the rest of his life in a country that had such contempt for him. He had to go to the U.S. where he could start anew.

Aunt Dahlia came for a short visit that had more to do with getting the money that she kept in her locked bedroom than with visiting the family. The few moments she would share with them were about how wonderful everything in the U.S. was, and the fascinating things she and her children had been doing: Violeta had gone ice skating, Marcelo was learning English, Dahlia had seen *My Fair Lady* on Broadway. She would show them the pictures taken in front of the White House, Lincoln's Memorial, and New York's Central Park, etc., etc., etc. Memo would suffer in silence hearing about the wonderful life they were living in Washington, D.C. María suffered also but she too did not show it. La Cheli would beam every minute Dahlia was back, and then go into an emotional dive as soon as Dahlia left. The house would return to its silent existence. María would go her way, Memo his, and La Cheli to her room. Little by little she became ill. Though María and Memo tried, they could not fill the void.

Memo and María were drifting apart. Sometimes they would not see each other for weeks. One Sunday, as he was preparing to go out with his friends, María told Memo he had not come home earlier than two a.m. for more than six months. He was shocked. He realized she was right and made her a promise that he would do better. It only took a couple of weeks to break his promise.

He was having fun. For the first time in his life he felt he was with people of his kind. By and large, the neighborhood kids were a rascally bunch. Memo had never felt quite comfortable with them. He aspired to better and thought he had now found it. He had a circle of friends who, a few short years ago, would not have given him the time of day and now welcomed him. But they all lived in the opposite side of town, where the nice houses were, where Memo wanted to be. This created a plight within him; who were his real friends? The old ones or the new ones? The truth was that he was very busy. He worked Monday though Saturday from eight a.m. until two or three p.m. Then, he would take a bus downtown to the National Theater to rehearse a play. Then return to the T.V. station to rehearse or perform his T.V. show. His neighborhood friends were not happy with him because he no longer spent time with them. Once in a while he would bump into them and they would have a brief and uneasy conversation. They never mentioned it but they resented his success. They thought he had become a snob. Memo sensed their unspoken recriminations but did nothing to ameliorate the situation. He was living his movie, and in it, there were no roles for his old friends. They felt he had betrayed them, but the truth was that he wanted desperately to get away from them. On the other hand, not all was well with his new friends. Many a time, in the wee hours of the morning, when the buses were no longer running, his friends would offer him a ride home. Memo was ashamed of the area in which he lived and found it difficult to have them see it. Memo would decline the ride and since there were no rotating cabs in the city, he would walk the empty streets alone rather than let his friends see his neighborhood. He knew it was dangerous to do so yet he didn't want to risk rejection from his new friends. The closer to his house he got, the more danger he was in. He learned to walk in the middle of the street, afraid that if he walked on the sidewalk he had no time to react if his neighborhood's hoodlums assaulted him. This street knowledge might have saved his life.

Once, late at night, as he was crossing a bridge about a block away from his house, he heard a whispered voice pierce the silence. Sound seems to travel much farther in darkened streets.

"Here comes one!" said the voice in the shadows.

"Let's get him!" said another voice.

Memo was getting ready to run away from them when the first voice said,

"Wait! It's Memo. He's from the barrio. Let him be."

He thought he recognized the owner of the voice and was grateful he had shown him mercy. He might have been one of the kids with whom he had played years before. *What if he had not stopped them? Would they have harmed me, or even killed me?* The experience underscored his dilemma; he could go party with his new friends because he was well known and had money to pay his way, but ultimately he had to come home where the carriage and the steeds turned into pumpkin and mice. *I cannot keep up the pretense; I have to get out of this barrio! I have to get out of this country!!*

FUTURE IMPERFECT

The pictures aunt Dahlia had shown spurred him. He sensed he didn't have time to waste. Though he was having fun with his friends he knew that some day these friends would leave him behind. In a few years they would be graduating from the university and soon thereafter they would be settling down and there would be no place for him in their lives. They wouldn't want him around because their wives would not want him around. It was okay now, but his days of partying were numbered as sure as his days as a teenager were. The acting thing he knew was not for him—not in El Salvador. He had plenty of examples in the older actors with whom he worked. And if that was not enough, there was his mother. He did not want to struggle as she had.

She had quit acting and had taken a job as record librarian in a radio station because the acting jobs were getting fewer and farther between. She hated the job yet was grateful she had it. She had no experience in that area but the station manager was letting her learn it as she went. She wasn't getting paid much, which was probably why the manager let her do it. It helped that it was a tedious job that no one else wanted to do. It all boiled down to security. She needed to know that money was coming in every week, thus she was willing to trade the happiness she experienced acting, singing, and dancing for the tedium of typing, sorting, and cataloging.

She worked in the back room of the radio station all by herself. For a woman who had been for more than twenty-five years in front of appreciative audiences who had showered her with applause, the silence and anonymity of her job was excruciating. Perhaps because she detested it so, she was slow at learning it. But learn it she would. She was a Taurus, and tenacity was a quality she could count on. She was unaccustomed to getting up early but every morning at six she would get up, get ready, and be the first one at the station working at her new job with turtle-like determination.

Memo could see his future in her present. He decided to press Violeta and have her change her someday to soon, and the soon to now! With this goal in mind, he started to write to her more often. At the end of each letter he would remind her of his hope. It probably wasn't subtle but he knew she was his only chance ever to realize his dream.

"I can't believe that it's been more than seven years since you left," he would write. Or, "How much longer before I can come?" Or, "When do you think I might come? Next year?" Eventually she said, "Soon."

"How soon?"

"Soon," she said.

When he pressed her further, and perhaps because he was beginning to annoy her, she wrote telling him the conditions he would have to meet.

"How much money have you got? I'm not going to pay for your trip, you know?"

"How much money do I need?" he asked.

"Well, enough to buy a round trip airfare, and enough to last you until you find a job; at least a hundred dollars a month."

"For how many months?"

"No less than three months."

"I'll get started on that immediately," Memo wrote back.

Why do I need a round trip ticket? Memo wondered. *I'm not coming back. I'll ask her in the next letter. It's enough for now that she has said soon.* The very same day Memo got the letter, he went to the Pan American Airlines office to ask how much the ticket would cost.

The doorman opened the glass door for him. Walking into Pan American Airlines' office was almost like being in the United States; the company's famous logo, the airplane model sitting on a counter, the American staff wearing the insignia on the lapels of their elegant dark blue uniforms. Someone was talking in English right next to him! It was almost unbearable. Everything was so clean, so well kept, and so orderly. *It's so quiet!* There weren't a lot of people there and those who were were wealthy. You had to be, to be able to afford to fly. It was intimidating. It was exciting!

Memo had had this same feeling when he had gone to the airport to see Violeta off, or to welcome her and his aunt. One had to drive to the airport which meant one had to have a car. If one didn't have a car, hiring a taxi cost a small fortune. No one rode the bus there, not passengers anyway. El Salvador's International Airport, a hyperbolic title if ever there was one, was several kilometers outside the city. Small, but nicely appointed, it was a dome-like building with two corridors leading from the main building; one to the left to gates one and two, and one to the right to gates three and four. El Salvador presented itself well to the world when visitors first set foot on it. It went down hill from there.

To Memo, the airport reeked of wealth. Unlike today, when everybody wears blue jeans, T-shirts, and Reeboks, then, everyone was well-dressed. It was *de rigueur*. Violeta and aunt Dahlia had traveling suits tailor-made when they first went to the U.S. Including a hat! Hats were worn only by the rich ladies in those teas Memo saw in La Prensa's society page photographs. The men all wore suits and ties. Some of them had overcoats draped on their arms. Since no one wore overcoats in El Salvador, having one meant you were going to or coming from a foreign land. Memo loved being at the airport because it was the gate to the world he dreamt to go. And yet, he felt out of place there, for he knew he didn't have the wherewithal to live at the level the travelers lived. Nor did his aunt for that matter, but she had enough to appear as if she did. His aunt, Memo suspected, had hoped to live in that style but had not found the man to take her there. Memo could not blame her, as he himself harbored the same hopes.

The Pan American Airlines' office gave him the same feelings the airport did. Excited, he approached the counter.

"What can I do for you?" the clerk asked.

"How much would it cost to fly to Washington, D.C.?"

Memo was well dressed enough to appear as if he could afford the cost of such a trip but in his heart he felt inadequate. She took a moment to find the tariff table, wrote the amount on a piece of paper, and slid it on the counter.

"Thank you," he said and looked at the paper.

Memo had braced himself for the cost and acted casually as he read it.

"Would you like to make a reservation?"

"Not today, thank you," said Memo, and left.

That's a lot of money. I'd better start saving now. That, plus the money he would need to live on until he got a job, was a princely amount to him. Memo walked to the park across the street and sat in one of the benches. The park occupied a square block and was located in the center of town. It was flanked on the west side by the National Cathedral and on the south side by the National Palace. On the east side were located some of the most expensive stores in the country, and on the north side were national and international banks, and Pan American Airlines. Memo did some arithmetic. *I'll have to save about half of my income for one year to be able to have enough for the round trip fare, and a few hundred more to take with me until I get a job. To do that, all frivolous expenses must be cut.* He was not happy about that. *It will be a long year before I can realize my dream.* Memo felt discouraged. *Change that! It will be a short year before I can realize my dream.* Memo was happy.

A sudden gust of wind made him shiver. It was the rainy season and even though it was hot, the chill he felt announced the quick approach of a tropical storm. Beyond the Cathedral's copula, he saw the swift moving dark clouds. He lowered his gaze and examined the old Spanish church. He had long been disappointed by the Catholic Church; *Religious repression.* He looked to his left at the Grecian pediment and Doric columns of the National Palace; *Political and military repression.* He turned and stared at the expensive stores that catered to the rich; *Social repression.* And then he turned north and saw Pan American Airlines again. *The United States,* he whispered to himself, *Freedom! In one short a year I'll be there.*

A silver-dollar-size raindrop hit his forehead, snapping him out of his reverie. *I got to get to work.* Tropical raindrops can get one drenched in less than a minute. He leapt to his feet and began running toward the bus stop. A block away he saw his bus pulling in. The silver dollar drops accelerated their attack. Everyone started to run.

"I can do it and I will!" He exclaimed.

He galloped toward the bus. The bus started to move away. Dodging traffic, Memo redoubled his efforts. He was now close to the bus' rear door. The bus picked up speed.

"I can do it and I will!" He yelled again.

He reached for the handle and did what he had done hundreds of times before; he grabbed the handle and swung himself onto the first step of the speeding bus. Triumphantly he yelled to all who could hear.

"I can do it and I will!"

Thunder cracked as the rain drops drowned his words.

The next day, he wrote to Violeta and told her what he had done and that it would take him a year to be ready. "What else do I need to do?" Violeta wrote back and told him to go to the American embassy and they would tell him what he needed to do. The next day on his way to the TV station he stopped at the embassy.

The TV and radio chain he worked for had built its own edifice. It was a first in Salvadorian broadcasting history. Up to that point, all radio stations had used houses already in existence. They would knock out a few walls, put in some sound proofing, install the necessary equipment and they were in business. The owner of the station had hoped to be the one to bring television to the country but had been beaten to the punch by a rival radio chain. He wanted to gain the upper hand and this was his way of doing so. As an added dig, he chose the best part of town to erect the expensive structure. This was the area where the U.S. had its embassy.

The embassy was a stately mansion with a circular drive. As Memo got off the bus he paused to admire the manicured lawns of the neighborhood. *I bet the rich in El Salvador live as well as the rich anywhere.* The Salvadorian upper crust is a closed society that allows few in, but the ambassador of the United States of America is ipso facto one of them. In fact, all American staff is automatically part of the elite. The embassy's location attested to that. It also attested to the fact that all foreigners are more easily accepted into El Salvador's upper class than equally accomplished Salvadorians. As Memo entered the mansion he felt he was in the U.S. and he was, for the embassy is American territory. But he did not know that, then. He waited patiently for his turn, day dreaming of a life that in a year would be his.

"To come as a resident of the United States they require: an application for residency, a valid passport, a police report stating I've never committed a crime, a medical report to prove I am in good health, an affidavit stating that I will serve in the U.S. armed forces if drafted, a round trip airline ticket, and a notarized affidavit from you, stating that you are responsible for me while I'm in the U.S. I'll start getting all the documents here but please send me your affidavit as soon as possible because, as you know, they have a quota system. It will take about nine months from the day I submit my application before I'm allowed to go."

Memo

"P.S. I'll be ready, don't you worry."

The cost of the preparation of the documents surprised him. *I will need to save more if I'm going to make it in one year.* He began to put money away every week. It cut into his style of living but it was worth it. He would buy no more shoes and clothes. Whatever he already had would have to do. *Fortunately, they don't need proof that I have the airline ticket until a couple of weeks before I leave.* Quietly, he started his preparations. Afraid it might jinx him, he didn't tell anyone about his plans, except his mother.

Maybe because he was eighteen years old, maybe because he had been paying his bills for several years, maybe because he told her rather than asked her, maybe because she knew how long he had dreamt about it, maybe because that was the way between them, but his mother acquiesced. She did not offer to help him in any way nor did she try to stop him. For that, he was grateful. La Cheli was not getting better. This shocked the two of them because she had been such a force of nature that it was hard to believe she would ever be sick. They let the family in the U.S. know about it. He had picked up the guitar because Marcelo played it; he wanted so much to be accepted by him. But Marcelo was at a stage of life in which there was no room for anyone or anything except himself. He taught himself a few songs and offered to sing them to her.

"You play the guitar Memo?" she asked incredulously.

The doubt in her voice shook the little confidence he had. He knew he was not as good as Marcelo and he knew she would compare the two and he knew he would come out a distant second.

"A little bit," he said. "Do you want me to play for you?"

"No," she said, "not now."

Memo left the room kicking himself for trying to win her over.

"I'll never be good enough for her, never."

If he had ever pleased her, she had kept it a secret.

Little by little, the paperwork was coming together. Since he had never been in trouble with the law, he didn't worry about the police report and sure enough they gave him a good one. The medical exam worried him a little bit for in his family no one ever went to the doctor unless they were sick, so just going to the doctor was enough to make him feel that something might be wrong. He passed that too. Without thinking twice, he signed the affidavit stating that he would serve in the U.S. Army. It never occurred to him he was putting his life in jeopardy. Violeta's affidavit was taking longer than he hoped and he gently pressed Violeta for it. One day, there it was! All in English and looking very official with a couple of fancy seals. He kissed the document. *I'm getting closer!*

He knew Violeta was taking a chance on him. Dahlia, he guessed, was not thrilled that her daughter was vouching for him. She must have had to stand up to her mother in order to do it. Not an easy task, because she was accustomed to having her way. Memo was grateful. He promised himself that, no matter what, he would not let Violeta down. If worse came to worse, he would return to El Salvador rather than cause her problems. He kept his promise.

Memo had a bright idea! *If my father would help me, I could go to the U.S. sooner.* The wound had healed enough to make him forget the humiliations suffered a few years back. Memo had received mail from Honduras from a fan that had seen him on television. Others in the cast had gotten mail from Guatemala and Nicaragua, so it seemed reasonable to him that perhaps his father might have seen him. His fame had made a positive difference in the way people were treating him in El Salvador; would his father accept him now that he was famous? *I will fly this time, and stay in the best hotel and I will be dressed well and I will treat him with respect and . . . and . . . maybe he will help me get to the United States.* The more he thought about it the more it seemed to make sense and so he decided to give it a try.

He told his mother his plans. She was against it.

"Why not?"

"I don't think your father will help."

"Why not?"

If María had reasons, this was the time to tell Memo. He waited. She said nothing.

"I've never asked him for anything. I think it's worth a try."

"It's up to you."

He went to Pan American Airlines and bought a ticket to Managua. It so happened that the girl who attended to him was the same he had spoken with a couple of months before. He smiled a smile that said: Remember me? She smiled back at him with a smile that said: No. He was about to remind her but thought better of it. He decided to be business-like. He thought he was doing well until she asked him a question he had never been asked before; "Aisle or window?"

"I beg your pardon?" He asked.

"Do you want a seat by the aisle, or by the window?"

"By the window," he answered, embarrassed that he might have betrayed his inexperience. He hated to be seen as a yokel.

He remembered when he was fourteen years old and Marcelo invited him to go to a party with him. It was the first and the only time his cousin had so honored him. He had no idea why he had done so, but the mere thought of spending time with him was so exciting that he was falling all over himself trying to get ready to go, afraid Marcelo might change his mind. He put on a wool coat Violeta had brought him from the US. Marcelo let him wear one of his own ties! It was so exciting.

"Don't do anything stupid," Marcelo warned as Memo, Marcelo, and Monty, Marcelo's best friend, got in the car.

"No, no. Don't worry."

Marcelo drove to a part of town where Memo had never been. He pulled up in front of a beautiful home. An equally beautiful young woman opened the door. It was obvious by the way she greeted Marcelo how much she liked him. Memo was going to take advantage of the opportunity to learn from the master. He thought he was doing great until he heard Marcelo's voice.

"Say, thank you."

The beautiful girl had just asked him if he wanted something to drink and he had said yes without saying thank you.

"Thank you," he said apologetically.

Altogether, Memo managed to forget to say thank you, or please, a total of seven times. Each time, his cousin reminded and each time Memo felt like an idiot. The last time it happened he could hear the irritation in Marcelo's voice. He had never been so embarrassed in his life. He hated the inadequacy he felt that day, and he promised to avoid feeling that way again. That was the last time Marcelo asked him to accompany him anywhere.

He was now 18 years old and aware that he had so much to learn but he didn't want to look as if he had so much to learn. *Of course by the window. Who would fly and not want to sit by the window?*

"Have a good flight," she said as she handed him the ticket. That was another sentence no one had ever spoken to him before. This time he caught it.

"Thank you," he said. He took the ticket from her and walked out with as much sophistication as he could muster. *I'm going to fly! I'm going to fly!*

OUR FATHER WHO ART IN MANAGUA

The following week he was boarding one of the most beautiful airplanes ever built; a Constellation. He had seen those planes in movies flying over New York City's Statue of Liberty. As he climbed the steps up to the plane his heart pounded so loudly he wondered if every heart in the plane was equally excited. Everyone seemed calm. He tried to act as if he had done this many times before. The plane looked just as he had seen in films but the smell he had not expected. It was an odor he had never experienced. *This is the way the United States smells,* he thought. Years later he learned that, in Third World countries, airlines routinely spray a disinfectant to rid the plane from any possible bugs or diseases brought into the plane by passengers or service crew. But he did not know that then.

Always fearful that he would make a social blunder, he had developed a modus operandi: Don't do anything, and keep your eyes peeled. That was the technique he had used with his new found friends. In their company, he had been to parties at fancy hotels, private clubs, and lovely homes, as well as outings to lake-front summer places, and moonlight beach excursions. The technique had served him well and he had managed to learn a lot. *Time to use it here*, he thought. After he found his seat, he stood around for a while watching what others were doing. He had no luggage to put up in the overhead compartment but observed how it was done and filed that bit of information away for future reference. He noticed how the passengers sat and immediately belted themselves, so he sat and did the same. The belt was a little tricky to open but after a bit he figured it out. He opened it and closed it several times to make sure he could do it with ease, all the while looking out the window so no one would notice he was practicing. He looked at the back of the seat in front of him. *What is this square thing?* He asked himself. He unlatched it and lowered it. *Aha, a little table*, he thought, *maybe we will have something to eat during the flight. How exciting! Let's not show that you're excited,* he reminded himself, and he took on a look of boredom he thought would be appropriate. He saw the magazine in the pocket in front of him, pulled it out and noticed there was a folded laminated card also. He opened it. It contained instructions on how to exit the plane in case of a crash. *Oh my God!* That possibility had not occurred to him. His heart, which had slowed down somewhat, picked up speed again. *What if . . .* he worried. He looked around and saw no one else seemed worried, which relaxed him a bit. He felt a bit ashamed to be such a greenhorn. Fortunately no one could read his mind. *It wouldn't hurt to study it though*. He spent sometime doing that. He saw the signs overhead that read: <u>Fasten your seatbelts</u> and <u>No smoking</u>. He pronounced the words silently. He knew how to pronounce the No smoking sign but the other one he had troubles figuring out. He tried different ways of saying the words. None of them sounded right. *Next year I will be speaking English,* he said to himself. He liked the prospect. The plane started to move back. The stewardesses paced the length of the plane making sure everyone was ready for take off. One of them stood in the aisle and began the routine which in time he would learn to ignore, but today he listened to every word in both, Spanish and English. The plane started to taxi toward the runway. Memo looked out the window and tried to stay calm. Finally the plane was in position for take off and the pilot revved up its engines. The plane shook! Memo worried but again he saw no one else was concerned so he deduced everything was normal. The plane began to speed forward. The roar of the turbines increased as the plane strained to reach the required velocity to leave land. The airport terminal ran past the window. Memo's heart pounded inside of him almost as loudly as the plane's engines. The lush tropical vegetation sped in the opposite direction and then . . . they were in the air. The big bird's noise abated as it broke free from the restraining earth. The plane lifted and lifted until the green turned to blue, and then to white as cumulus clouds enveloped the plane. Memo was flying!

Memo had not called his father or his godfather Ted to tell them that he was coming to Managua. It did not occur to him that they might not be there. He knew Ted would answer the phone when Memo called him. He knew that he would come to pick him up and help him find his father. At some level, he expected it all to work out like in a movie or a fairy tale. It was not so much confidence as innocence. This innocence would serve him well many a time.

Everything happened just as he had imagined. He got off the taxicab that had taken him to the best hotel in Managua, walked in and asked for a room.

"Do you have a reservation? The clerk asked.

"No." *I didn't know I was supposed to make a reservation. How stupid of me.*

"That's fine. How long would you be staying?"

"Ten days." The bellboy took him to his room.

Without bothering to unpack, he picked up the telephone and gave the operator his godfather's number to call. Just as he had imagined, his godfather answered.

"Ted, this is Guillermo Antonio, your godson. I'm in Managua. Can I see you?"

"Where are you staying?"

Memo told him. And just as he had hoped, his godfather was duly impressed.

"I'll be there in a half hour. We can have dinner at my home."

"I'll be waiting for you in the lobby."

Ted's wife and children received him as if he were family. Which in a way, he was. During dinner Memo told them his plan to try and mend fences with his father. He read doubt in Ted's face.

"I'm sure I can do it." Memo said.

Ted said nothing. It was a wonderful evening, just as Memo had imagined.

The next morning Ted called.

"Your father has a business. I've found out where it is. You want me to take you there?

"No Ted, thank you. Just give me the address and I'll take a taxi there."

"Are you sure? I don't mind taking you. It's not very far from where you're staying. You could walk there."

"I'll be alright, thanks."

"Here's his phone number. Call me and tell me what happens, okay?"

"I'll do that."

His godfather gave him the address and wished him luck. He did not know why he had not accepted Ted's offer. Memo was not as confident as he sounded. Somehow he hoped that this time he, who was now eighteen years old, could handle the situation alone. It was more dramatic this way. *Maybe I should call and tell him I want to see him. No. I better just surprise him.* It was more dramatic that way. It made him afraid and it also excited him. Acting made him feel the same way.

He began his preparations; he chose to wear all white because he knew he looked good in white but also because he knew it was his father's favorite color. He had brought two pairs of shoes. He picked the light brown shoes he had had his cobbler make for him. They matched the brown wristband on his gold watch. His mother had given him a gold ring for his last birthday which had an oval amethyst and the Salvadorian Crest inlaid on either side of the stone. It looked like a graduation ring. He did not know if his mother had been trying to remind him that he had not graduated from high school but he liked the fact that others assumed it was a graduation ring. He never said it was or it was not. He combed his hair carefully. He had nice hair which he now knew he had inherited from his mother. He looked at himself in the mirror and liked what he saw. He looked prosperous, even elegant in a tropical sort of way. He had come a long way since last he had seen his father. He hoped his father would notice and be proud of him. Though he smoked, he left the cigarettes on the bureau. He took one more look in the mirror then went downstairs. He exchanged a traveler's check into Córdoba's so he could pay the taxi waiting for him outside. He sat carefully on the back seat to make sure he did not wrinkle his clothes. He gave the address to the driver. *Soon, I'll see my father again.* He never thought that his father would not be waiting for him.

"Here you are," said the driver.

"Where?"

"Right there, across the street," he said pointing to a house.

"That's a private home."

"That's the address you gave me."

Memo got out and the taxi took off. He checked the number again. The excitement was giving way to fear. He looked at the open door, took a deep breath and crossed the street. Typically, the front door was open. He climbed the two steps up to the front door and entered. What should have been a living room was being used as an office. Straight ahead of him, about twelve feet away, sitting at his desk, was his father! Memo stood there for an interminable moment.

"May I help you?" said the young woman sitting at a desk to the left of the doorway. Memo looked at her and then back at his father.

"Elías Granda?"

His father looked up. "Yes?"

Memo waited for a recognition that did not come. He took three steps forward and stood in front of his father's desk, like a private standing before a general.

"Yes?" he repeated.

"Guillermo Antonio," he said, smiling.

His father did not return the smile. A moment passed.

"What are you doing here?"

"I came to visit you."

"What do you want?" he said dryly.

It was the question he had hoped for, but it came too soon. He felt he should talk about other things first before he asked his father for help.

"I just wanted to spend some time with you." As he said that, he realized he had used the familiar 'tu' form twice already. *It would be cowardly of me now to change to 'usted'. I'll show respect with my manner,* he thought.

"Sit over there while I finish this," said his father and went back to work.

Memo did as he was told. Several minutes of silence ensued, interrupted by the shuffling of papers and the cars passing by. *It wasn't exactly what I had imagined but he didn't kick me out,* Memo thought. The girl looked at Memo now and then but said nothing. Memo watched his father work. He noticed how serious he seemed. Memo realized he had yet to see his father smile. Not once did his father look up. Memo used the time to compose himself.

"Had you had lunch?" his father asked.

"No, not yet."

"Have lunch with us." Without waiting for an answer he turned to the secretary.

"Tell the maid there will be one more for lunch." He continued his work.

The secretary got up and walked passed his father's desk toward the back of the house. *I'm going to have lunch with my father.* He suddenly remembered that four years earlier his father had said they were going to have lunch. *Better late than never.* Time ticked away slowly inside of Memo's head. He wondered how much time had elapsed but did not dare to look at his watch afraid to appear impatient. The secretary returned. *Things are going to be alright,* he reassured himself.

I'm going to have my first meal with my father. It would be the only time he would ever share a meal with his father.

A few more minutes passed which Memo spent wondering with whom, besides his father, he was about to have lunch. He remembered his father had said he was married and had three children. *I have brothers and sisters, how about that.* Suddenly, his father got up, announced he was going to wash his hands and disappeared into the back of the house. Memo noticed he was as tall as his father, maybe a little taller. *He did not invite me to wash my hands. Maybe he will do so, later.* His father's behavior was baffling. Memo decided the lunch was not going to be easy, and braced himself for the experience. The secretary got up, picked up her purse and went out the front door. Memo sat there alone for several minutes. The maid appeared, said that lunch was ready and disappeared. Memo was left alone in the room. He walked toward the room she had gone into, which turned out to be a dimly lit dining room. On the left hand corner of the far wall was another door which led into the Spanish style patio. What little light filtered into the room came from this doorway and the house's front door about twenty feet away. As his eyes adapted to the penumbra they discovered a long, dark brown wooden table with three high-back chairs on either side, and one at each end. Two boys stood near the first two chairs on the right and a little girl stood near the first chair on the left. The children looked at Memo for a brief awkward moment. One of the boys was about to say something when his father entered. Memo thought the children came to attention. His father took the end chair and as he sat said to Memo, "You being the oldest sit at that end." Memo sat. Then the two boys sat, and then, the girl. The maid brought four large earthenware bowls which she placed near his father's end of the table, then left. Silently, the little girl got up and began to serve her father from the bowls. The boys stared down at their plates. Her father signaled when she had served him enough. She came around to do the same for her brothers but her father told her that Guillermo Antonio was to be served next.

    She obeyed. Memo tried to have eye contact with the little girl but she kept her gaze down while she served him. Memo said thank you. She then served the oldest of the boys, seated nearest to his father, and then the other boy. She then served herself. The only sounds heard were the ones she made while serving. The little girl sat down. No one spoke. Their father began to eat, thus signaling that it was alright for everybody else to do the same. Memo seated at the end felt isolated; one empty chair to his right, two empty chairs to his left. Equal but separate.

Memo wanted to make conversation but was afraid his father would think him impolite so he waited for his father to speak, which he did not do. They ate in solemn silence. Abruptly his father said, "This is Fletcher," pointing to the oldest, "that one is Kenneth, and she is Astrid." As acknowledgement, as their names were spoken, the children sneaked a look at Memo. He smiled at each of them in turn. His father went back to eating. More silence. Now and then, out of the corners of their eyes, the children would take a peek at him. He would smile at them hoping to encourage them to talk, but they would not. Memo looked at the bare walls. The table, but for the plates and utensils on it, was equally bare. The room had a monastic look. No feminine touch anywhere. Memo wondered where the children's mother was. As if he could read Memo's mind his father said, "Their mother died a while back." After a moment or two his father asked, "How long are you staying?"

"I'll be here nine days more."

"What are your plans?"

"I hoped to spend them with you." He cringed as he pronounced the 'tu' word.

His father said nothing. Having finished eating, his father stood up.

"I'm going to take my siesta." He left through a door on the right side of the room. The moment their father left, the children sprung to their feet and ran to Memo, who welcomed them warmly.

"We've heard about you."

"Your name is Guillermo Antonio."

"You are our older brother."

"I'm eight."

"I'm thirteen and he's eleven."

"I'm in the sixth grade, he's in the eighth."

"I'm in third. Do you wanna see my drawings?"

"I'll show you mine."

"I have some comic books. Do you wanna see'em?"

And as quickly as they had surrounded him, they disappeared. Memo was still reeling from the friendly assault when they returned bringing with them their drawings, comic books, and toys. They all wanted to share them with him.

"Look at this."
"Do you like Superman?"
"Play with my truck."
"Do you like my doll?"

Memo did his best to listen to them, see everything, admire and compliment what they were showing him. He had never felt so wanted, admired, or respected. He was touched by their acceptance, their innocence, their enthusiasm. He laughed and was told to laugh quietly as to not wake up their father. The hour passed swiftly and happily until the sounds coming from their father's room alerted them that he was coming. One of them whispered, "Will you come tomorrow?"

Memo whispered back, "Yes, I will."

The children picked up their belongings and by the time their father entered the room, they were sitting back at their chairs. He looked at them and told them to go to their rooms. They quietly obeyed.

"I'm going back to work." He went out of the room.

Memo understood this to mean that he should leave. He followed his father out of the dining room.

"Is it alright if I come tomorrow?"

His father, already busy at work spoke a perfunctory "Yes."

Full of ambivalence, Memo walked back to his hotel. He always had had a keen sense of direction and knew he could get back. Had he succeeded or failed? *Is my father accepting me or rejecting me?* It seemed his father had managed to do both. Maybe his godfather could explain. *I'll call him when I get to the hotel.* He tried to analyze the event. For it was an event; he had finally shared a meal with the man. Memo found it difficult to call him father, even to himself. *A father is a man who raises you, teaches you, cares and protects you. He will be my father when he has done something to earn the title.* He had been invited to lunch and an invitation is by definition a friendly act, but his father had not been friendly. If someone had witnessed that lunch, friendly would have been the last word used to describe it. Still, it was a step forward in the relationship he hoped to have with his father. *I have to see it as a positive. But why is he so dour, has he been like this always? Maybe the death of his wife has something to do with it. Maybe tomorrow he will be in a better mood.* He recognized a park he had passed on the way over.

The hotel must be that way to the right. Sure enough, there it was, across the street. It was an old and grand hotel with a European charm to it. Its better days were behind but still held itself proudly. Memo took in a deep breath as he looked around the surrounding area. He liked the old town, he liked the day, he even liked himself.

Memo had a problem liking himself. There was something lacking in him. He did not know what he lacked but he knew deep inside that he lacked. There, in a place he could not reach but could feel, there was a hole. He did not know when the hole had appeared but he knew it was sometime after he was five years old. The first five years of his life he did not remember. It was when the pain started, that his memories began. He had concluded those first five years must have been happy, for, if they had not, he would've remembered those too. Why did his mother abandon him for more than three years in that horrible Mexican boarding school? Why did his grandmother reject him from the first day she laid eyes on him? Why did his aunt Dahlia go out of her way to make him feel inferior? He knew why Violeta and Marcelo treated him the way they did, but did not blame them. After all, they were only following their mother's example. It hurt, but he understood. Most hurtful of all, why did his father reject him twice; when he was just a baby and four years ago when he met him for the first time? Why did the persons closest to him disdain him so? It had to be his fault. *What did I do?* He did not have an answer. But today, his father almost accepted him. Today, his two brothers and his sister had given him unconditional love, and their innocence and acceptance had healed the hole. For one magical hour he had belonged to them, and they to him. They liked him! That night during dinner, Memo told Ted and his family about his triumph. They were happy for him. He told them of his plan to go to the United States and his hopes that his father might help him. He looked at Ted for reassurance.

"He might," Ted said, "he just might."

The next morning, after breakfast, he got ready to go see his father. He did not want to get there too early so he wandered about the city. He looked at it with new eyes. It was after all, the city in which he was born, and for the first time he saw himself as its son and not as a visitor. The city seemed to embrace him and he embraced it back. He had never felt that way. In Mexico he had been a foreigner. El Salvador was his mother's country. At last he could say to himself; *this is my country.* Around noon, he found a restaurant to eat. He did not want his father to think he was forcing himself on him. With his meal, he ordered a stein of beer like the ones he had had more than four years ago. He had finally begun to enjoy having a beer with lunch. He noticed that Nicaraguan and Salvadorian food were very similar and yet they were different. He was both happy and anxious to see his father again. *It is going to be difficult to get close to him but I will give it my best.*

His father's house was on the corner of the block. The day before, the taxi driver had dropped him in front of the left side of the house. Today, as he walked toward it, he was seeing the right side of it. The fear he seemed to feel every time he was about to see his father, returned. He decided to sit on one of the benches of the little park near the house and collect himself. He looked at his father's house. There was a door on this side of it. To the right of the door there were two windows. He deduced that one of the rooms on that side was where his father had taken his siesta. He wondered where the children's rooms were. As he thought of them his fear abated. He realized how much he was looking forward to seeing them. Driven by that emotion, he got up and walked toward the left side of the house. The door was open and he braced himself to face his father. He prepared his smile as he climbed the two steps leading into the house. Memo was about to say good afternoon to his father when he realized he was not there. The secretary told him he was not in.

"When will he return?" Memo asked.

"I don't know."

For a moment Memo was at a loss as to what to do next.

"Are the children here?"

"Yes."

"May I see them?"

"Well, I don't know if . . ."

"Guillermo Antonio!" One of the boys was standing by the dining room door. "Come here," he said conspiratorially.

Memo walked to him. "How are you?"

"Go out and come around to the side door," he whispered.

Memo thought it was a game they were playing and whispered back, "Okay."

The boy ran into the house.

"Good bye," said the secretary as he went by.

Memo thought to tell her he was going around the house to be with the children but something told him that would not be wise.

"Good bye," he said as he went out.

Around the corner, by the door, the three children were waiting for him.

Just like the day before they brought the things they wanted to share with their oldest brother. Memo, as he had the day before, enjoyed them immensely. He was curious about his father and asked them if they knew where he might be. They said they did not know. Something in the way they answered made him ask them if he was always as serious as he was the day before. They looked at each other as if they were hoping the other one would answer first.

"Not always," one of the boys said.

Their guarded ways told him they were not sure if they should say more than that, so he said; "It seems to me he is strict, is he?"

Again they gave each other sidelong glances. "You think so?"

"I don't know, I was wondering."

"Well, sometimes he is very strict."

"How so?"

They glanced at each other again.

"He doesn't like us to cry," one boy said.

"He pinches us and if we cry, he tells us not to."

"Then, he'll pinch us again, and if we get angry he says we should never get angry at our father," said the other boy.

"Then, he'll pinch us again. If we pout, he tells us not to pout. And he'll pinch us again and if we start to cry he gets angry at us and tells us to stop crying."

"He does that?"

The three of them nodded yes. Memo was flabbergasted. "Once," said the other boy, "he picked me up and stood me upon a five foot wall and told me to fall forward and he'd catch me. I said I was afraid to do that and he said not to worry that he would catch me. I said that I was still afraid and he said 'I'm your father, don't you trust me?' and I said that I did. 'Well,' he said, 'jump.' And I jumped. But he didn't catch me. I began to cry and he told me not to cry. I said, 'You didn't catch me!' And he said, 'Let that be a lesson to you.

Never trust anybody. Not even your father.' That's the way he is," he said sadly.

"That's the way he is, ah? I see."

Memo knew that although he sympathized with them and was disturbed by what they had said, he could not criticize their father without risking losing the affection they had given him.

"Well, let's have fun. What game would you like to play?"

Soon the children were laughing and had forgotten about everything else, including their father. Memo could not forget it.

It began to get dark.

"It's time for us to go in. Are you coming back tomorrow?"

"Yes," Memo said, "see you tomorrow."

"See you tomorrow."

He waited for them to disappear into the house. Through the window's wooden shutters, they waived good bye. Memo turned on his heels and crossed the street into the park. All the way to the hotel he thought about what they had said. He debated weather to tell Ted or not. He was not sure. *Of one thing I am sure, I'm glad I wasn't brought up that way.* For the first time in his life he considered that perhaps it had been better not to have had a father.

He went to his godfather's for dinner. He liked Ted very much. He had been generous and supportive in every way. Memo wanted to tell him what he had learned but felt it would have been disloyal to his father if he did. Maybe it was not so much loyalty to his father as it was to his siblings. They had confided in him. Out of need or innocence, they had taken a chance and he could not betray their trust. When Ted asked what had happened, he told him he had had a great time with the children, and left it at that.

"Did you tell your father your plan to go to the United States?"

"No."
"Why not?"
"He wasn't there."
"Maybe he had business out of town. You'll see him tomorrow."
"Yeah, I'll see him tomorrow."

The next day when he came to the house, the secretary told him his father was not in, and to not bother waiting for him because he was out of town.
"Will he be back tomorrow?"
"I don't know. Maybe."
"Could I see the children?"
"No. They are not here."
"When will they return? I'll wait."
"I don't know."
"I'll sit here and wait for them."
"Suit yourself."
He sat on the same chair he had sat before. The secretary kept busy doing whatever she was doing. Memo watched her. He had the distinct impression she did not like him, or at least she was annoyed at him for waiting. Once in a while he thought he heard the children's voices. He would look toward the back of the house and strain to listen. He would look at the secretary wondering if she had heard anything but she would keep on working. He knew there was a side entrance to the house. *Maybe the children have returned and do not know I'm waiting for them.* He waited for sounds that did not come. He could not contain himself any longer.
"Do you think maybe the children are back?"
"No."
"Is it possible they could have come in through the side door?"
"No."
"Do you mind checking?"
She did mind and made sure Memo saw her displeasure before she got up from her desk chair. She went into the house. Memo waited impatiently.

"They are not back," she said, in a way that allowed no questions. She went back to work. Her annoyance at him made him think the children were home. He decided to investigate on his own.

"I'd better go. Please tell my father I came." And he left.

The secretary went on working.

He crossed the street and walked half a block into the park before he looked back to see if she had come out. She had not. He turned left to make sure she would not see him and left again toward the side of the house. The shutters in the windows were closed. He sat on the cement step where the day before the children and he had played. He waited for a few minutes but heard nothing. *Maybe they are not here.* He stood up to leave.

"Guillermo Antonio!" a voice whispered. He turned toward the voice. The shutter was open enough for Memo to see a pair of eyes. It was one of the boys.

"Hi," he whispered. "Come on out."

"We can't."

"Why not?"

"Our father won't allow it."

"Why not?"

"We don't know. He said we are not to see you or talk to you ever again."

"Why not?"

"We don't know. I've got to go. He'd punish me if he knew I talked to you. Bye."

The shutters closed and the hole in Memo's heart re-opened.

Memo staggered across the street and sat on a park bench. He was numb. He could not believe what had just happened. *I must have heard wrong,* he told himself. He stared at the window hoping the shutters would open again. He pushed himself off the bench and crossed the street determined to knock on the door. He raised his fist to knock. His fist hovered near the door. "He'd punish me if he knew I talked to you." He heard the boy's voice in his head. *The maid or the secretary would tell him.* He dropped his fist. *They should not be punished because of me.* He crossed the street again. This time he walked farther before he sat down under the lush canopy of the trees. A breeze wafted softly across his cheek. The birds singing happily above him made Memo look up. Through the leaves he could see the cloudless skies of Managua. *What a beautiful day*, he thought. *Why? Why doesn't he let me see them? Why doesn't he like me? Why?* Questions for which Memo would never receive answers.

He sat there for hours, pondering. The lights in the park came on, telling him dark had descended. He remembered his godfather was going to pick him up at the hotel at seven-thirty. He looked at his watch. *I'd better hurry.* Ted's jeep was waiting in front of the hotel. Memo needed to share his pain and knew he would not be able to hide his feelings. As he ran toward the jeep he saw Ted coming out of the hotel. Ted's smile disappeared the moment he saw Memo's face.

"What happened?"

He held his tears back and spewed all else. Ted could only shake his head.

During dinner, Ted told Penny and their children.

"What are you going to do?" she asked.

"I'm going back tomorrow to ask him why."

"He has a right to control who his kids see."

"But I didn't do anything wrong. We had a great time together. Why wouldn't he want me to see them?"

"I don't know," Ted said, "but if you confront him it's going to be impossible to ask him to help you."

"Yes, I know, But I didn't do anything wrong. I don't understand."

Memo wanted to confront his father, Ted and Penny advised against it.

"Sleep on it and decide tomorrow."

Memo could not sleep. *What is it about me that invites rejection? What did the children tell him that he felt it necessary to take such a drastic measure? I was respectful to him, and loving to his children. Why is he doing this?* In the wee hours, without an answer, he finally fell into slumber.

The next day, as he walked to his father's house, Memo rehearsed his lines. He would ask the question in a way his father would not take offense, but he would ask. He had to ask. *I'm an actor, I can do this. I have to do this.* At the park, he wanted to take a moment and collect himself but was afraid he would lose his courage so he kept going. He found it curious that a part of him was aware of the drama in the situation and it was taking notes. *I'm a better actor than I think if I can divide myself this way.* With the confidence this gave him, he entered his father's house as an actor enters a stage.

But his father was not there.

"He is out of town and I don't know when he will be back," said the secretary.

Memo came back the next day, "He's still out of town."

And the next day, "I don't know when he will be back."

With each day that passed it became clear to Memo his father was going to be out of town until after Memo left Managua. Ted and Penny reluctantly agreed. Memo had only two days left. Each of those two days, Memo called from his godfather's house only to be told by the secretary the same thing.

The morning of his departure arrived. Ted came by to take him to the airport. Memo felt, but for Ted and his family, his trip had been a failure. He got on the jeep and off they were. It so happened that his father's house was on the way to the airport.

"Pull over," Memo said as they passed the house. "Let me try one more time."

"Do you want me to come with you?" Ted said as he stopped the jeep.

"No, thank you. He's probably not even there."

Memo crossed the street and entered the house. There, working at his desk, was his father. Memo knew it was too late to ask all the questions he had. He decided to ask only one. He walked up to his father's desk, just as he had done nine days earlier, and stood in front of his father. His father looked up.

"Yes?"

"I'm on my way to the airport."

"What do you want?"

His heart racing inside of him, Memo said, "I've never asked you for anything. I'm planning to go to the United States to live. Would you help me get there?"

Memo's father stared at him for a long moment.

"No. Go to the United States. I hope you fail. Then, come back here and I'll make a man out of you."

The two of them stared at each other. Memo was stunned. He could believe his father would not help him, but he could not believe his father would wish him harm. Memo looked at his impassive face. It turned out to be the last time Memo would see his father. Deep behind his eyes, tears were forming. With all the dignity he could muster, Memo turned and walked out of his father's life.

Memo cried all the way to the airport. As he told his godfather what had happened, Ted could only shake his head. It was a long ride to the airport, which was a good thing for it gave him enough time to compose himself. He was ashamed of his tears. After all, he was eighteen years old. He apologized to Ted over and over again. His godfather tried but could not console him. They embraced at the gate. Memo gave Ted a wan smile and said goodbye. The young man that boarded the plane back to El Salvador was different than the one that had come to Nicaragua; the hole in his heart was bigger.

Back at home his mother asked and he told her, and he cried. Walking down the street, his best friend Luis asked and Memo told him, and he cried. If, in a moment of shared intimacy, he would tell a girlfriend, he cried. If he just thought about it, he would cry. This went on for years. Then some day, somewhere, he told someone and he did not cry. There are just so many tears allowed for each pain, and Memo had spent all he had for this one.

OF MICE AND MEN

The trip had cost him more money than expected and now he had to make it up. He redoubled his efforts by looking for more work opportunities. More than ever, he was sure his decision to go to the U.S. was the right one. Nothing would stop him from getting there, nothing! The thing about life is that it seems to take pleasure in surprising us. Memo had two surprises coming.

The last time his aunt Dahlia had come to visit, more than a year before, Memo had walked into her bedroom and found her counting little piles of brand new twenty dollar bills she had laying on her bed. He did not know how much it amounted to but it was more money than Memo had ever seen. He did not know his aunt had so much money, though he should have suspected she did since she had been able to send her two children to the United States, pay for their schooling and all their expenses. Violeta had a job now but aunt Dahlia was still taking care of all of Marcelo's expenses. Aunt Dahlia collected all the little bundles, put them into a suitcase and as she was locking it she said, "I am going to sell the car. Do you know of anybody who might want it?" It was a 1948 Pontiac which she had left sitting in the garage all the time she had been in the U.S. His aunt had been the first woman in the barrio to have a car. That car had made it appear as if the family had money. Aunt Dahlia had money; nobody else in the family had any. Still, it had given the family certain status in the neighborhood. Marcelo had learned to drive on that car and his mother would let him have it once in a while, which only made him even more popular with the girls. Memo had wanted to have a car ever since he started to work but could not save enough money to buy one. In those days, in El Salvador, there were no credit plans. You had to pay cash for what you wanted. Some of his new found friends had cars their parents had given them. Memo longed to have one.

"I want it!" said Memo. "Sell it to me."

"No," said his aunt.

"Why not?"

"You can't afford it."

"How much is it?"

His aunt told him. It was more than he expected.

"I'll give you half now, and I pay you the rest in installments."

"No."

"I can do it. I promise."

"No."

His aunt sold it within a week and returned to the United States. Memo was heartbroken. Unwittingly, his aunt was doing him a favor. In his youthful enthusiasm to have a car, he was forgetting about his longing to go to the U.S. Because of his desire to have a car he started bugging those friends who had cars to teach him how to drive. That led to surprise number one.

The parents of his friend Rolando had a 1947 green Studebaker, which they called the submarine because of its pointy nose. Rolando gave Memo a ten minute lesson here, and a fifteen minute lesson there. He got another fifteen minute lesson from Ernesto, whose family owned a beautiful 1951 Buick. From those three lessons he had picked up a little knowledge about how to keep the car in a straight line, turn signals, and the clutch. The clutch was the tricky part. You had to have a certain coordination to control the release of the clutch while depressing the accelerator. Memo noticed each of the cars he had driven had a different clutch tension to which you had to get accustomed in order to shift gears smoothly. If you did not, the car would jerk forward in lurches which made it easy to have an accident. Mastering the clutch was going to take some time and Memo was a young man in a hurry. Which is why he said yes when El Turco asked him if he knew how to drive.

El Turco was a friend of one of his new friends. He was a merchant's son. Many stores in El Salvador are owned by Turks. They are known as excellent traders who will beat you out in any deal you are unlucky enough to get involved in. For this they are both respected and suspected. Just about every Turk's son has the nickname of El Turco. Just about every Turk's son is a nouveau riche. They are looked down upon by the bluebloods but accepted by most others because of their money. Aware of this, the sons spread money around in a way their fathers would not. El Turco was one of those. He had an easy manner, deep pockets and a 1957 Plymouth! In other words, he had everything Memo had not.

El Turco liked Memo, and because Memo dressed well and could pay his share of the tab wherever the group happened to go, he assumed, as many did, that Memo was equally well off. Memo no longer lied about his family's financial status, he just did not talk about it. In any case, one Saturday afternoon the two of them were riding back from a wedding in El Turco's car, when he asked Memo if he knew how to drive. Memo could not say no.

"You drive then," he said as he pulled over, "I don't feel very good." The boys had been doing some heavy drinking at the party.

"Okay," said Memo and as he slid behind the wheel, El Turco went around the car and sat in the passenger's side.

"I just need to close my eyes for a minute and I'll be alright." And he promptly went to sleep.

Memo was ecstatic! Here he was behind the wheel of a 1957, long finned Plymouth! Just like in the movies. His mind told him he should not drive; his heart told him he should. *Where we're going is only a couple of kilometers away, straight down the road. There isn't much traffic because it's Saturday afternoon.* This was true. It was also true that his driving experience amounted to forty minutes. *I'll drive slowly and carefully. Nothing is going to happen.*

With his heart in his mouth, he pulled slowly onto the street. He managed to shift gears without too much jerking. Fortunately, El Turco was fast asleep. The car gained speed and now was cruising comfortably, but Memo was so worried about making a mistake that he was not enjoying it at all. He hoped he would not hit a stop light so he would not have to shift anymore. But it was not to be. The yellow light came on, then the red, and he was forced to come to a stop. The light changed and he started again. This time the tricky clutch got the better of him and the car jerked like a bucking horse as it crossed the intersection. He looked at El Turco to see if he had felt it but he was snoring happily. He did a better job shifting into second and third. He decided to drive at a speed that would allow him to time the lights so he would not have to stop again. He was able to manage this. He started to look for the street name where the place they were going to was located. There was the street up ahead! He had to make a right turn, and had very little practice doing that so he slowed down to a crawl and made the turn. There was a parking spot right there and he took it. He turned off the ignition and for the first time in many a minute he breathed easily. He had gotten away with it, which was good and it was bad. He tapped El Turco on the shoulder to wake him up. Unfortunately for Memo, the others had already arrived and when they saw Memo get out of driver's side of the car they made a big to do about it, which made Memo feel great. Unfortunately for Memo, El Turco had slept through it and had not seen Memo drive, for if he had, what happened later on that night would not have happened.

Drinking and partying seemed to be the two things his group of friends enjoyed doing the most. It was a behavior the Salvadorian middle class appeared to accept from its young men. The girls had to be good girls while the boys ran wild. There were two kinds of parties; the ones in private homes, private clubs or hotel ballrooms where the boys mixed with the good girls, and the other parties in bars and brothels, where the boys mixed with the bad girls. Invariably, the first kind of party was followed by the second. It was an open secret that this was what the boys were doing. Society sanctioned it; men should know about drinking and sex.

It was the second kind of party the boys were about to enjoy at this establishment. Each kind of party had a different drinking code. At the good girls' party the boys would order mixed drinks; rum and coke, bourbon and soda and mostly scotch and water. Most men preferred scotch and water because it was an American drink. It isn't, but most Salvadorians do not know this. It was the drink most often drunk in American movies and middle class Salvadorians, whether they admit it or not, like to drink what Americans drink. When in the company of the good girls, the young men would nurse the mixed drink for fifteen or twenty minutes before ordering another. Memo had learned this double standard from his new friends. At the bad girls party the men would order by the bottle. They would order a bottle of scotch and a bottle of Salvadorian rum for example, and shot glasses. Someone would fill the shot glasses, toast to something or other, and they would down the liquor in one fell swoop. Every ten minutes or less, someone at the table would 'do the honors' and serve another round. And down would go another shot. In this manner they could have six or eight drinks in an hour. If someone happened to arrive late and the group was already on its third or fourth drink, the code demanded he catch up by drinking as many drinks as he was behind. If there were bad girls about, every once in a while one of the men would disappear into a back or upstairs room, and return to the table when he had done what he had done. Upon his return he too would have to catch up. After a couple of hours of this, one by one the young men would pass out until only one would be left standing, or sitting, as long as he was somewhat awake. The idea was to see who could handle his drinking the best, and the one who did, was by implication the manliest of them. After a while, the group had a drinking pecking order, with everybody knowing who would normally pass out first and who last. Your status within the group was directly related to your drinking prowess. In Memo's group, Ernesto was the acknowledged man among men. Memo was in the upper half of this select group, but he could never out drink Ernesto. If you were able to keep up with the leader until the bitter end, the group would be most appreciative of your efforts. As long as you were not consistently the first man down, you were alright. Around three or four in the morning, the survivors, those who could still walk, would go to some greasy spoon and have a hearty hot soup before staggering to their respective homes before dawn. The next day, around noon, they would get together to have a hair of the dog that bit them and recount, if they could remember, in which order the men passed out and who made himself the biggest fool. They would derive great merriment from hearing all the unseemly things they had done. Invariably someone would ask how many bottles the group had 'killed'. Usually the champion would have that answer; the more bottles drunk, the more manly the group. If it was a weekend, the group would start the ritual all over again.

This afternoon, the group found a table, ordered the requisite bottles, and got down to some serious drinking. The drinking they had done at the good girls party was merely a warm up. They took off their coats and ties, rolled up their sleeves, and looked around to see if a new bad girl had joined the stable. Ernesto, or Neto, as his admirers called him, opened the bottles and did the honors. He usually served each round thus setting the pace at which the group had to drink. His implicit message being; see if you can keep up with me. After downing the first shot and eating the first hors d'oeuvre, someone would say; "Who's got a joke." Besides coffee, which is El Salvador's national product, this little country is the largest producer of jokes, relative to its size, than any country in the world. The jokes would start pouring in at about three jokes per one drink ratio. Every group has a joker who seems to tell them best and Memo's group was no exception. Still, it was bad form not to bring at least one or two jokes to share, so during the week each one of them would endeavor to learn a couple for the weekend; the dirtier the better. And so it would go; drink, joke-laughter, joke-laughter, joke-laughter, drink, joke-laughter, joke-laughter, joke-laughter until the arrival of a bad girl would interrupt the pattern, turning the group of six into six separate men in search of sex. She would hang around for a while. If they were no takers she would move on to another table and the jokes would start again; some of them at her expense. As the evening wore off, the jokes would slow down, the men would find company and disappear into rooms. One by one the group would reassemble and they would drink some more. And so it went until the wee hours.

Hard as he tried, Memo could not get it out of his mind that he had driven that beautiful car. The group had killed its first two bottles, Neto had ordered two more, and everybody was having a great time. Memo was feeling great.

"Turco," someone said, "how come Memo was driving your car?"

Maybe El Turco did not want the group to know he had asked Memo to drive because he had been tipsy, or maybe he was just feeling high but he said:

"Memo is my good friend and he can drive my car any time he wants."

And to prove it, he threw the keys to Memo, who caught them in mid air. Neto had just finished pouring another round, lifted his glass, the group raised theirs.

"To good friends!" he said.

They chased the drink with an hors d'oeuvre.

"Who's got the next joke?"

"I've got a joke!" said El Turco.

He started his joke and just when he got to the punch line . . . he passed out.

Everyone roared.

"Hey, that's not fair."

"At least finish the joke, Turco."

"Let him sleep."

"I've got a good one," someone else said.

Everybody leaned in to listen, except Memo. His hand was in his pocket, caressing the car keys. The group roared again, bringing him out of his reverie.

"I'll be right back." said Memo.

"Where are you going?"

"To the restroom."

"Wait, I'll go with you." said Jorge.

On the way to the restroom Memo said, "Actually, I 'm going outside for some fresh air."

"Okay," said Jorge. "See you."

Memo went outside. Across the street was the beige and orange Plymouth. Memo stared at the car. He took out the key and held it by his side. He began to giggle. He remembered what his best friend Luis had told him once. "When I want to impress a girl, I take out my apartment key and hold it by my side like this," he demonstrated, "and they think I have a car." *El loco Luis*, Memo smiled.

"What are you smiling about?" Jorge was standing next to him.

"I was remembering something."

"One of tonight's jokes?"

"Yeah."

"Boy, Neto is pushing the pace tonight."

"Yeah." Memo stared at the car.

"El Turco fell first. He's gonna hear about it at Vicky's party tomorrow."

"Yeah."

"I hate to fall first."

They stood side by side for a while.

"Pretty car. How did you like driving it?"

It was a question no one had ever asked Memo.

"Not bad," he said, sounding as if he was talking about his car.

"Let's go for a ride."

Memo looked at Jorge. He hesitated.

"Come on. El Turco is fast asleep. He won't even know."

Memo could not say no.

They got in the car. Memo tried for the smoothest of gear shifts. The car jerked out of the parking place. "I've had one too many," he said to cover up for his clumsy driving. The truth was that he had a *few* too many. In order to avoid having to stop, he kept making turns and going farther than he should. He began to get nervous. Whatever confidence he had gained that afternoon, vanished. He had never driven at night and that made matters worse. All at once he realized he was lost. His pride did not let him tell Jorge. He tried to find his way back. He found himself going down a steep hill. Jorge, tipsy and unaware of Memo's fears, was having a great time; yelling encouragement as the car picked up speed. Memo stepped on the brake to slow the car down. He did not know how much to press the pedal to counter the gravity pull the hill was exerting on the car. Memo could feel the power of the car on his foot as he vainly tried to slow the car down. His brain told him what his heart had denied; *You don't have the skill to control the car.* He knew at a theoretical level that downshifting would slow the car. He tried to downshift but his inexperience betrayed him. The car jerked as he tried to control the release of the clutch. The road decided to make a sharp left turn, surprising Memo. The screeching started. The rear of the car passed the car's front. Memo realized he was inside a mass of spinning steel. He saw the foot of the mountain coming up at them like a black whale. Jorge was still yelling but Memo did not know if it was from excitement or terror. Memo buried his right foot on the brake. The whale grew larger. The car spun one more time, stalled, hit the whale and . . . stopped. It all had happened faster than it takes to tell it. The screeching and the yelling gave way to a surprising silence. The silence grew longer as Memo's mind tried to return to his head. "Who! Who!" An owl asked, then flapped its wings and took flight. Though the bird was not accusing Memo, he felt that it was. Guilt is a weird thing.

"Jorge, are you alright?" Memo finally asked.

"Yes," said Jorge. "Are you?"

"I think so."

"What happened?"

"I don't know."

But of course he knew. Slowly, they got out of the car. Memo came around to look at Jorge and to be looked at by Jorge. The moonlight showed they were both fine. They turned their attention to the car. It was facing in the direction they had come. The back of the car was against the mountain. From what they could see, it seemed undamaged. Memo gave a sigh of relief. He got in the car and turned the ignition.

The car responded. Jorge got in. Ever so slowly Memo pulled away from the foothill. Somehow he found his way back to the brothel and parked in the same spot he had parked before. He got out, and stepped away from the car. It looked alright. He had gotten away with it again! Just then Jorge called out.

"Memo, come look at this."

He did not have to look to know what that meant. He forced himself to walk around and face the inevitable. The right rear fin had been pushed in by the mountain and the light was broken. Memo's chest caved in.

"Oh no!"

"Not too bad," said Jorge. "A few hundred bucks at most."

A few hundred bucks is all I have in the bank.

"At least we didn't get hurt." Jorge said, trying to cheer Memo up.

"I guess."

"What are you going to do?"

"I don't know."

The two stared at the damage for a long moment.

"I won't tell anybody if you don't," said Jorge.

Memo nodded numbly.

"Well, I'll see you inside," and he took off, like a thief leaves a crime scene.

I shouldn't have driven the car. I shouldn't have listened to Jorge. If El Turco had not thrown me the keys . . . if . . .

But he had. And there was no undoing it. Is it not always that way? *Maybe if Jorge does not say anything . . . maybe . . .* He was trying to formulate a plan in his dizzy brain. He decided he had better go inside and see what Jorge was doing.

Inside, Neto was serving Jorge a drink. El Turco was still asleep. Neto, seeing Memo, called out to him. As he walked toward him, Memo tried to erase the guilt he was feeling on his face.

"Come Memo, you're one behind," and he served him another.

"Where are the others?"

"One is in the men's room vomiting. You can guess where the others are. Salud!"

"Salud!" The three of them drank.

Memo gave Jorge a look. Jorge's look reassured Memo everything was okay. He sat next to El Turco and dropped the car keys in his coat's side pocket as soon as he had a chance. His party mood gone, he was ready to go home. He needed to think how to handle his problem. He had not decided what to do. He knew what he should do. He was not sure he was going to do it. Guilt filled his being. *I need to think!*

"Here comes Rogelio from the men's room," said Neto. "How do you feel, Rogelio? Ready for another drink?"

"No, thanks. I'm ready to go home."

"So early?" said Neto. "Come on, this is Saturday night."

"I'm going out of town tomorrow. Anybody needs a ride?"

"I do," said Memo.

"You too?" asked Neto. Memo nodded.

"See you at Vicky's tomorrow?"

"Yeah, see you."

"See you, Memo."

"See you, Jorge."

They exchanged a knowing look.

Memo could not go to sleep. He had not felt this guilty since he took some dimes from his mother's piggy bank ten years earlier. *Maybe El Turco will not know who did it. Only Jorge knows I drove the car. El Turco might forget he gave me the keys. And even if he does remember he gave me the keys, that doesn't mean I drove it.* Memo had never been in this kind of trouble before, which made his dilemma worse; he either had to pay for the damage or lie. *Because it was Jorge who instigated the idea to go for a ride, he might keep the secret. Somebody else could have hit it while it was parked.* The cost of fixing the car threatened Memo's future. His trip to the U.S. was in jeopardy. *Besides, El Turco is rich and can afford to get it fixed. It's no big deal to him.* He knew he was doing the wrong thing but there was no way out: He would have to lie.

He did not go to Vicky's party on Sunday. He decided he better slow down his social life, concentrate in saving all he could, and try to avoid running into El Turco. It was better to let things cool off. Memo hoped El Turco would shrug it off as a minor incident and move on. But Memo knew that the longer he stayed away from the group the guiltier he would look. He had to see his friends and act as if nothing had happened. He would pick his spots and go to some parties and pray El Turco would not be there. He hated the situation he was in. It could lead to a violent ending and Memo was not fond of fighting. He had only been in one fight in his whole life; many years earlier.

He used to visit a boys social club that had a ping pong table. Memo loved ping pong and was rather good at it. Because there was only one table, if the table was being used, you had to challenge the winner in order to play. Memo had challenged and was waiting to play the winner. Two of his friends were playing: Melgar and Mauricio. Melgar was a bit of a bully and was wont to lose his temper easily. Memo and Melgar had had several disagreements in the past but they had never come to blows. Mauricio was a skinny but smart kid with a sharp tongue which he used to offset his lack of physical attributes. Memo and Mauricio were very good friends. The game was close. Throughout the game, both of the players had been trading insults in order to intimidate each other. Mauricio was winning the verbal battle as well as the game. As the game neared its end, Melgar, trying to intimidate Mauricio, threatened to beat him if he won the game. Mauricio knew that, in a fight, he could not beat the bully, so he said, "If you try to beat me, Memo will defend me."

No one was more surprised than Memo. Melgar stopped the game and asked,

"Memo, is that true?"

Mauricio looked at Memo as if to say, I'm counting on you.

Memo had no other choice than to say, "Yes."

Mauricio proceeded to win the last two points and won the game.

Melgar put down his racket on the table and walked up to Memo. "Time to make good on your promise."

The reason the two of them had not fought before was because neither Melgar nor Memo was sure they could beat the other. They had done a lot of barking but no biting. Melgar had been in a few fights and seemed to enjoy them; Memo had never been in one. Memo was not looking forward to this at all. They squared off and began to circle each other. Memo decided to wait for Melgar to throw the first punch, which he did. Melgar missed and Memo, more as a reflex than anything else, threw one himself. It hit Melgar squarely in his left eye! Melgar went down on one knee, not from the power of the punch but from the pain of being hit in the eye. That was the end of the fight. Melgar covered his eye with his hands. Other kids came to see what was wrong with his eye. They pulled his hands away. His lower eyelid was swollen and already turning green. Cursing Memo for having hit him, Melgar left the building to the accompaniment of Mauricio's taunts. For days after, Mauricio was like a town crier chronicling the happening to anyone who would listen, while Memo tried to discourage him, not wanting to have to fight again if he could help it. Anyway, what was El Turco going to do? Would the joy ride have a violent ending?

A couple of weeks went by without incident and Memo began to relax. Then, at one of the parties the group seemed to have every weekend, Rogelio told Memo the bad news.
"El Turco wants to talk to you."
"What about?" Memo asked.
"I don't know. He's looking for you."
Memo had seen a lot of Western movies and was sure he had heard that line in more than one of them. *The Man Who Shot Liberty Valance* was one. Invariably that line led to a gunfight. Some of his concern was based on reality because several of his friends carried guns. Neto, for example, had a Colt 45 that he brought with him whenever the group went partying. In more than one occasion he had taken it out and threatened to shoot somebody with it. Fortunately he never had, but Memo had noticed that many rich young men carried guns and were not shy about brandishing them, especially when they had been drinking. Memo had read and heard stories about the sons of prominent citizens who had shot somebody. Their parents had sent them abroad until the affair blew over. Memo was hoping that El Turco was not one of those gun-toting guys.

Inevitably, Memo and El Turco ran into each other at a party.

"We have to talk," said El Turco. "Let's go outside."

Memo braced himself for the worst and followed El Turco.

"What happened to my car?"

"What do you mean?"

"You drove my car the last night we were together."

"Yes, you were with me."

"No, you drove it again later that night."

"No, I didn't."

"Then who did?"

The question told him that Jorge had kept his word. He decided to stick with his plan.

"I don' know."

"I gave you the keys."

"And I put them in your coat's pocket."

"You didn't drive it?"

"No. Why?"

"It has a dent in the right rear fin. Whoever did it, will pay for it."

Memo realized El Turco had not believed him but could not prove Memo had done it. He felt bad about lying but relieved. Maybe that was the end of it. El Turco went back inside and told the group what happened and that he suspected Memo and he would find a way of proving it. By the time Memo joined them, they had split into those who believed El Turco and those who believed Memo. One by one his supporters found time to question him. Each time they did Memo pled innocence. Each time he pled innocence he felt worse, but he had gone too far to turn back. The thought of losing his chance to go to the United States kept him from telling the truth. Here and there someone would tell him to look out for El Turco. This created more anxiety in Memo and motivated him to save his pennies. He wrote to Violeta telling her he was saving his money and as soon as the consulate told him his resident visa had come through he would be on his way. He could not wait to leave. Memo was still reeling from surprise number one, when surprise number two occurred.

Besides the resident visa, the last document Memo needed was a valid passport. When he entered El Salvador he was eight years old. His mother's Salvadorian passport showed the two of them smiling at the camera. But Memo's nationality was Nicaraguan and now that he was 18 years old he needed a Nicaraguan passport. He went to the Nicaraguan consulate and started the process. A couple of weeks later he had his passport. The clerk at the consulate told him that the last thing he needed to do was to get it stamped by the Ministry of Exterior so he could leave El Salvador. At the Ministry of Exterior he was told by a clerk, who seemed to have worked there too long and had the power to stamp the passport, that he owed 1,000.00 colónes; equal to $400.00. The clerk said that Memo had to pay it before he would stamp his passport. Memo almost fainted.

"Why do I have to pay so much money?"

"Taxes you owe."

"What taxes?"

"You are a foreigner and you have to pay taxes for living in this country. You haven't paid them and that, plus the penalty for being late, amounts to 1,000.00 colónes."

Memo explained that he had entered the country with his mother as a minor and that his mother was Salvadorian and . . .

"Since you are no longer a minor you can't leave this country without paying these taxes," said the clerk dismissing him.

"Please, you don't understand, I . . ."

"Next!" called the clerk.

Memo walked out of the Ministry in a daze. That was the first, and it would not be the last time Memo would come up against the power of the bureaucracy. If El Turco did not get him, this clerk would. *I'll never get out of this country.* He told his mother what happened and she was sympathetic but could not help.

"La Cheli has been sick for a couple of years now and I'm paying for her doctor bills and her medicine. She is not getting any better, which means I have to continue to pay her bills. Sorry."

"What am I going to do?"

"I don't know."

He was trapped.

For a whole week, wherever he was, whatever he was doing, he went over and over his situation and got the same answer; he was trapped.

Then, one day, while he was sitting at a table in the TV station's café absentmindedly watching the news, he thought he recognized a man who was being interviewed.

"Raise the volume, please," he asked the waitress.

"That was the Minister of Exterior, Mr. so and so and his wife . . ." the news reporter said.

Where have I met that man? Memo thought. *I know him, I know him.* All at once it came to him. *Connie and Teresa introduced me to him!*

Connie and Teresa were sisters. Memo had met them a couple of years back, on the beach, during Holy week. Holy week is a Catholic holiday that the whole country celebrates by going to a beach or a lake or a river; near some body of water. There is no religious meaning to this, is just hot that time of the year. The Church has rituals that it performs for the loyal few, comprised mostly by the poor who cannot afford to go anywhere. The rest of the population is just having a good time. Having a good time to most Salvadorian males means getting drunk, which is what Memo and his friends were planning on doing that particular Holy week. Entire families migrate to the beach and stay, depending on their station, in summer homes, hotels, and champas. A champa is a hut made out of palm tree fronds as a roof. Families sleep in hammocks, which they hang from the posts of the hut. They cook their food in barbecue pits, and swim and drink as much as they can. If they are lucky, the boys meet and frolic with girls under the heat of the sun and kiss and coo under the cool of the moon. That year, Memo and Neto got lucky.

Memo and Neto saw Teresa and Connie for the first time as the girls walked past their champa. They did not look like sisters because Connie was light skinned with straight reddish-blonde hair and green eyes while Teresa was dark skinned, with curly black hair and brown eyes. What they both had in common, however, was their beauty, a quality which both boys did not fail to notice. Their eyes followed the girls, saw them stop and play with the sea for a while, before starting back. Latin American men look at women boldly. Latin American women learn to ignore the bold looks. But if they are interested, the smallest flicker of the eyes tells the men all they need to know. The girls eyes flickered and the boys approached them. From that moment on they were inseparable; Teresa with Memo, and Connie with Neto. It was a magic week. For Neto and Connie the magic ended with the last kiss of the last day of Holy week. For Memo and Teresa the magic went on for almost a year. It was during that period that Memo and Teresa double dated with Connie and the future Minister of Exterior.

He came in his Volkswagen Beetle to pick the three of them up. What made Memo remember the date was that the man, Memo guessed, was in his mid-thirties and Connie had just turned seventeen. *Maybe he is younger but because he is losing his hair he looks older.* Memo wondered what Connie saw in him. Teresa answered the unspoken question when she whispered that he was a lawyer. *I see. He gets points for that. But why is a lawyer driving this tiny car? Usually these guys like to drive big ones.* When Teresa and Memo squeezed in the back Memo understood why the tiny car, and gave the lawyer points for that also. Taking advantage of the closeness the tiny car encouraged, the two couples paid very little attention to each other. After a couple of hours together the lawyer dropped them where he picked them up and took off. Memo and the future Minister of Exterior did not see each other again.

As Memo sat there watching the TV set, he began to formulate a plan. No doubt, the plan he came up with was again influenced by some movie he had seen: He would wait at the steps of the National Palace until the Minister of Exterior would arrive. Memo would approach the Minister of Exterior, and he would remember Memo and Memo would tell him his problem and the Minister of Exterior would sympathize with Memo and help him. It would all work out just like that! What could be simpler? That's what James Dean or Tony Curtis would do. Right?

Early the very next morning, Memo arrived at the National Palace and waited at the bottom of the steps. One by one the cars of all the important men pulled up and the important men would get out and walk up the steps. Finally the Minister of Exterior's car arrived and he stepped out of his chauffer driven car and started to walk up the steps. Memo ran up to him, calling out his name. Suddenly, one of the National Guardsmen was upon Memo, grabbed him by the collar and began to pull him away from the Minister of Exterior, who was being hustled away by another guard. Memo began to yell, "Remember me? We went out together with Teresa and Connie." The Minister of Exterior had reached the top of the steps, hurrying away from the madman that was Memo. Another guard had come over and both of them were now holding Memo and pulling him down the steps. Another guard opened one of the doors of the National Palace. The Minister of Exterior was about to disappear through the door when Memo yelling at the top of his lungs repeated, "Remember me? We went out together with Teresa and Connieeeeee." Memo sounded like Marlon Brando in *A Streetcar Named Desire* yelling his wife's name, Stella, "Stellaaaaa! Stellaaaaa!" The Minister of Exterior stopped, turned on his heels and stepped outside of the palace. "Let him go!" he ordered. "Come over here." The guards let Memo go and he ran up the steps. Memo was about to remind the Minister of Exterior of their date one more time but the Minister of Exterior said, "Follow me." Memo did as he was told and followed him into the palace and through various corridors and offices. Finally, they entered what Memo surmised was the Minister of Exterior's office. He marched right passed the secretary, saying, "Hold all my calls." Memo followed close behind. They entered his office. The Minister of Exterior closed the door and, wasting no time, said in a hostile tone, "What do you want?"

Memo spilled his story. When he was finished, the Minister of Exterior asked, "When do you want to leave?"

"As soon as possible," said Memo.

The Minister picked up the phone.

"Give me the visa department." A long pause ensued.

"This is the Minister of Exterior. I am sending . . ." He turned to Memo.

"What's your last name?" Memo told him.

"I am sending Mr. Castellon to you and I want you to give him a visa. He is not to pay any taxes or penalties. Give him the visa he requires, immediately." He hung up the phone. "You can leave the country anytime you want."

"Thank you," Memo said.

"Good bye," said the Minister of Exterior, and, picking up some papers, he went to work. Memo wanted to express his undying gratitude but it was clear the Minister of Exterior had no more time for Memo, so he opened the door and walked out.

Memo wanted to dance but the deed was not done yet. He kept his emotions under control and found his way to the visa department. The weary clerk, who had dismissed him a few days ago, rose respectfully when Memo entered.

"Mr. Castellon?"

"Yes."

"I'm so sorry. I didn't know who you were. Please give me your passport and I'll stamp it."

Memo gave it to the clerk who quickly stamped it.

"Here you are, sir. Please accept my apologies."

"Thank you."

"Anytime, sir. If there's anything else you require just come by."

It all worked out just like that. Just like in the movies. What could be simpler? Right?

Memo was astonished. As he walked through the maze of corridors that led to the front door of the palace, he stared at the 1,000 colónes stamp. *It only took a phone call. How lucky am I. How nice of him!* The guards who had roughed him up just a few minutes ago were very respectful to him. *The power of power!*

Many years later, after telling the story to a friend, Memo again said, "How lucky I was. How nice he was."

"You *were* lucky," his friend said, "but maybe he wasn't so nice."

"What do you mean?"

"Well, maybe he wanted you out of the country. He might have thought you wanted to blackmail him if he didn't help you. He was married, and you knew about Connie, and suddenly there you were."

Memo considered the possibility for a moment.

"Maybe, but regardless of his reasons, I will always be grateful to him."

Memo had dodged that bullet but feared he had not dodged El Turco yet. His fears came true a few days later when he answered the door and El Turco was standing right there! He pushed Memo aside and entered the house.

"You did it!"

Memo was not sure whether Jorge had said anything so he took a chance.

"Did what?"

"You know. You hit my car!" he yelled.

"How do you know? You were asleep." Memo yelled back.

"I don't know, but it had to be you. You had the keys."

"I put the keys back in your pocket."

"It had to be you."

"You passed out. How can you be so sure?"

"All I know is that you better come up with the money or you're going to regret it! My father is very angry and he wants the 850 colónes!"

Memo's heart sank. "Even if I did it, I couldn't pay you."

"Why not?"

"Because I'm saving to go to the U.S. and I need every penny." Memo pleaded. "Turco, give me a break!"

Even though he had not admitted he had done it, even though he was not going to pay him, Memo's plea somehow reached El Turco's heart.

"You better pay me before you go," he said the anger vanishing from his voice. And with that, he walked out of the house, slamming the door as he went.

Memo was crushed. He had all but admitted his guilt. The years of Catholic indoctrination came back full force to make him feel ashamed. What a terrible feeling is shame. Memo recognized that El Turco was right and that he was a nice guy who did not deserve to have been betrayed. But Memo also knew that if he paid him, another year would go by before he could fulfill the dream he was so close to realizing. Memo did not want to give up his dream and so he never paid him. El Turco never asked for the money again.

NOT A SHED OF TEAR

"Guillermo!" La Cheli called from her room. She did not like to call him Memo; she thought it was a sissy name. She was very sick now. He rushed to her side.

"What was all that slamming and yelling?" La Cheli asked.

"Nothing," Memo said. "Just a misunderstanding. Can I do something for you?"

"Yes," said La Cheli.

"What?"

"Sing me a song."

Memo was not in the mood to sing. *Now, she wants me to sing to her!?* Memo had waited for those words for so long.

"I'll be right back," he said. He went to his room and got the guitar.

"I only know a couple a songs," he said.

"Sing the one you do best," she said.

"*Vereda Tropical.* You like that one?"

"Just sing."

His fingers trembling with every chord change, Memo sang her the bolero. "Voy por la vereda tropical," Memo sang, hoping his voice would not crack. He knew there was only one great voice in the family, and it was not his. Over the course of the song, he forgot about El

Turco and by the time he finished he was enveloped in the poignancy of the moment.

"Not bad," the old lady said, "not bad at all."

"Thank you," Memo said, "thank you."

"Now, get out of here. I need to sleep."

He felt grateful. He backed away toward the door, as vassals withdraw from kings. A week later, La Cheli died.

He was watching an afternoon movie at the Cine Central when someone tapped him on the right shoulder. He turned to see his friend, Luis.

"Luis, what are you doing here?" Memo whispered.

"Your grandmother just died," Luis whispered back.

Memo sprang to his feet and he and Luis began to walk fast up the aisle.

"How did you find out?"

"Your mother called the TV station to tell you, but you had already left. She asked me to find you and tell you."

"How did you know I was here?"

"I didn't, but knowing you, I guessed you would be in a movie theater. I hired a taxi and started to go from theater to theater. This is the fifth one."

They got into the cab and Luis gave the driver the address. Though Memo had seen this coming, it was still a shock. It was the first time in his life someone in his family had died. He had seen movies in which this had happened. Crying and screaming usually followed. He was doing neither. He did not know how to interpret his reaction. *Shouldn't I be crying or something?* He looked at Luis who was looking at him. Luis' look of concern made Memo wonder what his friend was thinking. *Does he think I'm acting weird because I'm not crying? I am feeling something.* He searched within him to pinpoint what he was experiencing. *I'm feeling . . . nervous!* That surprised him. For some reason that had not been an emotion he expected. *But I don't feel tears coming.* Memo was puzzled at his reaction. No one prepares one for this. *I hope Luis doesn't think me callous.* "You're handling yourself well," Luis said with a sense of pride. Memo felt relieved. Maybe Memo was not Luis' best friend but Luis was Memo's best friend and his opinion counted. Memo looked up to Luis because he was so talented. Luis was a very popular young actor, only a few years older than Memo but light-years more accomplished. Luis had studied acting at a conservatory somewhere and was the most versatile actor in El Salvador. Memo wished he had half the talent Luis had. Luis, for his part, had been very supportive of Memo and had become like an older brother. *He thinks I'm handling myself well. I'm not trying to do that. I'm trying to figure out what it is that I'm supposed to be feeling at this moment. But to him, it seems that I'm being courageous. Maybe I am being courageous and I don't know it. I do have a sense of loss but not nearly as deep as I think I should have. How much is one supposed to feel at moments like this?* Most people tend to think that relatives automatically love each other, or at least, that they should. *La Cheli and I were never affectionate with each other. We never hugged. She never had a kind word for me. I don't hate her. I just don't have a lot of love for her.* Memo could not help but feel guilty about that. *I wish I could feel more deeply about her death but my heart is doing what it's doing.* She could be mean but he had gotten accustomed to her ways and accepted that it was not in her nature to be a loving person. It was not a loving family anyway. *I'm not happy she has died. I'm not sad either. I'm . . . I don't know what I am right now.* La Cheli and he had become, if not friends, not enemies.

"We're here," said Luis, patting Memo on the back and snapping him out of his trance. "You're doing great Memo. Great." Luis slapped him on the back.

He decided to deal with his lack of sentimentality at another time. He had things to get done. He did not know what those things were, but he was sure he had to help his mother deal with La Cheli's death.

It turned out he did not do much. His mother was grieved but in control. The Gomez', the neighbors from the corner house, had been helping and in the few hours since La Cheli had died what had to be done was being done. The family owned a burial plot and the cemetery had already been contacted. His mother had insurance that covered the burial expenses and a coffin would be delivered shortly. Dahlia, Violeta, and Marcelo had been called and were booking a flight for the next day. They would call the Gomez' to tell them the time of arrival. Memo's family did not have a telephone. Few families in his neighborhood did. It was a luxury to have a private telephone line but the Gomez' had a business line for their pharmacy. The burial would take place the day after their arrival. There would be a wake that night in the house and the Gomez' were helping with the preparations. Memo was ready to do something but there was little for him to do. He did bring something, lift another thing, and take away something else. All major decisions had been made. The women were in charge. Chairs were being brought by neighbors for the wake. Funeral homes were seldom used in El Salvador so everything would take place in their house. Food was being prepared, liquor bought. Memo's job was mostly to stay out of the way of the traffic. One of the Gomez' ladies came to say Dahlia had just called to say she and Violeta were arriving the next afternoon. Marcelo was not coming. No explanation why. Before he knew it, the afternoon turned into night and people began to arrive for the wake. Memo had an American style dark blue suit he had bought a year earlier. He put it on, and began to receive people. He was a combination of maitre'd and waiter. People he had never met showed up to pay their respects, or to see if La Cheli was really dead. Some of them, Memo knew, La Cheli would not have allowed in her house. She was fond of saying that so and so would never set foot in her house. La Cheli had grudges with people that went back fifty years. Forgiveness was not one of her qualities and she probably would have gotten out of her coffin if she could, to throw out some of the people who showed up that night. It would have been a long night but for the booze. After a while it was more like a party. People had to be reminded of the occasion in order to keep the laughter down. Memo, who usually did not drink in front of his mother, did so that night. That made him feel better because, hard as he tried, he could not muster the right amount of sorrow required by the occasion. He did a good job and played his part well as he accepted the condolences of friends and strangers. Around three o'clock, his mother, emotionally and physically drained, told Memo she was going to bed and for him to stay up as necessary. In the wee hours of the night there were still some who hung around to eat the last morsel and drink the last drop. It was almost daylight when the last man left. All the women had left long before. It's amazing how much the grievers enjoyed themselves that night. At last, Memo was able to go to bed.

But not to sleep. La Cheli was dead! He had not dealt with that reality. So many things had happened in so few hours—life changing things. La Cheli was not his grandmother, though to the world who knew him, she was. He had said she was so many times that he had come to believe it. When he arrived at her house from Mexico, more than ten years earlier, Memo was hungry for a family, hungry for love. It had been a long and exhausting trip; it had started in Mérida, the state capital of Yucatan, with a long bus ride that took them to the port of Campeche, where they boarded a cargo ship, with less than stellar accommodations, that would take them to Veracruz. During the voyage across the Gulf of Mexico, a three day hurricane all but sunk the ship. When they finally made it to shore they took an even longer bus ride to Mexico City where his aunt Dahlia was waiting. After three days rest, Dahlia got on a plane to El Salvador, leaving María and Memo to take a five day bus ride to get there. All together they covered a distance of two thousand kilometers. Years later, looking at a map of Mexico and Central America, Memo wondered why they had taken such a circuitous route when they could have traveled only seven hundred kilometers if they had gone straight down the Yucatan peninsula to Guatemala and then El Salvador. But Memo was only eight years old and did not question his mother. He was happy to be with her. He did ask her why was it that his aunt was flying while they were going by bus. His mother said, "That's the way things are," and left it at that. Though Memo did not understand the statement, he was so happy he was about to finally have a family that he, too, left it at that. After a few days in La Cheli's house, he understood how things were.

"Hurry up, Marcelo! Open the door!" Violeta was urging her brother. Sixteen year old Marcelo and seventeen year old Violeta had come down to open the street door to let them in. Violeta was effusive and embraced them both, Marcelo was friendly but guarded. The teenagers led María and Memo up the twenty-one meandering steps that led to the house's front door. Waiting at the top was the queen of the house; Dahlia, and just behind her, the queen mother; La Cheli. There they all were. *My family!* Memo thought. *An aunt, two cousins, a grandmother, and a house to call my own!* A glorious ending to the three nightmarish years he had spent at the boarding school his mother had seen fit to put him in. At last, Memo had his family. Or so he thought.

Memo opened his heart to all of them. It was not so much a conscious choice as it was a need—and a hope. The orphan years were over! The good life was about to begin; the family life. They showed them the L shape house: Marcelo's room, the living room, Dahlia's room, the bathroom, (which contained a bidet, a contraption he had never seen before), Violeta's room, La Cheli's room, and the dining room. The bedrooms and the living room all had balconies from which one could see the street below. All rooms, but the bathroom, opened into a corridor. All the rooms, including the corridor, were tied together by a nice tiled floor. Except for the kitchen, where the maid was busy cooking dinner, which had a cement floor. It was a nice house; clean, roomy, and homogeneous. In the dining room there was a Frigidaire refrigerator—a luxury in those days. The dining room started the second half of the L. Then they were led to their room. It did not take a genius to notice the homogeneity had stopped. The rectangular room had a cement floor, the walls, though newly painted, were rough-hewn, the wood of their door not as nice as the doors of the rest of the house. Next to their room was another room of the same quality where tenants lived. Next to that room was a tiny room where the maid lived. Farther down, there were two more rooms where two more families lived. To the right and downhill of the guava tree there were two smallish rooms. In one lived El Sapo Miguel and his family, and next to him lived Hilario. Near the bottom of the hill, along the third wall of the property, there were several banana trees. Near the banana trees there was a shack that turned out to be a bathroom. Up from the shack there were two mango trees and a cashew tree. The forth wall of the property abutted against Victor's lumber business. It was all sort of rustic but to Memo it looked like paradise. Memo could see himself climbing all those trees, eating all that fruit, playing in all that space.

The only thing that bothered him was the marked difference between the main house and the rest of the house where Memo and María were to live. Memo noticed the tenants' rooms had dirt floors, which served as consolation. Memo and María were not tile floor but neither were they dirt. They were cement!

It became clear that Memo and María were not on the same level as the rest of the family and, with every passing day, La Cheli and aunt Dahlia made that distinction clearer. La Cheli was a humorless woman prone to anger and not shy to verbalize it. This was not your every day grandmother. She let Memo know that he was not to climb up the guava tree or the two mango trees without her permission. And that the fruit from all trees belonged to her and she would decide which pieces of fruit he could eat and which were to be put aside for Dahlia and her children. At first Memo thought she was joking but he soon realized La Cheli never joked about anything. Dahlia made it clear that everything in the refrigerator was hers. Out of the goodness of her heart she would separate a corner of it for María to put some perishables in, but the rest was to be respected by both of them or else they would not be allowed to put anything in it. They were also told that the bathroom was not for them to use. They were to use the one down at the bottom of the hill which was used by the tenants and which consisted of a wooden box with a hole on top where you could crouch or seat if you wanted to relieve yourself. Memo never sat on the fetid box for as long as he lived in that house. Next to it was a cement basin where a gourd floated in the cold water and which Memo learned to use to wash his hands and body. It was an act of courage to splash your body with that cold water even in the warm summer days. The hovel's walls were made of rotting wood through which anyone who cared to could look in. No one did, not so much out of respect but because everyone had to endure the same lack of privacy, so everyone kept away when it was being used. The roof was made out of corrugated metal. It sat on top of the walls; gravity keeping it in place. It was full of holes and so when it rained, you could kill two birds with one stone; you could take a shower while you squatted over the box. These commandments were laid down within the first twenty-four hours of their arrival. The honeymoon was already over. Memo's hopes for a family were shattered. For as long as they lived in that house that was the way things were. Later on, when Dahlia and her children left to live in the U.S., aunt Dahlia's side of the house was locked so Memo and María never had access to the bathroom, the living room, or the dining room. Their dining room, their living room, and their bedroom was the little room they shared for ten years.

Lying in his bed on his side of the room, Memo pondered what was going to happen next, now that La Cheli was dead. Then, like a bolt of lightning it hit him. *What is going to happen next is that I'm going to the United States sooner than expected!* He was overcome with happiness. He was ready to go. He had all his papers ready and had saved his money. Not as much as he wanted to have but he had to grab the opportunity while it was here. It was not happening as he had planned, but why not go now? *Violeta is going to be here today. I could go with her when she returns.* That was perfect! In the middle of his ecstasy he was overcome with guilt. How could he be so selfish at such time? He was supposed to be grieving; instead here he was smiling from ear to ear. A moment ago he could not go to sleep. Now he did not want to go to sleep. *I will ask Violeta. I'll have to wait for the right moment.* He did not want to appear insensitive. *I will do it out of ear shot of aunt Dahlia, just in case.* He could not take the chance that, if in a bad mood, Dahlia would order Violeta to say no. From that moment on he could think of nothing else but the United States!

He heard his mother stirring in her bed and decided he might as well get up too since he could not sleep. His mother asked at what time he had gone to bed. Memo told her. His mother told Memo to go back to bed. He said he wanted to help her and after a quick breakfast he did just that. Dahlia had entrusted La Cheli with the keys to the main part of the house. María found them and the two of them set out to clean all the rooms except Dahlia's which needed another key. Before they knew it, the afternoon had come and it was time to go to the airport. His mother said that the night before someone had volunteered to pick them up and it wasn't necessary for them to go. "They'll be here any minute."

Sure enough, within a half hour there they were, elegantly dressed in mourning colors. They had taken but a few steps onto the corridor when both broke down. Violeta let out a scream, her knees buckled from the pain she was experiencing and had to lean against the wall or she would have fallen from grief. Dahlia had to sit down on one of the corridor's chairs before she could continue on to the dining room where La Cheli lay in her coffin. The people who had brought them ran to their aid. It was obvious to those present how much love the two of them had for La Cheli. Memo's mother had yet to shed a tear. She had been too busy doing all the necessary chores. María was shocked at the tragic display because she had been telling them for months about La Cheli's deteriorating condition and that if they wanted to see her alive one more time, to come and see her, and soon. Given how much they loved her she could not understand why they had not come. For several minutes, all who were there attended to the two arrivals. At last, with the help of those around, they were strong enough to walk the last steps to the coffin, where again another wail and another rush to aid them took place. María and Memo stood outside the dining room which was now crowded with people helping Violeta and Dahlia. María looked at Memo and said nothing. Nothing needed to be said. The neighbors, who had seen María doggedly and silently go about taking care of all the burial details, began to wonder if María loved La Cheli as much as Violeta and Dahlia did. Neither Memo nor María could bring themselves to tears. They suffered the judgment of their friends in silence. It was obvious to all who loved La Cheli most.

The next morning, the four of them stood around the grave as La Cheli's coffin was lowered into the gaping hole. Dahlia and Violeta threw a handful of dirt onto the coffin as it was being lowered. María followed suit. Memo assumed he, too, was supposed to, and did so. When the coffin was down and the straps that lowered it, out, each of them in turn threw a flower onto the coffin and spoke something unintelligible. Memo, who had also been given a flower, now understood what he was to do with it. Murmuring something even he did not understand, he threw in his flower. For an interminable moment they stood looking down at the coffin. Dahlia and Violeta had been crying since they got out of the car and were still doing so. Memo looked at his mother who was at last silently weeping. He had yet to cry. He realized this long moment was the last he would share with La Cheli and was touched, but tears would not come. As the moment wore on, he felt more pressured to cry. He felt the eyes of all the neighbors upon him, waiting, waiting. He began to admonish himself. He asked himself what was wrong with him. An actor friend of his had told him that, to make himself cry in a play he was doing, he would stare hard at an object on stage a few moments before the required tears were to come and thus he had managed to achieve this dramatic moment every performance. Memo was desperate to show his love for La Cheli and so he stared unblinkingly at the coffin as hard as he could. No tears. *Maybe I'm not staring hard enough.* He redoubled his efforts. Memo sensed that the moment, as long as it already was, was ending. *Please! At least one tear.* Nothing. In a desperate effort to show something, he brought a hand to his eyes and covered them. With his thumb and middle finger he squeezed his eyes hoping to at least show some redness in his eyes if someone looked at him. Finally Dahlia and Violeta thought it was time to leave and stepped away from the grave. Taking their cue from them, everybody started to scatter. Just to be safe, Memo kept his chin to his chest as he followed the group toward the car.

It had something to do with integrity, or social expectations. That was the only explanation he could manage. *I can't cry just because people want me to do so.* But this was not enough to absolve him. He felt guilty. He felt lacking. He did care about the unforgiving old lady. He sensed there was a good woman under all that bad temper.

Like Henry Higgins, she was indiscriminate in her abuse. La Cheli's half-sister had been the prettier of the two and had married more than once. La Cheli held a grudge against her for something that had happened decades ago, and the mere mention of her name would make La Cheli fly into a rage. Many people and many things would send her into a rage. She was comfortable with rage. It was her primary color. After a while one became inured and would ignore her. It took him a year or two, but Memo learned to accept her just as she was and became somewhat fond of her.

She might have, begrudgingly, taken them back ten years ago, and in doing so she had given them refuge, but not solace. She never forgot nor forgave María for having gone against her wishes. Somehow, Memo was also blamed by her. Or maybe he was just the reminder of her mother's straying. Memo could never understand why he was treated as he was; somewhere between a foster child and a stranger. Love, which he had hoped to receive from her, was never given; and if it was, he had been hard put to understand its expression. He always thought he was barely a step above the tenants who lived with them. That is not the way he thought family members should treat each other. He never got any expression of love from her until, maybe, the week before she died. Her asking him to sing had been maybe, in her eyes, her way to tell him that she did love him. Memo chose to think so.

But it was not enough to erase ten years of insults and slights. He wondered what had happened in La Cheli's childhood that so embittered her. Still, that day, by her grave, he felt the lack of tears reflected poorly on him. Maybe he, too, was neither forgetting nor forgiving. We learn from our families how to behave and La Cheli had taught him emotional distance.

Over the years that followed he had occasion to cry in plays he was in, and managed it. Not by staring at an object as his friend had counseled but merely by letting it happen. And yet, twenty-six years later, when his mother passed away, Memo was unable to wrench a tear. Was that La Cheli's legacy?

HOME, SWEET HOME

The tears pretty much stopped after that morning and the rest of their stay passed quite in the same way as the other visits they had made. *Life must go on, I suppose.* Memo was glad of this because it made it easier to find a moment of levity in which to broach the subject of going to the United States with Violeta. He waited patiently for the moment and chose it well.

"Are you ready?"
"Yes. I have everything except my plane ticket."
"How much money will you take with you?"
"Two hundred and fifty dollars."
"That's not a lot. You're going to have to find a job quickly."
"I will. I promise."
"Get your ticket, we leave in a week."

He could not believe it. Even though he had been dreaming about this for years he could not believe that in a week it would finally come to pass. Ironically, La Cheli's death had precipitated it. He had expected to leave in a few months. He would have more money and he would have been able to mentally prepare for the long awaited trip. Boom! Here it was. He told his mother and she accepted it with her usual stoicism.

She would have also preferred a smoother plan but she understood Memo's decision. Spite the fact that La Cheli had been a burden to her for endless months; she was also an anchor that gave her life meaning. Suddenly she was losing them both. She felt empty. She felt free. She could again fend for herself and no one else; no responsibilities. Not since she was single had she felt like this. No Elías, no La Cheli, no Memo. Only María.

Memo bought his ticket the next day. He gave notice at the station that he was leaving and said farewell to the company of radio actors with whom he had worked the last four years. No one seemed to be sorry to see him go. A few wished him well, most were happy to get the parts he was leaving behind. He told his closest friends and had a few drinks with them the night before he left.

That last night, as he lay in the best bed he had ever had, he took stock of his Salvadorian years. He recalled the arduous trip that brought him to El Salvador, made bearable by the hope his heart held: He was coming home to his country. He was coming to his family. He was coming home.

It was a chilly morning in Mexico City in the waning days of 1950. Christmas was a week away. Aunt Dahlia's bags were replete with presents she was taking to her children. The taxi driver was putting her bags in the trunk. "See you in San Salvador," aunt Dahlia said to them as she got into the taxi that would take her to Mexico City's International Airport. Memo was impressed with his aunt. His mother had told him she was beautiful, and she was. Apparently she was also rich, judging by the money she had spent in the three days they shared with her. They stood there watching the cab speed away.
"How long does it take to fly to El Salvador?" Memo asked.
"A few hours."
"How long will it take us to get there by bus?"
"A few days."
His mother's voice sounded annoyed. She knew what he was going to ask next. She had always encouraged him to ask questions, telling

him never to be afraid to ask anything. Many times she had regretted it. This was one of those times.

"Why is she flying while we are going by bus?"

"That's the way things are," she said in a tone of voice Memo knew meant, no more questions.

Something was wrong. He did not know what, but it seemed wrong for his aunt to leave them. *We are a family*, he thought, *we should be together.* Maybe he misunderstood the meaning of the word. It was not unusual for him to think he knew a word's meaning only to find out he did not. The whole family thing was new to him. *Be patient. In a few days it will all be alright.*

Early the next morning they boarded the bus that would take them home. He could not contain his enthusiasm. He asked if he could sit by the window and his mother, seeing him so happy, smiled as she said yes. He spent his time looking out of the window enjoying the adventure. He noticed his mother was preoccupied with something and asked her what was wrong. She told him it was nothing but he knew better. He had always been able to sense his mother's moods. Even after the three years of separation, he could tell when she was sad. He insisted and she, needing to unburden, told him.

"The last time I saw La Cheli she was extremely angry with me. I'm worried she might still be."

"When was that?"

"Eight years ago."

"That's as long as I've been alive. She can't be still angry."

"You don't know La Cheli."

"I know no one can be mad that long."

"You don't know La Cheli."

The bus stopped at a small town and vendors rushed to sell food and refreshments to the travelers.

"Can I have an horchata?"

"Sure," said his mother, reaching for some coins to give him. He paid the Indian woman and she handed him his refreshment. Everybody in the bus was buying something. This scene would repeat itself each time the bus stopped. The bus started up again. Memo noticed that the further away they got from a city or town, the worse the roads became. At first the bouncing was fun. At least Memo thought so. But even he began to find it uncomfortable after a few hundred kilometers.

"Are we going to stop at a hotel to sleep?"

"No, we'll ride through the night."

"Really?"

"Really."

The night began to fall and soon they were surrounded by the kind of darkness only those who live in the country get to see. It was fun and it was scary. With the night, it got cold in the drafty bus. That, and all the bouncing, made it difficult to fall asleep but eventually he did. From behind a cloud, the pale circle of the moon appeared, sending its silvery slivers down to the bus, through Memo's window and to his uplifted face. His mother, who was looking down at her son, caught the moment. It seemed as if the moon was reaching down to touch Memo's hopeful face with her ephemeral fingers. María was returning to her country for his sake. She hoped she had made the right decision. A large black cloud, jealous, covered the moon. The bus fell back into darkness.

The yelling and screaming that the vendors do to get the travelers to buy from them woke them up. Breakfast was right there at their window. While they waited for a new driver to arrive, they had time to eat, get off the bus and find a bathroom in which to wash their sleepy faces. Refreshed, they got back on the bus and started the second leg.

"I might as well tell you why La Cheli is mad at me. She's going to tell you in her way, and I want to be the one to tell you what happened."

María took a deep breath before continuing.

"She's mad at me because I married your father."

"Why?"

"Because she didn't like him."

"Why?"

"Because she thought he was arrogant."

"Was he?"

"Maybe. But it was more that that."

"What?"

"He didn't cow tow to them."

"What's wrong with that?"

"Nothing. I liked that about him. Between you and me, they were afraid to lose me. I had so many roles in so many plays that if I left the company they would have a tough time replacing me. They didn't want to have to do that and so Dahlia and Lalo convinced La Cheli that I shouldn't marry him."

Memo liked it when his mother said 'between you and me'. It made him feel that she trusted him. It made him feel adult.

"I loved your father and I did what I thought was right. Lalo and Dahlia were very upset and encouraged La Cheli to threaten to disown me if I didn't obey her."

"What does disown mean?"

"It means that they would turn their backs on me. Never again accept me as a member of the family."

"Oh, I see." Memo felt the import of what his mother had just told him.

She let it sink in. It was something she had wanted to tell him, should have told him a long time ago. It might have made the three years in the boarding school less painful. Maybe she thought he was too young to understand.

"That's why I haven't been back."

"And now?"

"Violeta begged La Cheli to forgive me and let me return.

La Cheli adores Violeta and that's why she has relented."

"What's that mean, relented?"

"She's given in."

"That's good, no?"

"Well, I know La Cheli. She's never changed her mind about anything. I'm afraid she's only doing it to please Violeta."

"She hasn't forgiven you."

"No. But there's nothing to forgive. I was 27 years old. I had a right to marry anyone I wanted. I did what I thought was right. I still think so. Anyway, sooner or later it's going to come out and when it does you'll know the truth."

"I understand."

He did seem to understand. She was always surprised at his apparent maturity.

"Good." And she never mentioned it again.

Two days later the driver stopped at a little town and told everyone to get off.

"Are we there?"

"No," said his mother. "We have arrived at the border with Guatemala. See that bridge? On this side is Mexico and the other side is Guatemala."

Memo was amazed. The idea that the little bridge separated the two countries seemed fantastic to him. On the other side of the bridge there was another little town. Memo could see no difference between one town and the other. In fact, it looked like any of the other towns they had seen that had bridges just like this one. For all intents and purposes it was one town, except that the two sides were in different countries. All the bags were taken down and everyone had to carry theirs to a little one-room house where a man wearing something like a uniform asked them for their passport. His mother gave him her passport. The little man looked at it for a moment and asked for money, which his mother gave him. He then stamped one of the pages and told them to go across the little bridge. They did as he said. Right in the middle of the bridge there was a painted yellowish line. His mother stopped and told him what the line meant.

"On this side of the line is Mexico. On the other side is Guatemala."

Memo could not believe that the line had such power. He stood there looking at the line. All the other passengers went by, seemingly in a hurry to get to the other side where a line was forming in front of another little house. His mother seemed amused. She understood his perplexity. Maybe it reminded her of the first time she had crossed a border. Memo put one foot on the other side of the line and stood there astride it.

"Look mamá, I'm in two countries at the same time." His mother laughed.

She looked at him the way parents do when they think their child is the greatest kid in the world. Memo loved to see her look at him that way.

"The dirt's the same, the vegetation's the same, the houses the same, the people the same, yet because someone has painted this line my right foot is in Guatemala and my left in Mexico."

"Incredible, isn't it?"

"Incredible!"

She let him stand there a little longer.

"We better go to the other side to get our bags inspected so we can pass customs and get on that other bus."

"Customs? What's that?"

She explained as they walked to the little house.

There, another little man that could have been the twin brother of the man in the other house, asked them to open their bags.

"Anything to declare?"

"No," said María.

The man looked through the bags then told Memo's mother she could close them. He asked for money which she gave him and he stamped their passport and told them they could get on the new bus. They were the last to get on it. Memo observed that even though it was a different bus, everyone had sat in the same seats as the first bus. Their seat was waiting for them. The group had been together for three days and some tribal law was at work. Everyone was buying food and refreshments. The food and refreshments were the same, yet different. Off they were toward Guatemala City.

The round Mayan faces of ancient Tikal were the same on both sides of the border but the way they spoke Spanish was different. The singsong characteristic to the Mexican dialects was replaced by the less musical Spanish spoken in Guatemala. Memo noticed that Guatemalans used the pronoun vos instead of the tu used in Mexico.

"They have a different way of talking."

"Yes," said María, "all Central Americans except for Panamanians use vos instead of tu."

"Why?"

"I don't really know. Preference, I guess. Both forms exist in the Spanish spoken in Spain. The Central Americans, except the Panamanians, chose the vos. Argentineans and Uruguayans also use it."

"Will I have to switch to vos?"
"Not if you don't want."
"Are you going to?"
"No."
"Then, I won't either."
There was an enormous price to be paid for making that decision.

María had learned to speak in the Mexican style and preferred it to the Central American. María viewed traveling as a living school. Although her formal education was limited, she had been traveling for almost two decades and had developed a cosmopolitan flair. Though she was coming back to El Salvador financially broke, what she had to show for all those years abroad was what she had become. The more than eight years, after she left the Compañia Encanto, had been very difficult. The last five years spent in Mexico more so. Mexico had a closed-door policy with regards to foreign artists. María had to lie in order to get work. She had to pretend she was Mexican in order to work, which was why she adopted the Mexican accent. Whereas with the Compañía Encanto she had second leads, in Mexico she had to take whatever she could get. She had managed to work because she was good. The ten years she spent with the Compañía Encanto had served her well, but it was difficult to develop a career with the constant threat of getting caught. Time was passing and she found her age working against her. Jobs were harder and harder to get and they were paying her less and less. She could not return to El Salvador broke *and* homeless. La Cheli was unforgiving and so María's exile continued. She had shared none of this with Memo. Maybe she did not want to burden him or maybe she thought there was no point in telling him. Now that she was returning she hoped her many years of travel and experience would give her an advantage over artists who had never left El Salvador. It should. Mexico was far more advanced than Central American countries industrially, economically and artistically. She knew Mexican artists were admired in El Salvador. Mexico dominated all Latin America with its thriving motion picture industry as well as its recording industry. No Central American artist could compete with Mexican stars. Salvadorian artists yearned to go to Mexico to prove themselves. She had held her own in Mexico and knew she could more than hold her own in El Salvador. She had to pretend, however, that she was coming back to her country on her own terms. Part of that pretense included keeping the Mexican accent she had acquired. It was a risky proposition. Some would say: "Isn't she Salvadorian? Why is she talking with that phony Mexican accent?" If she did not keep the Mexican accent, others would say: "All those years abroad. Didn't she learn anything?" She knew she would be vulnerable to those attacks. She decided that if it was going to be tough either way, she might as well do it her way. Memo would suffer attacks too, but he did not know it yet.

The whole of that day and night was spent crossing the length of Guatemala. The next morning they found themselves waiting to cross the border into El Salvador. Memo had the opportunity to straddle two countries again as he stood with one foot in Guatemala and the other in El Salvador. Just as they had the day before, they celebrated the event. After they cleared customs and boarded the new bus, Memo was exhilarated by the knowledge that he was just a few hours from San Salvador and his family. María was apprehensive. Soon her fears would be confirmed. Most painful of all was seeing Memo's gradual disappointment as he realized he was a second class citizen in his own family.

At last they arrived in San Salvador. Memo and María got off the bus. There was no one from the family to welcome them.

"Where are they?"

"Probably at the house."

"Don't they know we're arriving today?"

"Yes, but they don't know on which bus. We'll take a taxi to the house. San Salvador is not a large city. We'll be there in a few minutes."

At a stop light, while waiting for the light to change, María called out.

"There's the house on the left; the one sitting on top of that tall gray wall."

Memo looked up to see the yellow house with the burgundy red balconies. Out of the middle balcony two young faces poked out.

"That's Violeta and Marcelo. Your cousins."
The taxi pulled up in front of the house.
"We are coming down to help you with your bags," yelled Violeta.
María paid the taxi driver. She looked at Memo and gave him a kiss on his forehead.
"We're home," she whispered. She had made good on the promise she had made to him in Campeche to bring him home.
At last I'm in my home, with my family, in my country.
On the other side of the door they heard Violeta telling Marcelo to hurry up and open the door.

La Cheli made no attempt to disguise the fact that María and Memo were, in her estimation, inferior to Dahlia and her children. She had not forgiven María and though she had opened her house to her, she had not opened her heart. María withstood the barrage of insults, implicit and explicit, as the price to pay until she could get back on her feet. She was good at suffering in silence and had had plenty of practice over the years she had lived with Dahlia and La Cheli. Unfortunately she did not tell her son, perhaps in hopes La Cheli would not extend her displeasure to him and the boy would be given a chance. Maybe she did not want to prejudice him against the family so he would approach them with an open mind. Unaware of the undercurrents, Memo, who had a righteous streak in him, fought as well as he could by talking back whenever he thought he was unjustly treated. La Cheli would not tolerate this and wanted to punish Memo for daring to defy her. She would complain to María about her unruly son, admonishing her to punish him or else. In order to placate La Cheli, María would tell her son not to talk back to his grandmother, but deep in her heart she knew the boy was only defending himself, and she admired him for standing up to her. Somehow María, afraid La Cheli would break his spirit as she had broken to a great extent hers, managed to convey the message to him, without actually saying it; that he was within his rights to fight back if he thought he was being wronged.

If María would not corporally punished Memo, La Cheli would find a switch from one of the trees in the house and come after Memo when he was playing in the garden. She would sneak behind him but when she would be about to strike him, Memo, sensing someone behind him, would jump out of harm's way before the switch reached his back. La Cheli would run after him, swinging the switch, but Memo, being young, would avoid each strike. Perhaps out of nervousness or out of relief he would laugh every time she missed. This succeeded in enraging her further. She would yell at him to stay put so she could hit him, and he, realizing he was too quick for her, would stay just slightly out of her reach. After a little while, she would tire of chasing him and would throw rocks at him and yell; "Memo, you're just like your father, that no good so and so your mother married. You look just like him, you skinny little scamp." He would dance around her, daring her to hit him and delighting in her every miss. When María would come home from job hunting, La Cheli would complain to her about Memo's disrespectful behavior and would request María give him a beating. María never did.

Not so much to defy La Cheli but because she was against corporal punishment of any kind. Many a time La Cheli tried to sneak behind Memo with the switch, with the same result. Some of the tenants and their children who saw her attempts to hit him found it funny. La Cheli never saw the humor of it.

Marcelo and Violeta witnessed some of these shenanigans and they, too, thought it funny, but La Cheli loved them too much to resent them. Memo tried to ingratiate himself to Marcelo. He wanted desperately to please him and be his friend. One day Marcelo would give him some attention and Memo would be ecstatic. The next day Memo would come to Marcelo's room hoping to spend time with him and Marcelo would ignore him. If Memo insisted, Marcelo would tell him to get lost, using a dismissive voice that would make Memo feel insignificant. Memo never knew when he could approach him so he waited like a little puppy dog for Marcelo to call him and he would run to his side and soak up every moment Marcelo would give him. Marcelo was eight years older and already interested in girls, parties, and playing the guitar with his friends. Memo would hang around Marcelo and his friends when they would come to practice their songs.

Memo could see the other boys admired Marcelo, and marveled at the ease with which he led them. Memo wanted to grow up to be like Marcelo. He would sit in the corner of Marcelo's room hoping he would let him stay. Sometimes he would, and sometimes he would tell him to get out using that tone of voice that made Memo scurry away. Marcelo's friends thought it was funny. Memo never saw the humor of it.

Violeta, of all his new found family, was the one who showed him affection. Memo was grateful for her acceptance. She would include him when she went on outings with her friends. Often, La Cheli or Dahlia would oppose her decision, warning her that if something were to happen to Memo she would be held responsible, but she would insist that she wanted him to go with her and they would reluctantly give in. He would be like her mascot. Besides, all her friends got a kick out of his Mexican accent. Memo relished the attention. One Saturday afternoon, not long after they had arrived in San Salvador, their dire predictions almost came true. Violeta took Memo to El Campo de Marte where a fair was going on with rides and games and food stands. Violeta thought Memo would love it and she was right.

El Campo the Marte was a park which had at its center a large oval grassy area about the size of two football fields, where the fair was taking place. The park was about a four kilometer drive from their house and the group had taken the bus there. For a couple of hours everything went well until suddenly Memo found himself alone in the middle of the throng. He started to look for Violeta by going back to the place where he had seen her last. He was sure she would be there. But she was not. Although Memo was only eight years old, he did not panic; he just kept looking for her. But minutes became an hour and Memo, who by then had walked the oval more than once, began to realize he was lost. The afternoon began to darken into night. Even though he did not want to believe it, Memo concluded the group had left without him. He was right. Violeta was home telling her mother what had happened and La Cheli and Dahlia were telling her they had told her so. Violeta insisted Memo was smart and would find his way home. So sure was she of it that no one was sent to look for Memo. María did not know what was happening because she was out, looking for work.

In the meantime, Memo decided to walk his way back. Trusting his sense of direction, he kept walking and walking toward where he thought the house would be. Somehow after about forty-five minutes he recognized the neighborhood. There, about two blocks away, he could see the house. Out of the balconies he could see heads looking out in his direction. Someone yelled,
"There he is!"
"Where?"
"There!"
He ran toward the house. The group started to yell encouragement, as fans do when a runner approaches the finish line. They were probably yelling more out of relief than anything else, but Memo had never been so hailed. The group ran downstairs to open the door. Everyone was patting him in the back, mussing up his hair, hugging him. Violeta kept repeating, "I told you he would! I told you so! He's smart! He's smart!" Memo could not stop beaming.

The incident did wonders for Memo's confidence. For the first time someone in his family thought him smart. María had told him so, many a time, but that was his mother. Mothers are supposed to say that. A bond was established between Violeta and Memo that would never be broken. She was proud of him! He was proud that she was proud of him! Perhaps that was why, ten years later, Violeta would take a chance on Memo and help him get to the United States.

Another good thing that came out of the incident was that from that day on, Memo trusted his instincts. Years later, whenever he was in a new country or a new city, he knew he could find his way. Once, he arrived by train in Paris, France at two in the morning and by three he was in bed in a little hotel near La Sorbonne. From a small grain of sand a pearl grows.

Dahlia's relationship with Memo was stormy. She could be charming one moment and abusive the next. She had the power La Cheli bestowed on her and she would not hesitate to use it. They were supposed to be sisters, but some sisters are more equal than others. Dahlia knew that María was weakened by the decision she took marrying Elías and she also knew María's financial condition. This knowledge gave her tremendous power in the house. Years of living with La Cheli had taught Dahlia the gift of rage. So, whenever Dahlia did not like something María did, she would let insults fly. If later it turned out Dahlia was wrong, never did Memo hear Dahlia apologize to his mother, or to anyone else for that matter.

Dahlia was an expert on all subjects and could not be contradicted on any of them. She had an opinion on everything and to support her position she would say that all the great philosophers agreed with her, or all the great scientists, the great artists, the great historians. She never quoted a particular scientist, artist, or historian, and no one ever challenged her. Those who knew better were too polite, and those who did not know bowed to her apparent wisdom. It was always the same; once she had made her pronouncement, conversation on that particular subject was over. The result was that she went through her life thinking she was always right.

This baffled Memo. *Does she really believe that she's always right? If we start with the premise that no one is always right, then it must follow that she knows she's not always right. At some level she must know this. If we add to this the fact that she had an average education; I do not know exactly how much but I know she did not go to college. And if on top of that we add the fact that she never reads much of anything, other than magazines, one has to conclude that she knows she does not know, or she is totally self-deluded.* Memo eliminated the last thing out of hand. Which left him with this: *She knows she doesn't know much about anything.* Which left him with this thought: *What kink of a person knows that she does not know, and still goes ahead with the charade? What happens to her when she closes the door and she is alone with this terrible fact? Does she deal with it? Does she feel like a total idiot as she realizes that most everyone knows of her ignorance? Does she think the world is comprised of fools who are unable to see through her act? Is it all an elaborate self-defense mechanism that allows her to march through life totally blind to her reality?*

As he grew up he thought about this less and less. Eventually, as he came into adulthood, he learned to forgive her. He thought he understood her reasons. *And anyway, the past is the past, right? Let it go.* But he could not. *What about all the injustices she committed; the trampling of other people's feelings? The abuse and insults she heaped on María and me? What about the psychological damage she caused, not only to her sister and nephew, but to her own children. Is it all forgiven and forgotten? She pays no price for this? She gets to ripe old age with impunity? Where's the justice? What's the lesson? If you live long enough nobody remembers what a witch you were most of your life? What's the point of spending one's life being sensitive and thoughtful if in the end it makes no difference? Is there no day of reckoning?* He had trouble with this. All his life he would have trouble with injustice.

Marcelo's way of dealing with his mother's absolutism was to appear to agree with her and then go ahead and do whatever he wanted to do. He knew he could never win, so he, as did María, kept quiet when Dahlia ranted about something. He paid a price for this; by the time he was eighteen years old he had developed an ulcer. He also developed a life pattern; he would seldom, if ever, openly disagree with those around him. He would leave the room rather than argue. If he could not leave the room, he would say yes in order to end it there, or he would retreat mentally from the argument altogether, returning to the conversation when it was over. He was very intelligent and had opinions but he had learned from his mother the futility of expressing them, and so he suppressed them. This cost him dearly in intimate relationships when it would eventually lead to violent explosions in which he would throw things with intent to harm those around him. It did not happen very often but when it did, it was a frightening sight. He seemed to be saying, "If you push and push I will eventually do this." Worse than the lifetime ulcer it caused him; his mother's dominance turned Marcelo into a pessimist. His motto seemed to be: 'Why bother fighting for anything since, eventually, the world will have its way." This was a pity because Marcelo was, without any doubt, the most gifted member of their family.

Marcelo had his mother's charm, his father's comedic timing, and their combined intelligence. He had an easy sense of leadership, the looks of a matinee idol, and innate aristocratic style. Before he was fifteen years old and without a single art lesson, he had created full color adventure comic strips hundreds of pages thick about aerospace, WWII, the African jungles of Tarzan, to rival any professional newspaper strip. He had an uncanny gift for caricature and could draw the famous of the world, or anybody in the neighborhood, with such accuracy and humor that even those who were the subject of his fun, laughed. And he could do it spontaneously. All you had to do was hand him a piece of chalk and within moments he would have drawn a strip right on the sidewalk, with a beginning, middle and end. He taught himself how to play the lead guitar and formed a trio which was the hit of any party he attended. He was as good with numbers as he was with art and eventually became a reluctant architect. He was admired by men and adored by women. There seemed to be unlimited potential to him. He could have become anything he wanted, if he had tried. But he did not try and so he did not become. Alas.

If his mother ever took responsibility for thus shaping Marcelo's life, she never showed it. In the same way, La Cheli never gave a second thought to the fact that her behavior shaped, not only her daughters' but her grandchildren's lives. Both chose to believe that if Marcelo kept quiet, it was because he was in agreement with them. Nothing could have been further from the truth. In this, María and Marcelo were kindred spirits. Subliminally, they understood each other's reluctance to rant and rave in order to get their way, but in doing so, they validated La Cheli's and Dahlia's ways, and by extension, all others in the world who bully their way through life. They also, at some level, began to see themselves as powerless. Never once did they share these feelings with each other, but each knew that the other one knew. Marcelo was fond of his aunt and María returned the affection. The greatest compliment he ever paid her was when she died. He flew from Washington, D.C. to San Francisco to pay his respects. Memo never shared these thoughts with his cousins, afraid it would hurt them. Maybe he should have. This he will never know.

As acquiescent as Marcelo and María were, Violeta and Memo were spirited. Violeta would fight her mother every time if she felt she was right. Maybe he learned to fight back from her. Both, La Cheli and Dahlia, would tolerate disagreement from Violeta because they loved her so, but Memo was another matter. For his part, Memo had learned to deal with La Cheli, but aunt Dahlia was another matter.

She took pleasure in imposing her will on him. In the few occasions when the whole family, except La Cheli who did not like to leave her house, went out together to a restaurant, when it was time for Memo to order, Dahlia would tell the waiter that Memo would not be ordering anything; that he would be given a bit from others' plates. Even if the person who was hosting the dinner insisted that Memo be allowed to order, she would say that there was no reason to spend any money on him. To save face, Memo would say that he was not hungry. Dahlia would say, "You see, he's not hungry anyway."

Memo looked forward to the Sunday newspaper because he loved the colored comic strips section. Knowing that his aunt would get up late on Sundays, he would get up early and read the comics before she awoke. Once she caught him reading them and, in her imperial way, told him that the paper belonged to her and he was not to touch it until after she had disposed of it. This meant he would not read it until the afternoon or the next day when she would throw it out—which was her point; I decide if and when you read the comics. Memo understood the paper belonged to her but could not understand what harm was there if he read the comic strips while she was still asleep. He was careful with her paper, always leaving it the way he found it. He asked his mother who said,

"That's the way things are. Just accept it."

But he could not. Memo's way of fighting back was to get up even earlier, read the comics, and be back in bed before anyone in the house was up. You gotta do what you gotta do.

He had difficulty accepting his mother's compliance. She would encourage him to stand up to injustice but would not stand up for herself. He sometimes wished Dahlia were his mother and immediately felt guilty for having considered the idea. Memo was susceptible to guilt; after all, he was Catholic and had spent three years in Mexico being indoctrinated. But he had learned to rebel against doctrine because of those three years. Just the same, his sense of justice made him ask himself: *Why doesn't my mother fight back? Why does she take so much guff from my aunt?* One day his mother did not.

It happened one Sunday afternoon. His mother was in their room reading while listening to music on the radio. Dahlia came into the room and told María she did not like the music and to turn the radio off. María, without raising her voice, told Dahlia that *she* liked the music and would not turn it off.
"In that case, I will turn it off."
"Not if I can help it," said his mother.
"Well, you can't."
She went into La Cheli's room where the electric panel was and turned off the breaker that fed electricity to María's room. His mother was livid.
"Turn the electricity back on, Dahlia!"
"No, I pay for it and I can do with it what I want."
Memo had never seen his mother furious. It was true that Dahlia had contracted with the electric company that served the neighborhood. It was not true that she paid for María and Memo's electricity. She had told María, almost as soon as they had arrived from Mexico, that she was to pay her a certain amount of money a month if she wanted to have electricity in her room. María paid her monthly share.
"In that case I will get my own electricity."
"Ha!" said his aunt, "see if you can afford it."
"I will!"

His mother came back into their room muttering to herself.

"I'll show you. All my life I've put up with your abuses. Not this time, sister. I'm down but I'm not out. You'll see!"

She went on and on for quite a while before she calmed down.

Somehow his mother got the necessary money; she went to the Lempa Electric Company and got her own service. For three days they did not have electricity, which made Dahlia very happy, but never again could she dictate to María what kind of music she could hear. From that day on Memo knew she had the courage to stand up to anybody. He was so proud of his mother. For once, his mother had won.

The only other time Memo saw his mother furious happened several years later. Dahlia had come from the United States to visit. Memo came home to find his mother seething with resentment for her sister.

"What's wrong?"

"Your aunt has done it again."

"What did she do?"

"She convinced La Cheli to make her will. And she has done so."

"Are we included in the will?"

"Yes."

"Then, what's wrong?"

"La Cheli had told me she had planned to leave half the house to Dahlia and half the house to me."

"That seems fair."

"Dahlia didn't think so. She convinced La Cheli she should receive two thirds of the house, and I only one third."

"Why?'

"She said that she has two children and I have only one. Therefore she thought the fair thing was for La Cheli to give her twice as much."

"That's not right."

"That's what I said to La Cheli."

"What did she say?"

"She said that she argued with Dahlia but in the end she came to see her point and she had decided to do as Dahlia wanted."

"What did you say?"

"I asked La Cheli that if I had five children, would she have left me five sevenths of the property and only two sevenths to Dahlia?"

"What did she say?"

"She said that would not be fair."

"Then, how come this is?"

"Well, you know how headstrong your sister is. She insisted and..."

"And La Cheli agreed."

"Not only did she agree, she left it to Dahlia to divide the house as she sees fit."

"How did she divide the property?"

"I don't know yet. You remember Marco, the handsome young man who was one of Marcelo's classmates at the school of architecture here at the University?"

"Yes, I remember him."

"He's an architect now, and Dahlia has asked him to draw the plans of the property so she can have an exact count of the size of the lot. She then will take it to a lawyer friend of hers to draw the will according to the plan."

Two days later, Marco came by and measured the property. When he had made the plan he showed it to Dahlia who then told him how to divide the lot. María was not consulted on any of this. Marco returned a week later and gave the plan to Dahlia who took it to her lawyer friend who drew the will according to Dahlia's wishes, and brought it to the house for La Cheli's signature. It was then, when it was all done, that Dahlia handed a copy of the plan to María.

"Here's your inheritance," she said and left before María had time to look at it.

María unfurled the plan and was outraged by what she saw. When Memo came home, she showed it to him.

"Here's your inheritance," said his mother bitterly.

The property was more or less in the shape of a rectangle. One of the long sides faced directly to the street. It was a rather large lot about 100 meters long and eighty deep. Dahlia had taken 98 meters of the front side for herself, leaving María with just enough space for a door.

She had taken the front two thirds of the lot for herself, leaving María the back one third. A sliver, on the left side of the property allowed María to reach the street.

"La Cheli approved this?"

"She has signed the papers. It's done."

"Doesn't she realize how unfair this is? Not only has she taken two thirds of the property but she has taken the most valuable two thirds. Who's going to want to buy our third with only a few feet facing the street?"

"No one. And she knows it."

"We can't sell without her. We are at her mercy."

"That's the way things are. That's the way things have always been." María started to cry.

"Maybe Violeta and Marcelo will see how unfair this is and redress it some day."

No one was interested in buying María's third. As soon as a prospective buyer saw that the property was all but landlocked, they would turn away. When it sold, thirty years later, they sold it together with Violeta and Marcelo who took their two thirds. There was no mention by either one of them about the uneven partition. Some things never change. Dahlia had won again.

Dahlia did not like to lose to anyone, let alone a dog. When Memo and María arrived from Mexico the house had a dog named Cholito. Cholito was a mixture of mutt and terrier. There are no thoroughbred dogs in El Salvador; every dog is a mutt. Cholito was a typical Salvadorian dog. He was white and brown and happy and he was beloved by all, but most of all by Violeta. One day, someone ran up to the house yelling that Cholito had been hit by a car. Everyone poured out of the house to help Cholito. He died in Violeta's arms and she was heartbroken. Dahlia got another dog in hopes Violeta would stop grieving. He was a Labrador mixed with something. Dahlia named it Adonis and he was as handsome as his name indicated. Soon he grew big and strong and was loved by all because he was so friendly. Once in a while he would get out of the house and someone would always bring him back. One day he got out and no one brought him back. Dahlia was sure he had been stolen. Violeta was heartbroken but by this time she was preparing to go to the United States to study so Dahlia did not replace him. For months Memo asked his mother if he could have a dog. María reminded him that as things were, Dahlia would not allow it.

María had finally gotten a job as actress and record librarian at a new radio station run by two Mexican men. María thought it ironic that she had been given a chance to act in a Salvadorian station by Mexicans. The woman who owned the station brought the two men all the way from Mexico to open her station because she believed their superior expertise would thrust it into the top tier in a short time. Although the station was doing well, the competition for advertising sponsors was fierce. Television had yet to come to El Salvador and Radio was the most effective way to reach the Salvadorian consumer. The most popular programs were radio soaps and two other stations dominated the airways; YSEB and YSU. They both had their stable of studio players and some of them were quite famous. YSAX had its work cut out. The station attempted to develop its own stable of players, which was how María had gotten the break, but YSAX was having trouble muscling into the time slots dominated by the other two stations and had to cut back in the number of soaps it could air. That meant less work for its actors. Sympathetic to María, because she spoke with a Mexican accent and understood the Mexican culture, they offered her the less glamorous position of record librarian. To soften the blow, they told her that it would be a temporary job and that she could still act whenever the opportunity arose and that as YSAX grew she would grow with it. She did not want to, but it provided a steady income which she so badly needed so she took it.

All stations had a runner whose job was to take things to and from the stations on a bicycle. It was the lowliest job and paid the lowliest wages. Guayito was YSAX's runner. Whenever he was idle, he liked to hang around María. He would watch her work and keep her entertained with the gossip he gathered around town. One day he told her his next door neighbor's dog had a litter of puppies. Would she want one?

"Probably not."

"There are two I particularly like. They are the pick of the litter. I can bring them for you to choose from."

"How old are they?"

"Just a couple of weeks. They are too young to be taken away from their mother but in a couple of weeks they'll be ready. Think about it."

"I don't think so."

But she could not stop thinking about it. It would make Memo so happy. Dahlia was the problem. La Cheli liked dogs because she could yell at them, throw stones at them, even kick them, and they still loved her. Dahlia also loved dogs, but selling her on the idea to let Memo have one was the challenge. But if the dog were for her, would that be alright? The answer was in the question.

"Guayito offered me a dog today. Do you think Dahlia would want one?"

"What kind of dog?" asked La Cheli.

"I don't know, he says they are very cute."

"We haven't had a dog for a while. I'll ask her."

A couple of days later La Cheli told María that Dahlia was interested.

"There are two to pick from. Guayito says they are the best two."

"She'll have to look at them before she decides."

"If she wants, I'll ask Guayito to bring them here when they are ready."

A couple of days later La Cheli said to tell Guayito to bring them.

"I'll ask him to bring them next week."

"Fine."

María did not tell Memo about all this, afraid that if her plan did not work out, Memo would be disappointed. She hoped Dahlia would fall in love with one of them and then María would ask if Memo could keep the one she had rejected. That was the beauty of the plan; Dahlia would allow Memo the dog because it was the lesser of the two. María knew Memo would love any dog, and that if Dahlia was happy when she asked, there was a chance he could have his dog.

The day came and Guayito brought the puppies for Dahlia to choose. She chose the prettiest and friendliest of the two; the one that was wiggling its tail and licking her hand. It reminded her of Adonis.

"But that one is a female," said La Cheli. "Get the male."

"He doesn't have personality. Look at him. He just sits there."

"But when she's in heat, we'll have dogs from all over the neighborhood snooping around."

María grabbed the opportunity.

"Not if we keep the other one. They'll become a couple."

"But we'll have the problem of giving puppies away."

"That's no problem. Everybody likes dogs," said Dahlia.

"He's not very pretty."

"Memo won't mind."

Dahlia picked up the female.

"Her name is Diana," and walked away with her. She had not said yes to the idea of Memo keeping the dog, but she had not said no, which María chose to interpret as her way of saying yes.

"Call him El Sapo Miguel. He has very short legs," said La Cheli.

Miguel was one of La Cheli's tenants. He was a short legged man and La Cheli called him El Sapo Miguel when he was not around.

"I don't think Miguel would appreciate that," said María.

"Well, then call him Sapo. He'll never know it's because of him."

María had Memo's dog. It was no time to argue.

"Fine," she said, "The dog's name is Sapo."

Which brings up an interesting question. Sapo means frog in Spanish. If anything, frogs have very long legs which most of the time they keep folded under them. It is for this reason that they are so close to the ground. Still, the name was not meant to flatter. Memo always wondered if, given Sapo's temperament, he knew his name was an insult.

When Memo came home and saw his dog, he was too happy to object about its name. Sapo slept with him from that night on until he got too big. Just like in the movies, they became inseparable. Diana and Sapo got along very well and eventually they did become a couple. There was only one problem, as Diana was friendly, Sapo was not. Diana let anyone touch her. Sapo could be touched only by María and Memo.

Tried as she might, Dahlia could never touch him. Every time she would approach him he would growl. Sapo could only be fed by María or Memo. Dahlia tried to bribe him by bringing him pieces of leftover steak, but he would not come to her. She would have to leave the steak on the ground and step away before Sapo would come to eat it. This rankled Dahlia. She began to tell La Cheli that maybe Sapo was too vicious to be kept and should be sent away to a farm somewhere. Memo would tell them Sapo was a good guard dog and he had never bitten anyone. Dahlia decided that the dog could stay only if he was chained and muzzled. La Cheli agreed and Sapo was chained to the guava tree. This did not make Memo happy and Sapo even less so. Memo would be allowed to take him on walks but had to muzzle him. Memo felt sorry for Sapo and would take the muzzle off. Sometimes another dog would come around to sniff Sapo, and he would growl and soon they would be fighting. Although small in stature, Sapo never backed away from a fight and never lost one, no matter how big the other dog was. Once, this worked to Memo's advantage. Memo would walk to school to the Colegio Bautista which was about a kilometer and a half from his house. A couple of bullies would sometimes hassle him. Once, he brought his dog to school with him and when the bullies came he let go of Sapo who promptly chased them. The bullies never again bothered Memo. As his days of enchainment became months, Sapo began to live up to Dahlia's expectations; he became more mistrustful and angry. Dahlia would still try to win him over by bringing him a morsel and telling him she would free him if he only showed her some affection. Sapo never gave in to her charms.

One day, Memo came home from the Instituto Nacional Francisco Menéndez, the school he was by then attending, and as was his habit, came over to the guava tree to say hello to his dog. But Sapo was gone.
"Where's Sapo?" he asked La Cheli.
"I don't know."
"He was here when I left. What happened?"
"I don't know."
He went to his aunt and asked her.
"I don't know," she said. "Maybe he got loose."

"But he would still be in the house."

"Maybe he went out when one of the tenants opened the door.'

He asked the tenants but they had not seen him. He went around the neighborhood and asked if they had seen him. No one had.

"He was probably stolen. The same way that Adonis was," said his aunt.

"Nobody could steal Sapo. He wouldn't let them near him. He would have to be tied and muzzled before anyone could put a hand on him."

"Well, I don't know. Maybe he'll be back in a couple of days."

When his mother came home he told her everything he knew and had done.

"Is the chain broken?"

"No."

"And no one saw him?"

"No."

"Maybe he'll turn up. Let's wait a day or so."

Memo looked for his dog every day before going to school and after he returned.

"There's only one explanation," said his mother. "Your aunt sent the dog away to some farm."

"Or she had him poisoned. She never liked Sapo."

"But we can't prove it. You might as well resign yourself that he's gone."

Two months went by and he had lost hope that he would ever see his beloved friend. Then, one morning, while walking to school, two blocks from the Instituto Nacional, about twenty yards ahead of him was a mangy dog. He was missing hair from bites he had apparently suffered from many recent fights. He was creeping along the wall as canines do when stalking pray, but in his case he seemed so weary that the posture was more defensive than offensive. It looked like . . ., it could not be . . . Sapo? Uncertain, Memo called out Sapo's name. He didn't respond. He called him again. The dog looked warily at him. Memo could see in Sapo's eyes that the world had shown its worse side and he was prepared to go down fighting. The look both frightened and saddened Memo. He called a third time and the dog took a second look. His distrust turned to inquisitiveness, then to recognition, and finally to joy! Memo understood the sequence only too well. Sapo ran toward him like a dog out of hell. About five feet from him, Sapo leapt unto Memo's arms and knocked him down on the sidewalk. Sapo ran three circles around Memo in the time it took him to get up. Memo wasn't going to school that day!

Memo turned around and ran home. The dog ran ahead of him about half a block, turned, ran back to Memo, past him, ran a circle around him and again ahead of him half a block and repeated the operation again, and again and again for the one kilometer glorious run home. Memo has not seen happiness like that since.

Dahlia was not happy to see Sapo back. From that day on she kept her distance from him, until she left for the United States where she stayed a couple of years. La Cheli too did not like Sapo but she understood him. They both had a healthy mistrust of the world. She would have long conversations with him, usually complaining about something or someone. Sapo could see in her eyes the same look he had in his. So long as they left each other alone, they got along.

Sapo lived with his beloved Diana for many years. She would come visit him at the guava tree everyday. No one understood him better. With her he could let his scowl go and become mush. The world never saw a gentler dog. She was the love of his life and he hers. Every year, like the sparrows come to Capistrano, Diana would give birth to a new batch of sapitos. At last, Sapo had found his home, sweet home.

There was no home, sweet home for Memo in El Salvador. Many years later, Dahlia began to see something especial in him but by then it did not matter. As Sapo had learned, the only way to get along with Dahlia was by staying away from her. Although not by design, Memo achieved peace with her the same way.

THE SALVADORIANIZATÍON OF MEMO

But this night, his last in El Salvador, Memo had no peace. He writhed in his uncomfortable bed trying in vain to go to sleep. He remembered how proud his mother had been when she surprised him with the new bed. This bed was a larger version of the old one with the addition of a headboard. Other than that, it had the same construction; a wooden frame upon which strips of cowhide were nailed in a crisscross pattern upon which a two-inch thick cotton stuffed mattress lay. It looked good and it was definitely the best bed Memo had ever had. The problem was that after a few weeks, the strips of cowhide stretched and bowed so much that they forced him to sleep in the center of the bed. It was like sleeping in a hammock, without its conveniences. Memo did not complain, for he knew his mother's bed was worse. *I won't be missing this bed*. Memo thought as he tried to find a comfortable position in his bed. *Nor will I miss this country*. El Salvador did not treat him well either, at least initially.

Adults found his Mexican accent cute, but kids thought it weird and they made fun of him, especially the kids from the Escuela Costa

Rica. In Mexico, Memo had attended for three years the Colegio Mejicano; a Catholic boarding school. It had been a very sheltered existence that had left Memo completely innocent about the outside world. Because of that, María wanted to put him in another private school in El Salvador. Violeta and Marcelo had attended the Colegio Bautista, a very good elementary school that was run by an American lady, Miss Evalena McCutcheon, who had come to El Salvador many years before and had dedicated her life to her school. It was private but it was not expensive and María hoped to place Memo there, but it was too late to enroll him.

The Mexican school year coincides with the American school year but the Salvadorian school year starts in February and ends in October. Because of its good reputation, the Colegio Bautista had a waiting list of those who would like to study there. Memo arrived just before Christmas. Miss McCutcheon, in deference to Violeta and Marcelo who studied there, promised to accept Memo for the following year. For now, the Escuela Costa Rica would have to do. María enrolled him in the Escuela, which did not make her, nor Memo, happy. He was told he had to repeat the third grade to pick up Salvadorian history and geography. So far, coming home to country and family was not turning out to be the 'they lived happily ever after' he had expected.

The Escuela Costa Rica was a public school that served the barrio in which Memo lived; a tough and poor neighborhood where kids grew up mostly on the street. Like the neighborhood, the kids were also tough. Tough was the last thing Memo was. As soon as they heard him speak, they started to laugh and call him a sissy. And when they heard him use the word pisar, they laughed even more. This was something with which he had not reckoned.

It started the very first day of class and it kept going on for months. The kids loved to hear Memo speak so that they could make fun of him. Behind him sat one of the toughest boys; his name was Corea. He loved to make Memo say something in order to make the class laugh. Corea would shove his foot through the opening between the seat and the back of Memo's chair and stepped on him. At first, Memo tried to ignore Corea but that did not work. Then he turned to tell him to stop, but Corea would not stop and so Memo raised his hand to get the teacher's attention.

"Yes?" she said, "what is it?"

"Corea me esta pisando." A roar of laughter followed.

Pisar in Spanish means to step on something or someone.

In Salvadorian slang, however, it means to fuck. Unwittingly, Memo had said; "Corea is fucking me." From then on, Corea took every opportunity to step on Memo. It was the joke of the week. The incident went around the school like wild fire and soon every kid was stepping on Memo in hopes to hear him say pisando again. By the end of the day, one of the teachers pulled Memo aside and told him not to say that word anymore. Memo asked why and was told that it was a bad word, and so he stopped. But the damage was done. For days on end the kids made fun of him.

When he got home he asked his mother what was wrong with the word. He had used it in Mexico and no one thought it vulgar. María could not explain it to him because Memo still believed the stork brought babies to their parents. "Just don't say it," María said. Memo was bewildered and unhappy because, if this was the result of his first day of school, what else was in store for him. He did not want to continue attending that school but his mother said that he had to go there for one year.

"One year! I barely made it through one day."

"Just don't say that word and the kids will stop bothering you. You'll see."

A reputation is made in one day at the third grade level. The kids had decided Memo was either an idiot or a sissy. It took a few days for Memo to prove he was not an idiot. It took much longer to prove he was not a sissy. In the meantime he was the butt of the jokes. This was not how he had expected his country to treat him. He was disappointed, to say the least.

Salvadorians have ambivalent feelings toward Mexicans; on the one hand they admire them because Mexico is a more advanced nation, on the other hand they find their way of speaking effeminate. Memo was the recipient of this ambivalence. In addition, there was one more thing some kids did not like about him: the color of his skin. Light skin in El Salvador is equated with the rich upper classes. He was amid the poor and they were having a great time making him feel he did not belong with them. There was nothing he could do about his skin.

Little by little Memo figured out that since they were not going back to Mexico, he had to learn to speak in the Salvadorian dialect in order to be accepted. This was his mother's country and thus it was his country. *As long as I am going to live here I am going to have to change the way I speak.* But he felt that in doing so, he was betraying the promise he made to his mother and for a while he tried to speak at home like a Mexican and in school like a Salvadorian. After a few months it became increasingly difficult to keep that up and eventually he absorbed the dialect and spoke like a Salvadorian.

Well . . . sort of. He was still too innocent, too refined, too something. Memo did not know that in addition to the dialect, he also had to learn the body language. The way one speaks reflects upon the way one moves. Learning this would take longer. The poor kids of the neighborhood viewed him with suspicion. To top it all, they could not believe he did not know the things he said he did not know. Having been for the last three years in a private school also separated him from them. They did not trust anybody who attended a private school. They also did not like that he did not swear. Was he trying to be superior or something? Or was he a sissy? Memo took pride in the way he spoke Spanish. His mother had instilled in him that swearing was for the uneducated and the vulgar, not for him. "You are different," she would say. Although he believed his mother, holding on to that difference was getting more and more difficult.

But he *was* different. In the eight short years he had lived he had been to seven different countries, seen many different cities, and met many different people. Some of those countries he had been too young to remember what they were like, but his mother would tell him. "When we were in Panama you did this. When we got to Honduras we saw that." She would show pictures of him in those places and tell him the stories that came with them. So even if he did not remember first hand, he had been there. As recently as a couple of months before, he had been in Mexico and Guatemala. The kids in his school had never left the country or even the city. If they had gone anywhere, they had been to a farm or the little town from which they had emigrated. Nothing as glamorous as the places he had been. Memo did not brag about where he had been but his accent made kids inquire about his past. Some kids liked him because of it; most kids disliked him. He learned to stay away from those who disliked him and after a while he had a small circle of friends. As he acquired the Salvadorian dialect, those who met him ceased to ask him where he came from, which was a relief. By the time he started to study at the Colegio Bautista he had totally assimilated the accent and no one any longer asked: "Where are you from?" Until he went to the United States.

But Memo *was* different and would be different the rest of his life. He never quite figured out what made him different. He had a certain grace or elegance that created the impression that he was highborn. Even after years of living in El Salvador, something about the way he talked, or the way he dressed, isolated him from the rest and there was no getting rid of it. It was a blessing and it was a curse. Between you and me, I think he liked being different. It cost him friendships, and later on it cost him jobs, but he preferred being different than ordinary. Eventually he was able to say, "So what if I'm different." But it took him years to accept himself as he was.

But not while he was still a kid. He learned to curse as well as the rest of the neighborhood kids. He did not like it but, such is life. He only did it when he was with the neighborhood kids as a survival technique more than anything else. Still, while he learned to be a Salvadorian he had to put up with the ridicule. Memo could not wait for that year to end because he hoped the kids in the Colegio Bautista might be more like him. Mercifully, the year ended. As soon as he started to attend the Colegio Bautista, he was happy to see that the kids hardly ever swore, which was more to his liking. He would enjoy the three years he was there; perhaps the happiest years of his childhood.

In contrast to the Escuela Costa Rica, which was nothing more than a house being used as a school, the Colegio Bautista had a large building erected for the expressed purpose. While the Escuela Costa Rica was situated right off a main thoroughfare with cars, buses, and trucks roaring by, the Colegio Bautista was located in a very nice upper middle class residential area off a narrow and quiet lane. Half a block away you could smell the Colegio Bautista because it was separated from the lane by a fence made of cypress bushes. There was no gate; just a breach between the cypress bushes that opened to a huge grassy area as big as a football field. At la Escuela Costa Rica, during recess, a couple of hundred kids crowded into the house's concrete floor courtyard. There was no room to play anything, which was probably why a fight erupted at least once a day. At the Colegio Bautista, as Memo walked along the cypress fence, he could admire the gray rectangular building with its four steps that led to a wide entrance. An even wider corridor ran right down the center of the building. On either side there were six classrooms; two per grade. Except for the sixth grade; there was only one of those and it was taught by Miss McCutcheon herself. The first time Memo walked down that corridor he could not believe how large and airy and clean the school rooms were, with lots of windows and sturdy wooden desks in the style of American schools. The checker patterned tiled corridor opened to the back playing field which was even larger than the front one!

A kid could look forward to attending such a school. Memo did.

It was probably here that Memo fell in love with the United Sates. Here he learned to play softball, baseball and a bit of basketball. Here he heard, for the first time, in person, English spoken. Miss McCutcheon would have American visitors and he would love to hang around to listen to them speak. It sounded softer that Spanish and it seemed to have a lot of sh sounds in it. He did not understand anything they said of course, but he could imagine that he was in the United States. He wondered how it would feel to speak it. It was magical.

Miss McCutcheon was magical. Her hair, which she wore in a bun, was mostly white with streaks of gray, made her look like Katharine Hepburn, only neater. Sometimes, Memo would stay after school and play on the front field with his schoolmates and once in a while he would see Miss McCutcheon in her private quarters brushing her hair by her window. She would bend her neck to one side so that her long hair would hang down, and she would brush it slowly with long strokes. Her skin was so white, it was pink. She wore dresses with little collars buttoned up to her neck. Short sleeved summer cotton dresses that came down to just below her knee. When Memo came to the U.S. he learned the term "little old lady" and to some degree she could have been described that way, except that no one thought of her as a little old lady for she held herself up and walked with the energy of a woman half her age. She did wear little old lady booties that came up to her ankles. She would walk briskly about the school giving a compliment here, an admonition there. She spoke excellent Spanish with an American accent that only added to her charm. Miss McCutcheon ruled her school with a firm but gentle hand and was loved and admired by all. She was America at its finest. She was a beautiful American.

The Colegio Bautista was about a kilometer and a half from Memo's house so his mother would give Memo twenty cents for the bus: ten cents each way. He would take the bus across the street from his house and he'd get off at El Polvorin's stop. El Polvorin was an army fort that sat on top of a hill from where it overlooked the city. About 150 feet below the fort there was a large soccer field which had at the far end a cement basketball court. Another fifty feet below the field and across the street was the Presidential House. Memo would get off the bus and walk uphill about a block before turning left into a narrow street, then, after another short block, he would turn right into the lane that led to the school. There was a small store where the two streets met and he would run into students there who were always buying candy. You could easily recognize the Colegio Bautista students because they were all dressed in white. Memo did not have money to buy candy so he would watch the other kids buy some and then, together, they would walk the last few meters into the Colegio Bautista's front field. Sometimes the kids would give him candy, sometimes they would not.

One day, Memo decided he would walk the kilometer and a half home and buy candy with his ten cents. He went in and pointed to the candy he wanted.
"That's fifty cents," the lady told him.
"Fifty cents? Why so much?"
"It's made in the United States."
"How about that one?"
"The same."
"And that one?"
"Forty cents."
"What can I buy for ten cents?"
"That and that and that." She pointed to the unwrapped candy.
"How come it's less?"
"It's made here, in El Salvador."
"What's the least expensive of the American candy?"
"This one here is twenty-five cents."
"I see. Well, give me ten cents of the Salvadorian candy then."
He enjoyed his candy as he walked home. Fortunately, it was all downhill and Memo decided it was worth the long walk.

He did this for several days but after a while it was not as much fun. The candy was good, but it was not American candy. His friends had given him a taste of it and it definitely was better. *If I don't take the bus at all, I can have enough to buy American candy every other day.* It meant he had to get up earlier to allow for the time it would take him to walk to school. He decided to try it. The walk to school was harder because it was all up hill but it was worth it if he could have the candy he wanted. His mother did not know he was doing this because she was at work when he got home. And anyway, Memo did not see any harm in what he was doing. On the second day he had enough to buy the twenty-five cents or the forty cents candy. He tried the twenty-five cents candy and it was great. Not only because it was better but also because he could buy it before school and have it during recess when the other kids were having theirs. *If the twenty-five cents is this good, I wonder how delicious the forty cents candy must be.* So he tried that, and it was delicious but he had to walk to and from school for two days to be able to buy it. That took some of the fun out of it. The other thing was that, as good as the candy was, it lasted such a short time, while the walk lasted so long. Every day it was a tough choice between the candy and the bus. *If only I could have both, like the other kids can.*

One day, when his mother was at work, he was rummaging in her closet when he found an alarm clock. Only it was not an alarm clock. It was a red plastic piggy bank in the shape of an alarm clock. Memo picked it up and as he did he heard a rattle inside. He turned it in his hand and saw a circular knob in the back. He twisted it and it came off. He pored out its contents: More than a hundred American dimes fell on the cement floor. Even though El Salvador has its own currency—the colón—for some reason American dimes are in circulation and are worth twenty-five Salvadorian cents. Among the dimes, there were two American silver dollars. Memo looked at one of them and put them back inside. Memo took one of the dimes and put the rest in the clock. *Here's my candy*, he thought. He knew he was doing wrong but there were so many more dimes there that he thought, *she'll never miss one*. This would have been true if he had stopped at one. But he did not. After a couple of days he took another one, a few days later one more, and one more a few days after. This went on for about a month. Then he got caught.

He ran into their room and suddenly stopped in his tracks. Standing there holding the red plastic clock, was his mother. The expression on her face said it all. Memo did not even try to lie. He told her everything including the feelings of inadequacy he experienced seeing his peers buying candy every day.
"I'm sorry."
"You should be. I trusted you and you betrayed my trust. You are a thief. As such you will be punished."
"What are you going to do?"

"You are going to pay it all back. You will not get an allowance for one year."

"One year!"

"And since you don't seem to need to ride the bus, you will walk to school from now on. Any questions?"

"No."

And so it was.

Though he felt the punishment was harsh, he also felt he had it coming. The part he never forgave his mother for was that in her anger she told La Cheli what he had done and from then on La Cheli called him a thief. If she could not find something she blamed it on the thief. He never took anything from anybody in the house but if anything was missing both La Cheli and Dahlia would blame the thief. The thief label really hurt him and it stuck to him for several years. It did a lot of damage to his self image. Memo never complained and never forgot.

How does the saying go? "When a door closes, a window opens." Memo could no longer go to his beloved Sunday movies so he took up basketball. On his way to school he had seen kids playing basketball on the cement court at the far end of El Polvorin. He would come and sit on the grass and watch. One day, a player was needed and they asked him if he wanted to play. And of course he said yes. It was love at first play. From then on, whenever someone would get tired or leave, Memo was there ready to jump in. He was not very good at it but he loved it. He convinced friends from the barrio to come with him on weekends. Ricardo and David would take the long walk to play basketball. In due course, the one year punishment was over and María began to give Memo his allowance. He decided to save it until he could have enough to buy his own basketball. This he did. After several months of saving he was able to buy a basketball. From then on, he would dribble it all the way up to El Polvorin, organize his own game, and play until he dropped. Eventually he saved enough to buy a pair of basketball shoes. In the summer he would leave home at eight in the morning and play until the sun set. For the next four years, basketball was his life.

One of those years, Bill Russell, the great American basketball star, toured Latin America and visited El Salvador for a day. Memo could not wait to see him. In typical Salvadorian fashion, only the rich kids were invited to the game, and Memo could not get in. Russell probably thought he was performing for the average Salvadorian kid. This did not dampen his enthusiasm for the game. Memo's love for basketball would last all of his life.

The piggy bank incident notwithstanding, in his three years there Memo grew scholastically, physically, and socially. Scholastically, the Colegio Bautista gave him the three best teachers he had in El Salvador: Miss Berta in the fourth grade, Miss Ofelia in the fifth, and Miss McCutcheon in the sixth. Miss Berta was a brown haired, plain looking woman of ineffable intelligence whose forte was math and biology. Miss Ofelia was a black haired woman of ineffable beauty whose forte was that she could get any student to do anything she wanted. All the boys wanted to grow up to marry a woman like her. One could not not learn from a teacher like Miss Ofelia. And Miss McCutcheon was the reward one got for making it to the sixth grade.

Physically, Memo blossomed. He reveled playing on the school's grass all the games he had never been allowed to play, like Tag and Leapfrog. Here he had the first opportunity to play organized games. He learned to play softball and, as his confidence grew, he participated in baseball as well. For the first time in his life he was in a school where he could run, fall, and roll without getting hurt. It was here that Memo touched his first basketball. Although the school did not have a basketball court, some boys had basketballs and would bring them to school, giving Memo a chance to play catch with them. The joy that had been stifled in the Colegio Mejicano returned to his heart in the Colegio Bautista.

And socially, he found kids of his ilk with whom he could play and joke without fear of ridicule. He had to do a lot of catching up in all fronts to make up for the three years he spent in the private catholic school in Mexico. Those times had been so oppressive, confining, and lonely that years later he would refer to them half-jokingly as 'my Jane Eyre years.'

MA, GOD, DOGMA

His Jane Eyre years started when he was five years old, in the city of Mérida, Yucatan. His mother told Memo the Monday she left him at the Colegio Mejicano that it was necessary that he start his education.

"It is going to be very exciting, you'll see. I will miss you very much but I will visit you soon."

"How soon?" he asked.

"Soon," she said. As Memo's mother explained, she would give furtive glances to a woman standing by the large dark brown wooden door. So large was the door that it had within it a smaller door near the opening of which the woman was standing.

"How soon is soon?" He wanted to cry but not in front of the woman, who Memo suspected was waiting for him.

They were standing in the school's reception area which had the shape of a car garage. It probably used to be a garage. Against each of the two walls there was a long brown wooden bench where two other mothers were saying goodbye to their sons. One of the boys started to cry, giving Memo cause for concern.

"Be brave, be brave," María said, and as she kissed him she motioned to the woman to take Memo. The woman extended her hand. He did not wish to go with her but he did not want to embarrass his mother so he gave his hand to the woman who took him inside through the smaller door. As the woman started to close the door, Memo turned to take one more look at his mother, but she was already gone. The door closed, separating Memo from the outside world. He would not see his mother for almost a year.

Memo looked at his surroundings. They were standing it the middle of an office. There were a couple of desks and chairs to their left.

"See that door across from that desk? That's the Directora's office, Doña Belisa. Next to her office, in that corner, is where she lives. You'll meet her later."

The woman took Memo out of the office and into the school. It was a typical Spanish architecture building with three concentrical squares: a large courtyard at its center, a tiled corridor framing the courtyard formed the second square, and the third square was the building itself. The tiled roof sloped down and covered the corridor, but not the cement courtyard, which had a working well in the center. The mid-afternoon sun pored down the roofless courtyard, bouncing off the white cement and into Memo's eyes, causing him to squint.

"Over there," said the woman as she pointed to the right side of the beige colored building, "are two first grade classrooms and one second grade. On this side, there is a second and two third grade classrooms, and on the left side over there are the fourth grade classrooms."

A doorway demarcated each classroom. Memo noticed that right in the middle of the wall in front of them was an opening which divided that side of the building into two halves. The woman followed Memo's gaze and answered his question before he could ask it.

"The left half of that side is the comedor where you'll be having your meals with all the other children, and the right half is the dormitory where you'll hang your hammock." She looked down at his belongings, "You have a hammock, don't you?"

"Yes, right in there," Memo said pointing to his suitcase.

"I'll take you there and show you where to hang it. My name is Melinda."

They started to cross the sun drenched courtyard.

"There's water in the well?"

"Yeah, take a look." Memo peeked down the well.

"It's very deep." His voice echoed in the well.

"We get all our potable water from there. Come on, let's go. I've things to do."

They stood at the opening between the comedor and the dormitory.

"Take a look," she said, pointing at the door to their left. Memo stepped into the comedor. Four rows of long wooden tables and benches that could seat twenty children on each side of each table filled the long hall; a dining room worthy of a Dickens novel.

"The door at the far end of the comedor on the left leads to the kitchen. The other door on the right side leads to the servants' quarters. You are not to go in there. Ever."

"Why not?"

"That's one of the rules. I'll show you the dormitory."

The same as the comedor but instead of tables, four rows of empty hammocks filled the length of the room. They took a few steps into the room.

"Hang your hammock there," she said, point to her right. "Put your things in there." She pointed at a black box sitting against the right wall.

Later, when Memo lived in the United States and was drafted into the Army, he had a similar box to put his things in; the army called it a footlocker.

"Where are the other boys?"

"They are at afternoon prayers."

"Afternoon prayers?"

"Yes. You'll pray every day; once in the morning, and once in the afternoon. That reminds me. If you pee during the night while you're asleep, you must clean it up before you can go to morning prayers."

"Pee?" said Memo, not wanting to believe his ears.

"Yeah, you have peed in your bed, haven't you, boy?"

How do I answer that question from a total stranger? Fortunately she did not wait for his answer.

"You peed. Every kid pees. When you do, there will be a telltale puddle right under your hammock. Now, see that door on the left at the end of the room?"

Memo, still in shock from the personal turn the conversation had taken, stammered, "Er, where? Ah, yes, yes," he said quickly, trying not to stutter. He was a pee-r already, he did not want to add stutterer to his rapidly falling image.

"That's the latrine. There's a mop in there. After you mop your pee *completely*, rinse the mop in the showers in there. You can't have breakfast until you clean the pee. Any questions?"

"Yes."

"What?"

"About the praying?"

"What about?"

"Do I have to pray?"

"Yeah, aren't you Catholic?"

"I think so."

"Were you baptized?"

"I think so."

"Then you pray."

"But my mamá and I don't pray. We . . ."

"This is a Catholic school. Didn't your mamá tell you? If you didn't before, you'll pray now. Have you studied your catechism?"

"Uh, what's that?"

"Don't worry. Saturday mornings you'll study it and when you're ready, you'll have your First Communion. That's probably why your mamá put you here."

"First Communion?"

"Yeah, Doña Belisa will teach you. Once you have your First Communion you'll confess every Saturday and commune every Sunday."

"Confess?"

"Enough with the questions! Ask Doña Belisa. Hang your hammock, put away your things, and put your uniform on. I'll be back in a while." And she left.

Memo found himself alone in the silent room full of empty hammocks. The room was lit by the sunlight that filtered through the two doorways that faced the courtyard. The hammocks seemed frozen in the gray eerie space. Memo stared at his new home. All energy drained from him and his fingers dropped the suitcase. It groaned as it hit the floor. The silence brought him face to face with his loneliness. Softly, Memo began to cry. His whimpering echoed down along the bare adobe walls. His little chest convulsed with pain. He had not moved from the spot the woman had left him. Memo had never been away from his mother's side. Slowly, the significance of his situation knifed his heart.

"Don't cry."

Memo turned toward the voice and saw a slender boy with sandy brown hair looking kindly at him.

"Your mother will be here Saturday morning to pick you up."

"She will?"

"All mothers pick their sons up on Saturdays. Now, stop crying because afternoon prayers are over and the rest of the boys will be here soon. What's your name?"

"Memo."

"I'm Carlitos. I'll help you set up."

They were putting up the hammock when the rest of the boys began to rush in bringing with them the noise of their numbers. Memo was glad nobody seemed to be aware of him. Carlitos opened the box and showed Memo how everything was supposed to be placed. Memo looked at Carlitos and marveled at his strength. Not his physical strength, for he looked weaker than Memo, but the strength that he saw in his light brown eyes; a mixture of pain and determination that seemed to say: 'I have shed my last tear.' Over the three years they spent together they became more than friends; they became brothers.

"Put your uniform on before we go to dinner."

"Where should I change?"

"Right here."

"In front of everybody?"

"It's better you do it here and show them you're not a mamá's boy."

"I am my mamá's boy."

Carlitos looked at Memo, not sure what to think of the remark. He decided this was not the time to explain it.

"You trust me?"

"Yes."
"Change here."

Thus began Memo's education. Up to this point he had seen the world through his mother's eyes. Sometimes her explanations were meant to teach, others to protect. Now he was about to see it though his own eyes. He was totally unprepared for what was about to happen. His mother had made the arrangements without telling him anything about them, and the sudden change had shocked him out of the cocoon in which he had been living. His first visit to the dentist had been handled the same way. His mother told him this nice man was going to look at his teeth and it was going to be fun. When he was led into the room with the ominous dentist chair in it, Memo panicked. It took the combined strength of the dentist, his assistant, the receptionist, and his mother to keep him on the chair long enough for the doctor to do what he had to do. That nightmare stayed with both of them for a long time. Maybe María, fearing another panic attack, decided it was better to do it in the secretive way that she did. And that was why she scurried away as she did. Fortunately for Memo, he had found in Carlitos a kindred soul.

Carlitos had been at the Colegio Mejicano for one year and knew the ropes. He was only a year older than Memo but was a world weary veteran of the boarding school wars that Memo would soon experience. The constant pushing, yelling, pulling, bickering, shoving, and competing for everything would take its toll on Memo. The children were always making lines, and every line led to more pushing and bickering and shoving. This led to some yelling on the part of the teachers which led to some sort of group disciplinary action which included a lot of silence. But it was silence as punishment not silence as peace. Still, Memo preferred it to the infernal racket.
"Why do those kids fight so much?"
"That's what bullies do."
"What's a bully?"
"It's a guy who enjoys beating on others."
"Why?"

"I don't know. Just stay away from them and their friends."
There was so much to learn. Luckily, he had Carlitos.
"Why are they bullies?"
"Because they don't want to be here."
"Then why are they here?"
"Because their parents make them."
"Why do their parents make them?"
"Because they are bullies."
Some of it he did not understand, but luckily he had Carlitos.
"Is the food always this bad?"
"It can get worse."
"Really?"
"Really. You'll get accustomed to it."
"Never!"
"Yes, you will."
"That oatmeal is like eating puke."
Breakfast was always a blob of oatmeal that was splattered on the pewter plate which by the time the boys sat down to eat it, was cold and lumpy. Memo had it every day for more than three years and never again after he left the school.

But there were some good things. Carlitos showed him where to hide, told him how to deal with his first grade teacher, and if he needed something done, to ask Melinda.
"Melinda?"
"Yes. Get on her good side."
"Why? She's just a servant."
"She's more than a servant. She runs the school."
"I though Doña Belisa ran the school."
"She runs the office and leads the prayers, but all other things Melinda runs."
The servant runs the school. How about that? Memo had trouble with that one.

There were some very bad things. Even Carlitos could not help him with those.

"I hate the praying. Why do we pray so much?"
"To pay for our sins."
"What are sins?"
"Bad things we do every day."
"We haven't done any bad things."
"We must have, otherwise we wouldn't have to pray."
"But, what if I hadn't sinned, would I still have to pray?"
"You must've sinned."
"Wouldn't I know if I had sinned?"
"I guess."
"If I told Doña Belisa that I hadn't sinned, would I still have to pray?"
"Even more so."
"Why?"
"Because she would say you are lying. And lying is a sin."

The boys were woken up at six a.m. and after they had cleaned the pees and themselves, they would put on their khaki uniforms and go assemble in the patio and wait for Doña Belisa to lead them in prayer. At six thirty sharp she would appear, dressed in black from head to toe, including her shawl, and she would sit on her hammock. She would get her rosary out and say:
"Good morning."
"Good morning, Doña Belisa."
"Let us pray." All the children would kneel on the dirt to pray along with her. Memo did not know how to pray.

María was a Catholic but never went to church. Actually, Memo knew she had gone to church once, right after he was born. She had taken baby Memo with her. María told Memo she was grateful he had been given unto her and that she had brought him to the Virgin of Guadalupe to thank her for her healthy boy, and to ask the Virgin to protect him all of his life. Other than that, Memo could not remember going to church. María did pray every night when putting him to sleep but it was more like a conversation she had with God than a prayer. She talked to Him about her day and ended always by asking Him and the

Virgin to take care of Memo. She would ask him if he wanted to say something to God and Memo would have his little conversation with the Lord, and then both would say amen. He'd go to sleep and she'd go to the theater to work.

That was her way.

Doña Belisa's way was very formal and very long. She would have her rosary with a lot of beads on it, and the praying went on for as long as there were beads; which was entirely too long. Especially if you were a little boy wearing short pants. Memo marveled at how many little stones his knees could find. The tiny little things would dig deeply into his flesh causing him great discomfort. All the children spent the interminable twenty-five minutes of prayer, squirming. This torture took place twice a day. It was not long before the children developed an aversion to praying; praying equaled pain. It was difficult to understand why one should go through the agony if one had not sinned.

"Did you sin today?" Memo asked Carlitos.
"I don't know. Maybe."
"What do you mean maybe?"
"Maybe I sinned and I didn't know it."
"How could that be?"
"Maybe I thought something bad."
"Like what?"
"Maybe I thought that I would like to drown one of the bullies in the well."
"And thinking it is a sin?"
"Yes, thinking can be a sin."
Memo could not wait for Saturday to arrive so he could tell his mother all he had learned.
"You sure my mother is coming tomorrow?"
"Most mothers will be here Saturday, except for the kids whose parents put them here as punishment."
"Punishment? Like who?"
"Like some of the bullies for example. They put them in here because regular schools don't want them. They've been bad."

"Well, I haven't been bad, so my mother should be here, right?"
"Right."
"You'll get to meet my mamá, and I'll get to meet yours?"
"Probably."
"What do you mean probably?"
"Sometimes she's too busy to come; an emergency or something."
"What do you do when that happens?"
"Sometimes there are a few other kids to play with. Most times there's no one."
"What do you do then?'
"Roam around."
"It must be lonely."
"Yes, but at least is quiet, and sometimes you get a goodie."
"A goodie?"
"Melinda takes pity on you and gives you an arroz con leche."

Saturday morning arrived. Memo saw there was a line forming by the front door. He ran up to it.
"What's going on?"
"We're going to confession."
"Can I come too?"
"Have you had your first communion?"
"No."
"Then you can't come. You go to catechism instead."
Even though Doña Belisa was a humorless woman, the stories he heard that morning he enjoyed. He learned about the creation of the world, Adam, Eve, the serpent, and sin, Cain, Abel, and sin, God, Satan, and sin. *It's like a fairy tale, with a lot of sins.* Surprisingly he had survived his first week and was looking forward to his mother's visit.

"Come," whispered Carlitos, "the best place to wait for our mothers is in the third grade classrooms."
Those rooms had windows that protruded about six inches out, just enough for the boys to stand on. Through the wrought iron bars the boys could see the parents coming to pick up their sons. The boys craned their necks in anticipation. Interminable minutes went by.

"There she is!" cried Carlitos and he ran out, leaving Memo by the window. Almost immediately Carlitos popped his head back in the door frame, "Don't worry; your mother will be here soon. See you tomorrow night!" He was off again.

Memo watched Carlitos and his mother walk away until they disappeared around the corner. He waited, and waited, and waited. Once in a while he would run into the courtyard to see how many boys were still left and he would run right back in case he missed her arrival. Every woman who walked toward the school was his mother, and every woman turned into a stranger as she got closer to him. Each hopeful high was followed by a disappointing low, taking so much out of him that eventually he crumpled down on the floor.

"Memoo . . . Memoo"

He heard the voice call.

"Memoo . . . Memoo."

"My mother! She's calling me."

That's how his mother always called him in the mornings, when it was time to get out of bed; in a sweet soft tone. "Memoo . . . Memoo . . ." The oo of the second Memo sung a third higher than the first one.

He sprung to his feet and ran toward his mother's voice.

"There you are," said Melinda. I've been looking all over for you. What are you doing in that classroom? Don't you know you're not supposed to be in there?"

"I was waiting for my mother."

"She's not coming today."

"How do you know?"

"I know," she said, in a way that brooked no argument.

He looked around the courtyard.

"All the boys . . . ?"

"Gone." She took him by the hand and walked him to the empty comedor.

"You'll have lunch with me."

They sat at the first long table, nearest to the kitchen. She tried to make conversation but Memo could not manage more than a grunt or two. She looked at him. He looked at his plate.

"I have a surprise for you." She went into the kitchen.

"There." She put down a dish of arroz con leche.

Memo could not help but smile. Next to flan, this was his favorite dessert. *I hope it's good.* So far, every meal had had the dubious distinction of being worse than the last one. Cautiously, Memo took half a spoonful into his mouth.

"It's good!" He said incredulously.

"Course it's good. I made it myself." She let out a belly laugh that surprised him.

Memo giggled. She laughed louder. Memo giggled again. She laughed uproariously. They laughed uproariously together. Their laughter reverberated all over the empty school.

That night Memo talked to God and asked Him why his mother had forsaken him. God did not answer. In his hammock, quietly at first then less and less so, Memo cried the tears he had been holding back since the day he met Carlitos. Carlitos was not there to tell him not to cry.

Sunday morning Memo roamed. He went into the first grade classroom and walked around it. He sat at his desk and traced, with the nail of his index finger, the names of other kids scratched into the wooden surface. He thought about them and wondered if they had been as unhappy as he was. For a moment he considered scratching his name in too. *I wonder if that's a sin. Maybe I have already sinned since I thought about it.* He decided he better leave the room before something worse happened. He walked through the second grade classrooms. Just more of the same. He listened to the silence. *Carlitos is right, at least it is quiet.* The quiet made him sad so he decided he needed a distraction. He went to the third grade classroom and stared out of one the windows at the empty street. After a while he went to the other window and after another while to the other one. Nothing is more silent than a Sunday street. He told himself he was just killing time but, deep inside, he clung to the hope that his mother might still come. He started to feel sorry for himself so he decided to go somewhere else. He stood outside the classroom and stared at the sun-soaked courtyard. His gaze scanned the four-sided corridor. He stared at the rust colored stains that came from the bottom of the four drain pipes which hung down from the four corners of the roof. *How beautiful they are,* he thought. The stains ran toward the center of the courtyard and softly faded at about the same distance from the well. *Well, what else can I do?* He had never been inside the fourth grade classrooms and considered going there but decided that all classrooms were the same; boring. *The most interesting part of the school is the patio!* He decided to go there. He started to cross the cement courtyard but, on a whim, he stopped by the well. He leaned in and looked into its darkness. The dank smell of water filled his nostrils. He could see the water bucket bobbing gently upon the water like a little ship. He called out, "Bucket . . . bucket . . . what are you doing?" The echo repeated his question. Memo decided to talk to the echo.

"Echo . . . echo . . . do you like me?"

"Do you like mee?" asked the echo.

"I asked you first."

"I asked you first," said the echo.

"No, *I* asked you first."

"*I* asked you first." said the echo.

At last he had someone to talk to. He decided this was worth exploring further.

"What is your name echo?"

"Echoo," the echo answered. *That makes sense,* Memo thought.

"My name is Memo."

"Memoo," said the echo.

"That's right, Memo."

"Memoo."

Memo liked his name. He did not know anyone whose name was Memo.

"My real name is Guillermo Antonio, but my mother calls me Memo."

"Memoo."

"Memoo!"

Memo turned around and saw Melinda standing by one of the comedor's doors.

"Memo, what are you doing?"

"Nothing."

"We'll have lunch at noon. I don't want to have to go find you."
"How will I know it's twelve?"
"You'll hear the church bell. Got it?"
"Got it."
There is always a church nearby, in Mexico.
"Don't lean too far into the well, you might fall in," and she disappeared into the comedor. Memo remembered the patio. "Bye," he said to the echo and left without waiting for echo to answer.

The patio's plants grew wildly in the shape of a horseshoe. There was no design to it. The horseshoe shape was the result of years of praying assemblies that had left the center of the patio bare. The children knelt in front of Doña Belisa's hammock, which hung from two large trees that grew in the center of the patio. Behind the hammock grew some banana trees and other assorted trees. In between them there were bushes that grew willy-nilly. The only water they received came from the sky during the rainy season. Fortunately, the canopy formed by the trees provided a shade which protected the prayers from the merciless Mérida sun. Memo looked at Doña Belisa's hammock which sat in the silent shade, still. He walked toward it. He wanted to sit on it but wondered if he would be breaking a rule if he did. He looked back toward the building. Melinda was nowhere in sight. It was a sturdy hammock; it had to be because Doña Belisa was a heavy woman. He sat on it. He hardly made a dent on it, which surprised him because when she sat on it the hammock sagged noticeably. *Either I don't weigh much or she weighs a lot,* he thought. He began to swing in the hammock by pushing it back then jumping on it. It was very nice, very comfortable. *Easy to pray from here.* He thought he heard Melinda coming so he jumped off the hammock and moved away from it. He stood still and listened. Only silence. *I must be doing something bad because I feel guilty. I better stay away from the hammock.* He went around the patio looking for places to hide. *It's always a good idea to have at least one place to hide, Carlitos told me.* Memo could see the wisdom in that. He climbed up one of the trees. It was the first time he had ever climbed a tree and it took more effort than he thought it would. He got about half way up and decided not to push his luck. *I'll rest a little while before I climb down.* He sat on a sturdy branch and looked down at the hammock. A soft breeze wafted his face; a welcome change in the oppressive humid heat. He was pleased about his climbing feat. He looked at the hammock again. His mind kept returning to the one thought; *easy to pray when you're comfortably sitting on a nice hammock.* It did not seem right somehow. The church bell began to toll twelve.

"Memoo."

He had completely forgotten about lunch.

"Coming," he yelled and began to climb down as fast and as carefully as he could. He jumped down from the lowest branch and ran to the comedor.

"What were you doing?"

"Nothing."

"You've been doing a lot of nothing today."

"I guess."

"Well," she said as she mussed his hair, "let's eat."

He followed her into the comedor.

"What are you going to do the rest of the afternoon?" asked Melinda after lunch.

"Well, uh maybe I . . ."

"I know. Nothing. Go ahead and go, wherever you were before, and do some more nothing. Just don't get into trouble doing it."

"Thanks for the arroz con leche." And he ran off to the patio.

He went right back up his tree and sat on the same branch. He tried to go higher but he could not reach the next branch. He was afraid he might fall, harm himself and worse, cause trouble for Melinda. He liked Melinda. He did not want to make her mad at him. She had made his loneliness bearable. He had Carlitos and now he had Melinda. He sat and he sat as the afternoon slowly wore on.

Little by little the boys began to return to school. By the time it was dark enough to turn the yellow lights on, most of them were back. He had dinner with them. This time there was no arroz con leche. All the boys were telling each other their stories. Carlitos was telling his to Memo. He was happy his friend was happy but he was sad he did not have similar stories. In the middle of his listening, Memo became aware of how sad the yellow lights made him. He had never before minded the yellow quality of certain electric lights, but from then on yellow lights would make him sad. When he went to El Salvador he noticed that the street lights had that yellow quality. And again they made him sad. Was it the lights or was it his loneliness? He did not know. For many years he dreaded the night because it brought with it the yellow lights.

The second week started. The learning he liked. Carlitos he liked. And Melinda he liked. Religion he did not. The woman who was teaching it to him he did not. And the god he was learning about he did not. With each week that passed he disliked all three more. His mind told him that something was not right.

Over the course of the year, every Saturday morning would be dedicated to the Bible. At first he was full of whys and asked Doña Belisa, but soon he learned she did not like it when he questioned her answers and, like the rest of the boys, he ended up listening without listening. As a result, he began to dislike what he saw as two-facedness: Abstinence and sacrifice preached by an overweight woman sitting on a comfortable hammock. "If something doesn't make sense to you—ask," his mother had taught him. Dona Belisa was the first, in a line of religious authority figures, who seemed intolerant of inquiry. Something was not right.

The god, in the Bible Doña Belisa read from, was full of wrath and vengeance. This was a stern god, a demanding god, a punishing god. Why would anyone love such a god? This was not the God of love and understanding his mother had told him about. Something was not right.

Every weekend Memo would wait by the balcony and every weekend his mother would not come, and every weekend he would roam the school. About once a month or so, he would receive a letter from his mother and he would write back asking her when she would come visit him and she would write back, "Soon." But soon never came.

Night after night, before going to sleep, he would ask his mother's God why was his mother not coming to see him, but He would not answer and eventually Memo grew disenchanted with both; mother and God. This would cause him great anxiety and guilt. The teachings of the church were taking hold. Sins were everywhere. Memo had to be on the lookout for them. His mother had led him to believe he was good but it seemed to him that, at the school, adults were always assuming that children were naturally inclined to be bad. Punishment, punishment, punishment followed by prayer, prayer, prayer. His mother's abandonment seemed to support the idea that he must have done something wrong and this was his punishment. He began to doubt he was good. *But I am good. I believe in my heart that I am. I have not changed. I have been good and I cannot believe that all of a sudden I am not. Something has gone wrong but I haven't. But then, why isn't my mother here? What's she doing that's more important to her than I am? What did I do to deserve this punishment?*

How does a mother tell this to her child: "I am thirty-three years young. I am an actress with a career I like. I am a woman with a lover I love. I need to work in order to take care of you. That means I have to travel. You cannot travel with me because you must go to school. I have to leave you behind even if it hurts you or me. I love you, but I love my freedom too." She does not. She lies to him.

The weeks turned into months. He was doing well enough in the first grade but his troubles with religion, Doña Belisa, and God were mounting. He had given up on all three of them. One day he was told that soon he would take his First Communion. This was good and it was bad because catechism would end but confession and communion would begin.

"Do you know if your mother is coming to see you for this important event?"

"I wrote to her asking her, but she hasn't answered. So, I don't know."

He was embarrassed to say he did not know. The day of his First Communion came. In his fairytalish heart he hoped she would surprise him and be at church for the occasion. At the church, the boys, all dressed in white, stood in the first row. All the parents stood in the row behind, beaming with pride. Only Memo's mother was missing.

Thus the school year ended and vacation started. One by one, all the boys were picked up and soon the school was empty; including the dormitory. Only Memo's hammock hung silently in the void.

"Your mother can't come pick you up," said Doña Belisa. "You'll spend the summer with me." *Not if I can avoid it,* Memo thought.

He counted his blessings. *At least I know she's not coming so I won't bother spending every day waiting by the window. Melinda is still here so I can have arroz con leche with her. And I know every hiding place in the school and Doña Belisa will never find me.* This ability to be where she was not came handy years later when he was in the U.S. Army. He noticed many soldiers had the same skill. Memo wondered where they had honed theirs.

And so the weeks passed. The long lonely days made longer by the sweltering summer heat. Memo got good at being alone. Day dreaming became his favorite pastime. He would lie in Doña Belisa's hammock, stare up into the tree's canopy and let his imagination dream. He could climb every tree and knew which birds had nests where. He knew which parts of the building were cooler at which times of the day. He would sit by the window for hours to watch people go by; a sort of live television. He knew when the paletero would come by to sell his popsicles. He liked to watch the kids in the street run up to him to buy their favorite flavors. He knew what flavors each of them liked. He knew the children's names and the paletero's name. He ate all his meals with Melinda and learned which topics she liked and which she did not. He also learned when she wanted him around and when it was better to leave her alone. Doña Belisa would go away for a week to visit somebody, leaving Melinda in charge. Memo found it amusing that Doña Belisa did not know Melinda was always in charge. The days blended into sameness. As the summer droned on he would not have been able to tell you the difference between one week and another, let alone between one day and another. Then, two weeks before the end of the summer, it happened!

"Memoo, Memoo . . ." he heard Melinda call. *It's too early for lunch time.* "Memoo . . . Memoo . . ." she called again. "Coming," he yelled. He crawled out of his hiding place and ran toward her voice. "Memoo . . . Memoo . . ." called the woman standing next to Melinda. Memo stopped in his tracks. The woman was his mother! He ran and leapt into his mother's arms almost knocking her down, just as his dog Sapo would do years later when he found him all beaten up but alive. Memo threw his arms around her neck, buried his head in her chest and cried. He did not want to cry but he could not stop crying. He was so happy!

"Let me see you," his mother said as she tried to put him down.

Memo shook his head. He would not let go of her. He was ashamed of his tears.

"Don't cry," she said, echoing the words Carlitos had said to him almost a year ago. Moments passed before the tears began to subside. Somewhat calmed, he lifted his head, looked at her face to make sure he was not dreaming and burst into tears once again. Sometimes life exceeds our dreams.

"I'm sorry, I'm sorry," he whispered.

"I'm sorry, I'm sorry," she whispered.

Tenderly she patted him on the back. They stayed like that for a while. When María thought he was composed she put him down and said, "Come on, we have a lot of wonderful things to do!"

The next two weeks were a whirlwind of happiness. She took him to Campeche, a port southwest of Mérida known for the friendliness of its people, and fed him love. He gobbled that up. She also fed him his favorite meal; crab legs. He gobbled that up. And flan and Orange Crush. And he gobbled them up too. In between bites and sips, he told her all that had happened in the last fifty weeks. She listened sympathetically. She did all the things that made him love her so much. She made him feel special again. She soothed his wounds. She made him the center of her life—for two weeks.

On their return from heaven the two of them sat silently on the back of the bus. There was nothing to say. He knew he was going back to jail. She knew what he had gone through and yet she was the one taking him there again. He understood now the look he had seen in Carlitos' eyes one year ago. There was no pretense this time. He knew he had touched her heart. He had hoped that it would have made a difference. He could not believe that in spite of all that, she was going to put him back in hell. He knew about hell; he had studied the catechism. She knew there was no use of trying to explain. She had to take him back to school, whether he like it or not. Whether *she* liked it or not. She knew she had taken a chunk of innocence from his heart. She had caused irreparable damage and was about to cause more. There were no words worth saying. He now regretted the two weeks. She probably felt the same way. He had to go back, and she had to go away. There was no other choice. *What kind of world is this?* He asked himself. *Is everybody's world like this? How did I get so lucky?* Why had he been so chosen? What had he done to deserve another year of loneliness? *If my own mother doesn't care, I can't expect anyone else to care. Who decides these things?*

They got off the bus and, in silence, walked the few blocks to the school. She knocked on the door. The little door opened. He walked in and did not stop until he was in his hiding place. This time he did not turn to take one more look at his mother. What for? In his little hiding place he daydreamed the ending he hoped had happened. His mother said the things he had hoped she would say. He dreamt away his loneliness.

MORE DOGMA, LESS MA

The second year started: The same thing, but different. A different classroom, a different teacher, the lumpy oatmeal. The same thing. The pushing and shoving, the praying and squirming, Doña Belisa and her hammock. The same thing. Melinda and Carlitos, the long lone weekends, the roaming. The same thing.

Memo was different. He knew that happiness is fleeting and loneliness permanent. Like Carlitos before him, and he was sure many other children, he had no tears to shed. There were others who did, but Carlitos and Memo were not among them. He still went to the window to see the mothers pick up their sons, but he held no hopes for himself. He did not envy the boys who went away on Saturday morning because he knew they had to come back Sunday night to the yellow lights.

Saturdays were different. Instead of the catechism game he now had the confession game. It was a more complex game than the catechism game. In the catechism game all you had to do was to appear to be listening. The confession game was another matter.

First you have to stand in line waiting to go to church. At church, you have to stand in another line to go into the confessional; a small enclosed place where there is a screen. On one side of it sits a man dressed in black, on the other side is you, kneeling. He had learned the sitting and the kneeling parts from Doña Belisa. Then the tricky part started. The man asked Memo to tell him his sins. Memo made the novice's mistake of answering truthfully.

"I haven't any sins to tell, sir."

"Call me Father. You haven't committed any sins?"

"No, sir."

Why does he say committed? It sounds like a crime. Is a sin a crime?

"When was the last time you went to confession?"

"Never, sir."

"Call me Father."

"Yes, sir. I mean Father." *Why do I have to call him father? I don't know him.*

"Is this your first confession?"

"Yes, Father."

"And you have no sins to tell me?"

"No."

"Hmm, are you sure?"

"I'm pretty sure, Father."

"Not even one?"

"No, sir, I mean Father."

"I'll tell you what. All this next week every time you commit a sin try to remember it and at the end of the week you'll have sins to tell me."

"What happens if I don't sin?"

"You will. Two Hail Mary's and two Our Fathers."

"What do you mean?"

"Go out there, kneel and say two Hail Mary's and two Our Fathers."

"And why do I do that?"

"For your sins. Go!"

"But I didn't . . ."

"Go!"

"Yes sir, er, Father." And Memo scrambled out of there.

The kid who was next in line, seeing Memo run out of the confessional and looking very concerned for his immediate fate, asked Memo, "What happened?"

"I had no sins to tell him."

"Oh, that's bad."

"Next!" Called the Father.

The kid, fearing he just might have added to his burden by being late, ran in.

Memo walked to a pew, knelt, and said his penitence. *I need to talk to Carlitos about this. He'll be back Sunday night. Until then I'll be very careful and watch myself for any sins I may commit.* Religion is an unfathomable thing.

Sunday night, after Carlitos told him about his weekend, Memo told him about his problems in the confessional.

"How does it work?"

"Let's get in our hammocks before Melinda calls lights out."

They brushed their teeth and got in their hammocks.

"First of all, you never tell the truth."

"Why not?"

"They don't want the truth."

"What do they want?"

"They want sinners."

"If I haven't sinned and I can't tell them that, what do I tell them?"

"You tell them you sinned."

"But, I'll be lying."

"Yes. And if you are lying you are sinning. So you are telling the truth."

"Huh?"

"If you tell them you haven't sinned, they think you are lying. If you tell them you have sinned then you are sinning, so you're telling the truth. You're both right. They give you your penitence and it's over."

"What if they ask what the sins are?"

"That's when it gets a little tricky. You make up the sins."

"I make up the sins? But that's a sin."

"Exactly. This is fine, because they are going to give you penitence no matter what. You just have to be careful about two things."

"What two things?"

"How many sins, and how serious. Don't make them too serious or too many or you'll spend an hour praying."

"It's all a big lie."

"Yes it is. But lying is good. Stealing is more serious. If you tell them you stole something, make it something small. I'd recommend you start with lying."

"How many lies?"

"Two or three. Once in a while I do four, just to make it sound like I'm telling the truth."

"Huh?"

"Don't worry, after a while you'll get good at it. Lying is my favorite sin."

"What about the penitence?"

"What about it?"

"How do they know that you did it?"

"They don't. That's why I love penitence."

"You love penitence?"

"No. I just don't do it."

"Not at all?"

"Just enough to make it look as if I did it."

"Isn't that a sin?"

"That's the beauty of it. It's your first sin for next week."

"But God knows you didn't do it."

"Exactly. God knows I didn't do it but He also knows I didn't sin, so it all works out for everybody."

"So that's the way it works."

"Lights out!" Melinda shouted from the door as she flicked down the switch. The room quieted down somewhat.

"Oh, one more thing," Carlitos lowered his voice.

"There's more?"

"Yes. When you are in line waiting to confess, ask the boy in front and the boy behind what sins they are going to tell."

"Why?"

"You don't want to tell the same sins. It doesn't look good."
"You mean all the boys know?"
"Everybody knows."
"Do the priests know?"
"Of course they know."
"They do?"
"They played the game when they were kids. They probably sit there chuckling."
"Really?"
"It's been around from the beginning. It's a very popular game."
"Does everybody play the game?"
"No. Only Catholics play it. Other religions have their games."
"And God knows about the game?"
"Of course. He created it."
"He created it?"
"Of course!"
"Why would He do that?"
"To see how we play it. Remember the story of Adam and Eve?"
Memo nodded.
"God knew they were going to eat the fruit."
"He knew?"
"Sure. That's why he told them not to."
"He tricked them!" Memo whispered.
"You don't have to whisper. He hears everything."
"There's no escape."
"None." Carlitos yawned, "Just play the game and don't worry too much about it. Good night."
"Good night." Memo turned over in his hammock.

His eyelids began to get heavy with sleep. The blue silvery light of the moon shone on the cement outside the dorm. *So, that's how it works. Well, I'll be . . .* And he fell asleep.

The following Saturday Memo had his lies all lined up. He repeated them to himself, like an actor preparing for a performance, over and over again. The kid behind him tapped him on the shoulder. Memo turned to a chubby little boy named Lito, who looked frazzled.

"Are you alright?"

"No. This confession business makes me nervous."

"Me too. How many sins have you got?"

"I've got fourteen."

"Fourteen? Are you crazy? Why so many?"

"How many do you have?"

"Three plus a back-up just in case," said Memo, sounding very professional.

"You think that's enough?"

Memo nodded.

"Tell me your sins."

Memo told him.

"I have three of your four. That leaves me with nine. Is that still too many?"

"You mean eleven."

"What?"

"You still have eleven left."

"I do? Oh, yeah. Is that still too many?"

"Definitely. Four is plenty."

"I'll choose the worst four."

"Don't embroider too much or he won't believe you."

"Thanks," Lito said, sounding somewhat relieved.

Memo tapped the shoulder of the boy in front and asked, "Emilio these are my sins," Memo told him his sins. "Have you got any of them?"

"No, you're clear. But, I like your number three. I have to remember that one."

"Thanks," Memo said proudly.

Just then a kid came out of the confessional.

"Wish me luck," said Emilio. He took a deep breath and disappeared into the confessional.

In a few moments Emilio came out and gave Memo a wink. Memo went in, played his part perfectly, and got his penitence. He went to a pew, did half his prayers, crossed himself and went out to join the rest of the boys. Kids were bragging about their lies, some were a little concerned about them, and all were relieved it was over for another week. Memo was amazed at the whole thing. He was also disappointed. *Carlitos was right; it's just a game. I hope God doesn't punish me.*

God did. At least that was how Memo interpreted it. A month later he found himself in the hospital, quarantined with the measles. It was a horrible time. His skin erupted with a hundred ulcers, his throat and nose so full of mucus he could hardly breathe, and a fever so high he hallucinated. It was especially bad at night when nightmare and reality seemed to mix together. The rectangular ward had windows on three of its four sides. The fourth side had a door that connected it to the rest of the hospital. Through the windows Memo could see the clothesline which, during the day, the hospital used to dry uniforms, patients' pajamas, sheets, towels and whatnot. During the night, in Memo's feverish mind, the clothes became ghosts dancing in the air outside the windows. The first week or so he was not as frightened because he shared the isolation ward with another boy who was on the side nearest to the door. After that, he was left alone. It was then that he began to experience a recurring nightmare that would wake him up several times during the night.

He would see himself standing erect, feet together, hands by his sides. Little by little he would start to grow taller and taller and taller until he would become a giant. He would continue to grow until he was taller than the trees and taller still until his head would touch the clouds. He then would look down at his feet and see the earth below. The earth would be rotating clockwise on its axis. He would continue to grow so tall that he would be bigger than the earth. So big in fact, that, as it rotated, the earth's gravitational pull would be unable to keep him on it and, when the earth had rotated one quarter of its circumference, he would inexorably fall into the blue-black cosmic void. At that very moment he would wake up screaming. The nurses, assuming he would sleep all night long, were too far away to hear him. It was then that his feverish eyes would see the ghosts dancing in the moonlight. He would yell for the nurses but none would come. At some point he would fall asleep again and the nightmare would start again.

How long was he in the hospital Memo never knew. Eventually the disease desisted and he was well enough to be released. He never thought he would ever be happy to go back to school but for him it was his home, and the kids, his family. For years after, even into his twenties, whenever he got a fever, he had the recurring nightmare. For the next few weeks, Memo had to study hard to make up for the time lost, but he was one of the better students in his class and soon life in the school droned on as before.

The illness had a positive effect on him. He had never been so sick in his life and now that he was healthy again he found that, by comparison, the school life was not as bad as he used to think. He was not happy; he was content. Again the days blended into weeks and months. There was some measure of comfort in the monotony of routine.

"Doña Belisa wants to talk to you," said Melinda.
"What does she want?"
"I don't know. Come with me."
It was usually bad news to be called into her office. Memo began to go over the last few days to see if he had done something wrong. He could not think of anything, which made him worry more; the unknown being scarier than the known.
"Go in," Melinda said, "she's waiting for you."
Memo went into her office and stood not too far from the door.
"Come closer, young man," said Doña Belisa.
Memo walked up to the front of her desk and stood there at attention, awaiting his fate.
"The school year is almost over and I hear you've done well enough that you will be promoted to the third grade."
"Thank you ma'am," said Memo, feeling confused. *She wouldn't call me just to give me good news.*
"This is the problem. I'm going to close the school for two months during the summer. That means you can't stay here like you did last year. I've already sent your mother a letter informing her of this. However, I think you better write to her also. Maybe when she hears it from you she'll realize she has to make arrangements now. Do you understand?"
"Yes ma'am."

"Fine, go do it."

Two weeks later, classes were over and the school was left empty, except for Memo, Melinda, and Doña Belisa.

"Doña Belisa wants to talk to you." said Melinda

"What does she want?"

"I don't know. Come with me."

"Go in," Melinda said, "she's waiting for you."

Memo went into her office and stood not too far from the door.

"Come here, young man," said Doña Belisa. "Melinda tells me your birthday is next week?"

"Yes, ma'am."

"How old would you be, young man?"

"I'll be seven, ma'am."

"I'll tell Melinda to make you arroz con leche."

"Thank you, ma'am." *She wouldn't call me just to tell me this.*

"This is the problem. I've just received a letter from your mother. She says she's in the northern part of Mexico and doesn't think she can be here before I close the school. I think you better write her and tell her that if she doesn't come I will put you in an orphanage. She might take this more seriously if she hears it from you. Do you understand?"

"Yes, ma'am. What's an orphanage ma'am?"

"It's a place where children who have no parents live. You'd better write that letter today. With the mail being slow, and your mother always traveling, it will take a couple of weeks before your letter reaches her. Do you understand?"

"Yes, ma'am."

Two weeks later he had yet to hear from his mother.

"Doña Belisa wants to talk to you." said Melinda. "Don't ask me what she wants because I don't know."

Memo walked to her office in worried silence.

"Go in," Melinda said, "she's waiting for you."

Memo went into her office and stood not too far from the door.

"Did Melinda make you arroz con leche for you birthday?" "Yes, ma'am."

"This is the problem. I'm closing the school in three days. Your mother has not answered my letter so you better start packing your things. In three days I will send you to the orphanage. Do you understand?"

"Yes, ma'am."

"Happy birthday."

"Thank you, ma'am."

Memo spent each of the next three days by the window hoping his mother would pick him up. He had not heard from her. His only hope was that she had not written because she was on her way.

"Doña Belisa wants to see you," said Melinda.

Memo did not ask her because he already knew it was going to be bad news.

"Here he is, Doña Belisa."

"Are you all packed?"

"Yes, ma'am."

"At noon today someone will come from the orphanage to pick you up. Bring your things to the front door."

"Yes ma'am."

Memo brought his things to the front door and ran to the window hoping to see his mother arrive. The orphanage frightened him. He had learned to live with the boys of the school who, with few exceptions, were just like him; children whose parents, for whatever reasons, had seen fit to put them in a boarding school. He did not know what kind of child ended up in an orphanage. Carlitos said they were poor kids who had lost their parents. Carlitos had also said not to worry; that Memo's mother would come pick him up. But here he was just minutes from being sent away and there was no sign of his mother. He stared at every woman he saw coming toward the school thinking he could will her into being his mother. *Where is my mother? She's not going to let me go to an orphanage. She's not. She's not.* He kept an ear fixed in the direction of the nearby church. It was the church in which he made his First Communion and where he went to confession every week. The bell would soon toll twelve. In the distance he saw a man on a black bicycle. The church bell began to toll. Bong. The straight and narrow street was almost deserted, telling Memo it was almost lunch time. Bong. The man on the bicycle neared. A boy and his mother walked right past Memo's window. Bong. His eyes followed them until they disappeared. Bong. The man on the bicycle stopped in front of the school's door. Bong. He got off, left the bicycle leaning against the wall, and entered the building. Bong. *I hope he is not the man from the orphanage.* Bong. He heard the door open. Bong. Memo clung to the window's iron bars. Bong. He heard the muffled voice of the man. Bong.

"Memoo . . . Memoo . . ." Melinda called. Bong.

He took one last look. The street was empty. Bong.

Reluctantly, he let go of the bars and started to walk slowly out of the room.

"This young man is going to take you."

The man was already holding Memo's things.

"See you in September," said Melinda. She gave Memo a hug.

It took all of Memo's will not to cry.

"See you." He let go of her.

"You'll ride on the bar," said the man. "Have you ever done that?"

"No." Memo sat on the bicycle's bar.

"Hang on tight to the handlebar. Carmencita's is not far."

Memo sat uncomfortably on the metal bar and hung tightly to the handlebar.

The man pushed off the curb. There was a wobbly moment but as the bicycle gained speed, it rode straight forward.

"Is Carmencita's the name of the orphanage?"

"No. Carmencita is my aunt. She and your mother are friends. I'm taking you to her house."

"Her house?"

"Yes. You're going to spend the rest of the summer with her."

He could not believe it. His mother had come through after all. He was ecstatic.

"You'll like her. She has a couple of kids about your age. You'll have fun."

It was not as fun as he hoped but it was much better than an orphanage. Carmencita was nice to him but she was not his mother.

He had never lived in a house before and he did not know what the right thing to do was, and what was not. He was a guest but he had not been invited; he had been taken in. Probably his mother was paying the lady to keep him. Maybe Memo was too sensitive but it was an uncomfortable situation. It was somewhat akin to what he would experience later on in El Salvador with La Cheli; he was not an equal. The toys were their toys, the furniture was their furniture, and the house was their house. But it was much better than an orphanage. The kids were nice to him but if something went awry they would say something to remind him of his status. Still, it gave him the opportunity to see a family up close. It made him long for the day he would have a house and a family of his own. It was an uneasy state of affairs, but it was much better than an orphanage.

About ten days before the end of the summer, María showed up. Memo was happy but cautious. His mother was eternally grateful to Carmencita. For as long as María lived, every Christmas and every birthday, his mother sent a card to Carmencita. After a day or so, María told her she wanted to spend some time alone with Memo and, as they had the year before, they spent the few days they had left in Campeche. Memo enjoyed each and every day but not with the abandon with which he had the first time. He had learned that each happy day brought closer his return to school. He kept his happiness in check. He wanted to discuss his grievances with his mother but he was afraid this would spoil their time together. One day, after a wonderful lunch by the beach, his mother asked him if he wanted to go walk on the pier. He said he did. It was a lovely sunny day. The breeze from the sea cooled their faces as they walked toward the end of the pier. *How can I talk to my mom about my future and not ruin this beautiful afternoon?* Their time together was running short so he decided to take a chance. They arrived at the end of the pier and stood silently for a few moments, admiring the emerald green Caribbean Sea.

"Mamá, I don't want to spoil this beautiful day but . . ."

"What is it?" His mother asked, concerned.

"I know our time together is about to end and I must go back to school . . ."

"I'm sorry, but I have . . ."

"I know you don't want to do it and that you have to do it. I understand that now, but I need to ask you a question. May I?"

"Go ahead." María braced herself.

"This is going to be my third year there. How many more years do you think, I mean, is this the way it's going to be for the rest of my school life?"

María was stunned. It had been a day to day thing for her. From her perspective it was a short term solution. From his, it was a long term problem. For the first time she understood the bleakness of Memo's perception.

"I mean . . . is this what I can expect my future to be? You, somewhere working and me, in some boarding school?"

She had no answer for him. She realized the impact her answer would have on him. She needed to think. Emboldened by her silence, Memo continued.

"Because right now, I can't see an end to it. Is there going to be?"

María looked at her son as if she was discovering him. This was not the little five year old boy she remembered. The maturity of his questions surprised her. She recognized that he was changing and she was missing her son's growth. There was a good mind in her little boy and her little boy was asking profound questions. She had to reconsider her life and put some kind of plan in motion that would bring her and her son together.

"When do I get to live with my family, in my house?"

She stared at the immensity of the sea.

"I mean, I want to feel what it's like to be part of a loving family. I don't like being always surrounded by strangers. When do I stop being an outsider? Never?"

Never is a long time, but to a child never is even longer. She suddenly realized that never is hopelessness. She had to give her son hope. She looked into his eyes and saw in Memo what he had seen in Carlitos' eyes two years ago; she saw strength, and she saw pain. It was then that she became aware of how much she was damaging him.

"You are right. There has to be an end to this. I don't know when and I don't know how but we will change it. I promise you."

"You promise? Really?"

"Yes. It's going to take a while. You still have to spend this year here but I'll find a way to bring us home." She paused for a moment as she looked at him appreciatively. "You have become quite the little man, haven't you?"

"Have I, mamá?"

"You have." She caressed his cheek. "Shall we go back to the hotel?"

They walked slowly back toward the beach. María looked at her mature little boy. *Too mature*, she thought. *At what price?* She put her arm on his shoulders. A tear slid softly down her cheek.

The last few days were joyous. Even though it was coming to an end, the conversation they had, had cleared the air. They had been honest with each other. She no longer saw Memo as a problem she had to solve but as a person to love and respect. He regained the trust in her he felt had been lost. They were a team once again, working together toward a common goal; getting back home. They had found each other again as two human beings who were inextricably linked. María realized she had a higher calling: more than an artist, she was a mother. She came to the realization that it was she who had taken away his Nicaraguan family and his Salvadorian family. Unwittingly, he was forcing her to her day of reckoning. Maybe she thought she could push that day to a vague formless future. Her son was telling her that day had arrived, prematurely perhaps, but nevertheless it was here and it had to be dealt with now. She had told herself that she had time to resolve the issue. Maybe she did, but her son's questions were telling her the time had been used up. Her boy was claiming his mother and all that that entailed. She could not deny him anymore. Besides, she liked what she saw. The boy had promise and she had to honor that promise. She did not want to lose Memo as she had lost Hector.

Hector was Memo's little brother. When his mother had left the hospital where Memo had been born, she had joined The Santillanas, a company of four siblings: Two brothers: Amaury and Mario, and two sisters: Hilda and Gladys. While the Compañía Encanto did operettas and zarzuelas, The Santillanas did vaudeville. In theatrical hierarchy

La Compañía Encanto was champagne, The Santillanas beer. María and Dahlia had known The Santillanas since they were children in El Salvador and, through the years, their paths had crossed when the two companies found themselves playing the same town. As luck would have it, The Santillanas were playing Managua when Elías was giving María his ultimatum. They heard her predicament and offered her a job. The Santillanas did not need her; after years of touring Central America, their act was set. It was a drastic drop for María but she was in no position to be choosey. Gratefully, she took their offer.

This decision further exacerbated her relationship with La Cheli, who looked down upon them as low comedians, which they were, and theater trash, which they were not. In La Cheli's puritanical mind, María was going to hell; a woman with a child, gallivanting around with a troupe that included two single men? Unconscionable! Unfortunately, La Cheli turned out to be right.

It was with The Santillanas that María went to Mexico. María and Mario became lovers and had a child out of wedlock: Hector. Having a lover was bad, having a child with him was worse. María had crossed the line that would keep her in Mexico a lot longer than she might have wanted. There is nothing more inflexible than a righteous spinster. As far as La Cheli was concerned, María was dead! This was the situation María had to repair to be able to bring Memo home.

Memo did not know he had a brother. His brother was born while he was in el Colegio Mejicano. For all he knew, his mother was already pregnant when she took Memo to the boarding school. The boy was born sickly and within months of his birth he contracted whooping cough. The little child had fought valiantly for his life but had lost the battle. It was a great loss to María and Mario and it might have soured their relationship. Memo did not know any of this. María probably thought it wise to keep him in the dark, but apparently La Cheli found out and even the little boy's death did not soften her heart. If anything, it confirmed her belief that she was right, and María wrong. The boy's death was her punishment for having strayed. At some point María and The Santillanas separated and she was forced to freelance from company to company in order to make a living. It was a tough time for her personally and professionally.

María had made some bad decisions and she had paid dearly for them. Memo's questions could be taken as a warning. That was not his intention, but given how she had been faring lately, she did not want to lose Memo. She decided she needed to rehabilitate her image with La Cheli and if that meant swallowing her pride and humbling herself before La Cheli in order to give Memo the family he wanted, she would do so. But it was not going to be easy, and it was going to take time. As they walked toward the hotel, María's mind considered her options. She did not like any of them but she had to do it for her son's sake. Besides, touring Mexico was leading nowhere. It was time to come home.

The bus ride back to school was not joyous but it was not nearly as painful as the year before. This time they talked about the day when he would be able to leave the school and live with her again. The hope of better times to come made the last few hours bearable. When he entered the little door, he turned around to say one more goodbye and his mother was still there to blow him a kiss. He returned the gesture. As the door closed they both clung to each other's eyes for as long as the door allowed. They were both smiling through their sadness. As she had the last two years before, Melinda was there waiting for him.

"Back for more, eh?" She said, smiling at him.

"You think you can take it?"

"I can, if you can."

"One more time," he said as he took her hand. "Let's get started."

Buoyed by his mother's promise, Memo tackled the school year. It would make her happy to see him do well and he was determined to please her. He had made peace with his mother and to some degree he had made peace with the Colegio Mejicano. He was a veteran of the wars now, having learned how to play the teacher-student game, the Doña Belisa game, and the confession game. He still had trouble with the praying game; too often, too long, and too painful. But he could see one good thing coming from it; by the time he would leave the Colegio Mejicano, he would have prayed for a lifetime and, since he hardly ever sinned, he would have plenty of reserves in the religious bank. Oh yes, he had one more thing to do; he needed to make peace with God.

For her part, María had a lot of work to do. She started by sending a birthday card to La Cheli that included a one page letter telling her about how well Memo was coming along. La Cheli did not answer. Christmas time she sent cards to all. Violeta responded, giving María the opportunity to write back. Before María had gone to Mexico she had stopped in El Salvador and Dahlia, Violeta and Marcelo had met Memo. A picture was taken of that occasion, and that frozen moment showed the five of them happy together. It was a picture taken in a studio by a professional photographer which indicated the two sisters had to have planned the event. Dahlia had agreed to it and that showed María that perhaps the door if not fully open, it was, at least, ajar. The fact that Violeta remembered that moment fondly increased María's hopes. Could La Cheli and Dahlia forgive and forget? María knew the answer to that. Still, could the family reunite? That was the unanswered question.

Memo wrote to his mother wanting to know if progress had been made. María told him what had happened and that she would continue her efforts but not to expect something to happen right away. "Please be patient," she cautioned, "I'll tell you of any progress I make."

Back in Mérida, he was talking to God again. He would pray with Doña Belisa during the day but at night in his hammock, he would talk to his mother's God. He apologized for having been angry at Him but he hoped that since He knew everything, He would know what Memo was going through and forgive him.

"I know you are very busy taking care of the universe, and maybe that is why you didn't hear me before, but I know you are listening now. Help us get back to El Salvador and our family. I'll be talking to you every night. Thank you, God."

"P.S. Lord, could you please make it happen by the end of this school year?"

As each member of the family's birthday came along, María would send cards and letters. Violeta would write telling her that she had asked her mother and La Cheli about letting them come and she hoped soon La Cheli would allow it. Dahlia was showing signs of softening her position. It was not yet yes but it was no longer no. María was afraid to tell Memo that it was going to happen, so she would tell him it might happen, but only not yet.

Dahlia decided to come to Mexico City to study at a beauty school. She thought she could make money doing that because she was a beautiful woman and perhaps other women would patronize her salon in search of her secrets. María made an effort to find work in Mexico City to allow her to be with her sister. If she could mend fences with Dahlia, she could help María with La Cheli.

Memo wrote to his mother to tell her what she already knew; the school year was almost over, when would she come get him? "Please be patient, it's going to happen. However, you might have to stay in school one more summer. God willing, it'll be soon."

"Dear God,

I'm sorry to bother you but I had hoped you would get me out of here by summer. I know you're busy and all, but I really would appreciate it if you could help my mother do whatever it is she needs to get done, as soon as you can. Thank you, God."

"P. S. School year is almost over; please don't let me spend the summer here."

In San Salvador, Violeta was pressing La Cheli, in Mexico City, María was pressing Dahlia, and in Mérida, Memo was pressing God. Still, La Cheli would not relent. She was not a God fearing woman.

The summer came and went. Memo started the fourth grade. He was doing everything right. At school he was earning the best grades, he was confessing, communing, and praying morning, afternoon, and night.

"Dear God,

Please don't keep me here another year. Please help my mother. Please God, please. You know I've been good. As you know, I'm even saying all my penitence every Saturday. Please don't let me down Lord."

Maybe God inspired Violeta to ask La Cheli that María and Memo be her Christmas present. Maybe God inspired La Cheli to grant Violeta's wish. But at last, La Cheli said yes. There were to be conditions but she would allow María to return. Violeta wrote María and María wrote Memo: "I'll be there to pick you up the second week of December! We're going home! María" That was the way she signed her letters to her son. Never: Your mother. Always: María.

"You did it, God! You were listening after all. I'll spend Christmas with my family. What a present! Sorry I ever doubted you but as you know the last three years haven't been great. Thank you, God. I'll never forget it. You're wonderful!"

It was time to prepare for his departure. Leaving the school and Doña Belisa was cause for joy. The more than three years spent there had been the worse of his young life. They would forever alter his relationship with the Church. *Why does the Pope, who is the symbol of God on earth, wear such lavish robes? Why does he live in a palace in Castelgandolfo?* Questions like these were always at the root of his displeasure with the church establishment. Many years later, in Lima, Peru, while he was on a goodwill tour of Latin America for the U.S. State Department, he happened to enter a modest little church. Just inside the entrance, to the right, was a wall entirely devoted to the display of Inca artifacts made of solid gold. Just outside the church were several Incan beggars. *Why would the church have all that gold while the poor are begging just a few feet outside?* He could not reconcile why the Church got so rich taking from the poor it purported to serve. Those questions had started with Doña Belisa. And they would haunt him the rest of his life.

God was a different matter. Memo made peace with the God his mother believed in, the good God. The avenging God, the smiting

God, the punishing God would reenter his life in the shape of La Cheli in less that a month.

He had said goodbye to Carlitos at the end of the last school year when his mother took him to another school. Carlitos had been his best and most trusted friend. *I would never have survived the last three years here without him. God, please bless Carlitos.* And then there was Melinda, whose no-nonsense affection sustained him through all those lonely weekends. Her arroz con leche was more than just a treat he looked forward to having, it was a hopeful reminder that he could trust to find a friend in the unlikeliest of places. *God, please bless Melinda.*

The appointed day came and Memo, as he had numerous times, waited for his mother by the third grade window. Because of the many disenchantments suffered, doubt gnawed at him. He waited the morning long. *This time she will come, she must come.* Then he saw her! No, it was not his mother. In an effort to see better, he squinted his eyes. The lady looked like his mother. He did not recognize the dress. *Is it she? Is it? It is!* His heart exploded with happiness! He ran out of the classroom and almost fell turning the corner of the room. He got to the big door. He could hear her voice inquiring for him. He was jumping up and down in anticipation and calling out: "Mamá! Mamá!" Finally the little door opened and he burst out of the Colegio Mejicano and into his mother's arms. His Jane Eyre years were over!

A RITE OF PASSAGE?

They stood before the pier where a little more than a year before they had the heart to heart talk that led to today's trip. At the end of the pier waited the black cargo ship. A strong breeze blew in from the sea as they started to walk gingerly toward the vessel. Through the planks of the wooden pier, they could see the murky sea below which, stirred by the wind, crashed forcefully against the wood pillars and made the old pier sway. The wind, and the weight of the luggage they carried, unsteadied their walk. Beyond the ship, dark clouds gathered against a gray afternoon sky. Memo felt a shiver crawl up his spine into his nape and up the back of his head. He looked at his mother for reassurance but she was busy collecting her balance with every step. His happy heart struggled against his qualms. He had waited so long for this day that he did not want to darken it with doubt. He decided not to share his misgivings with her. Unbeknownst to him, she was doing exactly the same. They leaned resolutely into the wind.

At the end of the pier, a man waited impatiently for them. Brusquely, the man took their baggage.

"Quickly, come with me, I'll show you to your cabin." He started up the plank.

"Is everything alright?" asked María, following him.

"Yes, but we must sail before the wind gathers more force." They reached the ship's deck.

"Is the wind expected to increase?" His mother asked with more than a little concern.

"Don't be alarmed. It should abate once we're at sea. Be careful with the steps. They are slippery." The steps clanked as they went down the rusted iron ladder.

"This is your cabin," he said, entering the narrow space. "Let me get out of your way," he put the bags on the lower berth and squeezed out the door. "I'll tell the captain we can sail."

Glamorous would be the last word one could use to describe the cabin.

"Which bunk do you want?" said María with hollow enthusiasm.

"The one on top," said Memo, playing along.

The ship began to lumber away from the pier.

"We're leaving!" said Memo.

"Do you want to go up on deck?"

"Yes. I want to see Campeche for the last time."

They climbed up the narrow stairs and rushed to the side of the ship. The vessel had left the pier, heading out to sea. They stood there for a moment.

"Come up here," a voice called.

They looked up to their left. A man was beckoning them. "Come up here."

They climbed one more flight of steps. Up on top, the man extended his hand to María and helped her up the last two steps.

"You can see better from here." he said, taking off his cap. "I'm Captain Miro."

"I'm María Castellon and this is my son Memo."

"Well, Memo, is this your first time on a ship?"

"Yes, sir," said Memo respectfully. He had never met a real captain before.

"Well sailor, let me give you a quick lesson. Where we are is called the helm. Where you were a moment ago is called the starboard side, the left side is called port, the front of the ship is called the bow, and the back the stern. You got it?"

He did not get it all but the situation called for certainty.

"Yes, sir!"

"Now, you memorize that and I'll teach you other things."

"Yes, sir!"

"We are heading SSW to the port of Veracruz and we should be there in a couple of days, weather permitting."

"Will the weather get worse?" asked María.

"Don't worry, ma'am, this old lady can handle it."

Memo and María stood side by side looking at the receding Campeche shore. *I hope I return someday to see you again and have crab legs, Orange Crush and flan. Goodbye Campeche.*

María looked toward the bow; toward Veracruz and from there to El Salvador. She suddenly realized that El Salvador means the Savior. She looked at the stormy skies ahead. *I hope you protect us, Savior. Please, bring us safely home. Please, permit us to be a family again.*

The ship sailed slowly toward the threatening sky.

It was the darkest of the darkest of nights. They had just had dinner and were going to their cabin when Memo had asked if they could go on deck for just a little while before going to bed. They stood on the bow looking straight ahead into the void. Not a star in the sky. Only sailors get to see black nights like these. There was no horizon. The black sky melted into the black sea; as if the boat was in the center of a limitless black bubble. The yellow light from below deck seemed to be afraid to venture outside. The salty wind gusts slapped their faces. *How does the Captain know where Veracruz is? I can't see anything.*

"You better go to your cabin soon, ma'am," said the sailor who had carried their bags before.

"Is the sea sky always this black?" asked Memo.

"No," said the sailor, "the clouds are covering the stars."

"I can hear the sea, but I can't see it."

"It's a rare night. A storm is coming our way and when it arrives, I advise you to stay below."

They watched as he walked toward stern like a drunkard leaving a bar. The wind whistling by their ears told them to hurry to their cabin.

They got into their bunks and wished each other happy dreams. But there were no dreams to be had that night, or the next night, or the next. Outside, the wind howled, then hollered, and then shrieked through the night. Neither spoke. They pretended they were asleep, afraid that if they shared their fears they would frighten each other even more. The night went on and on and on. Both hoped the sunlight would bring with it warmth and peace. The morning came, but not the sun. The black night turned into a gray day and the black sea turned brown. Through the porthole they could see the sea above them. So high were the waves, that it was inconceivable the ship could stand their weight when they crashed down upon it. The next moment, the sea was below them. The ship seemed like a half of a walnut shell bobbing helplessly in the immensity of the deep drink. Wails rose from the passengers in the cabins on either side of them. Again, no one left their berths all day; no one ate or drank anything. María was seasick, so Memo climbed down to see what he could do. The crew was tending to the survival of the ship; the passengers had to fend for themselves. Miraculously, Memo was not seasick but could do nothing to lessen his mother's discomfort. They waited all day for the hurricane to hie away. The night came again, and again the ship was enveloped in total darkness. At least at night they could not see the size of the waves crashing down upon them. If the first night was interminable, the second one was even more so. Memo and María suffered in silence in their bunks. The howling of the hurricane, the crashing of the waves, and the groaning of the ship made it impossible to hear anything else. Once in a while someone would come by, stick his head in to see if they were alright. If no one was dying, that was considered alright. By night it was the fear of the unseen, by day, the fear of the seen. They did not know what was worse. The next morning when Memo got down to see how his mother was doing, he stepped into a foot of sea water. María was too sick to care about anything. A sailor came by and Memo pointed out that the water was up to his knees.

"It's like that all over," he hollered. "The ship can handle it. Stay inside. This can't last much more."

Though the sailor's words were reassuring, the fear in his eyes was not.

Memo no longer wanted to look outside. The size of the waves terrified him. By now he could tell, by the angle of the ship in relation to the sky, how big the waves were. The wailing from the adjacent cabins had ceased. Judging by how he felt, Memo guessed everybody was too tired to even complain. Ironically, the third night, due to a combination of exhaustion and resignation, Memo and María fell asleep while the roaring went on and on.

Memo woke up to an eerie silence. He looked through the porthole and saw the blue sky. The ship was moving gently upon the green sea. Memo got down from his bunk to share the good news with María but she was fast asleep. He decided to let her be. He opened the door and, for the first time in eons, it seemed to him, he stepped outside the cabin. It was as if nothing had happened. The yellow sun, the blue sky, and the green sea all had returned. Memo wondered, *Why had we been tortured? Why had we been spared?* Was Doña Belisa's God making a point? Was his mother's God making a point? The hurricane had gone somewhere else to inflict pain on another ship. One by one the passengers came out with wan smiles on their faces. Even the crew looked ashen; their eyes bleary, their hair disheveled. They all stared incredulously at the calm sea. One thing had been true; the old lady had handled it.

For some reason, Memo felt the need to brush his teeth. He went into the cabin and got the tooth brush and paste. He was standing by the port side, brushing his teeth, when a seagull landed near him on the rail of the ship. The bird startled him and he dropped the brush. He watched it fall and fall until it splashed softly into the sea. It floated gently then slowly sank into the green until it disappeared.

"See what you made me do? I've lost my toothbrush because of you."

The seagull stared at Memo with icy blue eyes. Memo shook his fist at it. The seagull squawked an insult and took flight. Memo laughed. His laugher surprised him. He had thought he would never laugh again. One of the passengers giggled, and then he too laughed. Little by little all eight of the passengers were laughing. All at once, they all started to talk. The bird flew up and away past the bow of the ship. In the distant horizon Memo saw land. They had been closer to Veracruz than they had known.

From Veracruz they took the long bus ride to Mexico City where they met aunt Dahlia. Though they were exhausted, they still had the five day ride to El Salvador ahead of them. Memo's Mexican years were about to end. They had been hard years. Years that had left a hole in his heart. El Salvador, he hoped, would heal the hole. He looked with anticipation to a new beginning. At last, he was going to belong. His Salvadorian family awaited him!

LAST DAY, FIRST SEX

Unable to sleep, Memo kept reflecting upon his Salvadorian years. *The family I came to find did not turn out to be what I had hoped,* Memo thought as he tried to find a comfortable position in his bed. *I won't be missing this bed that's for sure. In a few hours I will leave for the United States. What will I find there? Will my search end there? Will the United States fulfill what Mexico, Nicaragua, and El Salvador have not? What do I want? I don't know. I only know something is missing inside me that urges me forward on another trip to another place where I can become one again.*

By the time he fell asleep it was almost morning. Normally after just a couple of hours of sleep, he would have been dead tired. Not the day he was leaving for the United States of America! Violeta burst in.

"We have to be at the airport by one for a two-thirty departure and that means we have to leave the house by noon." Violeta burst out.

María always kept things inside so that it was impossible to tell if she was nervous or sad. Dahlia and Violeta were exactly the opposite, so the house had been in an uproar from daybreak. Memo was somewhere in the middle, but today's level of excitement was difficult to control. After all, it had taken eight years for this day to arrive. He had always been more mature than his age and he was trying to handle the event with a certain degree of sophistication. He decided to stay close to his mother for two reasons; to stay away from the tension on the other side of the house and to spend his last hours with María.

María was doing her best to appear normal. She was about to lose her son. Memo, she knew, was going to the United States to stay. She agreed with his decision. "Nadie es profeta en su tierra," she had said on many occasions. She thought she was a living example of it; she had never been appreciated in her own country. Maybe her son would be more appreciated somewhere else. She had other reasons. Although she had not made much ado about it, she had been worried about Memo's night life. The libertine life allowed to men in her country could cost him. It was so easy for a young man to take the wrong turn and ruin his life. If she only knew how close her son had been to doing just that.

Besides the accident with El Turco's car, Memo had had two brushes with death. One had happened in Dario's white Packard convertible. Memo, Neto, Armando and Dario were coming from a good girls' party on the way to a bad girls' place a few kilometers out of town. They had all had been drinking more than they should and Dario was driving faster than he should. There were no freeways or four lane highways in El Salvador. As soon as one left the capital, all roads were narrow and not in the best condition. Suddenly, from the right side of the road, an oxen-driven cart appeared and blocked most of the narrow road. Trying not to crash into them, Dario veered to the right and into a trench on the side of the road. The trench was as deep as the car was wide and because the top was down, it fitted perfectly into the ditch. The Packard slipped sideways into the trench and slid about twenty meters along the length of the trench until it finally came to a stop. Just before the accident, Memo, who was riding on the front passenger seat, had had his right arm dangling outside of the car. Instinctively, all four young men had ducked their heads down. The movement brought Memo's arm into the car. Had that not happened, his arm would have been torn off. After a long moment in which no one spoke, one by one the boys started to call to each other; a cloud of beige dust enveloped the car. Everybody was shaken up but alright. In order to get out of the car, Dario stepped on Memo's left side and Neto on Armando's. Once out, they pulled the other two up and out. When the cloud of dust settled, they could see the damage to the car. It was totaled.

"Oh, my God," said Dario, "my father is going to kill me when he sees this."

"It wasn't your fault," said Armando, who was in his first year of law school.

"No, it wasn't, but that's not going to stop him from killing me."

"It wasn't your fault," repeated Armando.

"We know it wasn't his fault," said Neto. "If that stupid cart . . ."

"What I mean is that it wasn't his fault because he wasn't driving it."

"Of course I was driving it. You must have hit your head hard, or something."

"I'm perfectly fine, and you were not driving it."

"No? Then who was driving? Mandrake the Magician?"

"The thief."

"What thief?"

"The one who stole the car."

There was a long silence. They all spoke at once.

"Yeah!"

"The thief!"

"He stole the car when we were at the party!"

"When we came out, the car was gone!"

"You looked everywhere and couldn't find the car."

"Hey, you're not wasting your time in law school."

"Hey! What about the witness?"

"What witness?"

"The peon who was driving the cart?"

"What about it?"

They looked around to see that the cart had disappeared into the brush on the other side of the road.

"Okay Pilgrims," said Armando in his worst John Wayne imitation, "first, we have to get back to town."

"Let's walk back to that little roadside store we passed about a kilometer back."

"We can call a compadre to come get us," said Armando.

"Please Armando, stick to the law, you do a terrible Wayne."

They all laughed. They started to walk back as they dusted themselves off.

"Once in town, we'll report that car stolen."

"You know what Armando? You're going to be a very successful lawyer."

"We were learning about alibis in class just this week, pilgrims."

"Oh, shut up."

"I'll wait a while before I call my father."

"Yeah! Do I have any scratches on my face?"

"No. How about me?"

"I got a joke I was going to tell you guys at the cathouse."

"Let's hear it."

Joking and laughing the boys walked down the middle of the road. They had already forgotten how close they had been to dying.

The other incident also involved Neto and Armando. Whenever he went partying, Neto liked to bring with him a gun. It was a status symbol and many rich boys had one. Neto was proud of it, often showing it to his friends. He was the son of a sweet lady whose husband had passed away years earlier; Neto was accustomed to getting his way with her. She had problems denying him anything, including the gun. He liked to put it inside his cowboy boots. Of all Memo's friends, Neto was the only one who had a pair of boots. They were part of his paint-the-town-red party getup. Memo had handled the gun once or twice. It was a nickel-plated gun with white ivory handles, at the bottom of which the 45 caliber magazine was inserted. It was a beautiful gun, and on several drinking occasions Neto had pulled it out and fired a few rounds up into the night sky. On this night, the boys were on the way to a party. It was a hot summer Saturday night and all three of them were standing outside the car while Neto filled up his mother's dark gray Buick at a corner gas station.

A drunken man watched the three boys laugh and carry on. He neared the car and stared at them.

"What are you looking at," demanded Neto, who, at over six feet tall when wearing his boots, was an imposing lad.

The drunk stood there smiling at the boys, in what Neto interpreted as a condescending manner. It was not one of the best neighborhoods and the man seemed to be one of the local winos.

"Are you rich boys slumming?" said the man continuing to smile.

"You want me to wipe that smile off your face?" Neto said impudently.

"Are you the one to do that?" said the man giggling.

"Yes!" said Neto and pulled out of his boot, the 45 caliber.

"I'm so scared," said the man continuing to smile.

Ernesto's machismo challenged, he lifted the gun and pointed it at the man.

"Go ahead, boy," said the drunk, still smiling.

Neto pulled the trigger!

The gun did not go off.

"Did mamá forget to teach you how to load it?" The man giggled.

Neto pulled the trigger again!

Again, the gun did not go off.

The man laughed!

Neto ejected the magazine. It was full of bullets. He cocked the gun and looked into the bullet chamber. A bullet was in it.

The man took off running.

Neto fired three more times at the running drunk.

Three more times the gun did not go off.

The man disappeared into the shadows.

Neto was livid.

Armando and Memo were aghast.

"Let's go!" yelled Neto, furious at his failure.

Armando and Memo quickly hopped in.

Neto drove off in a huff. Out of anger, or pride, Ernesto stuck the gun out the window and pulled the trigger three times. Three bullets flew into the sky.

The boys laughed hysterically, finally realizing how close they had come to killing the drunk.

In the dark, Death watched the boys drive away.

Memo never told his mom any of this, but maybe she knew; the way mothers know without knowing. She sensed that he was better off leaving El Salvador. She was also concerned for his artistic career. She knew her country's prejudices; she had been victimized by them. He was doing well now, but how long would it last? Memo could make a complete new start in the United States. Lastly, she felt she owed it to him. Her decisions had taken away opportunities he might have had. She could not stand in his way.

Memo was finishing packing his suitcase. His mother had taught him to pack by looking at himself; starting with his feet and ending with his head.

"You look at that part of your body," she had said, "and whatever goes there, you pack."

He found that was excellent advice and used it every time he traveled. He was only taking with him the best of what he owned: Four suits; two of them tailor made and two American made, four pairs of shoes, especially made for him to match the color of his suits, his Italian shirts, his American ties, and two Hitchcock belts. He had made Hitchcock TV commercials and they had given the belts. Some socks, underwear, and he was ready to go.

"Take these with you," she said. María gave him the two silver dollars she had saved in her piggy bank. Memo recognized them. "I know it isn't much, but I hope they help." On one side the coin read proudly: UNITED STATES OF AMERICA. He understood that. Under, in smaller letters, it said: E PLURIBUS UNUM. He did not understand that. He flipped the coin over. It read: LIBERTY. He understood that. He repeated the word several times. *That's what I want: LIBERTAD.* Below, also in smaller letters, it said: IN GOD WE TRUST. He did not understand that. *This English language is going to be tough. But I'm going to learn it, and fast!* Memo put the two coins in the inside pocket of his suit coat with his passport, his plane ticket, and two hundred and fifty dollars in travelers checks. He promised himself that no matter how difficult things would get, he would never spend those two dollars. He kept his promise.

Violeta burst into their room. "It's time to go. Are you ready?"

"I've been ready for years. Let's go."

At the airport to see him off were his mother María, and his two best friends: Neto and Luis. They had never met before but Neto knew who Luis was because of his television appearances. A couple of Violeta's friends and her mother Dahlia were there to see her off. The Gomez' sisters were there too. For reasons she did not say, Dahlia was staying in El Salvador.

No one noticed when Memo came to El Salvador more than ten years before, and almost no one noticed when he left. As if his life there had been written on the sand and a wayward wave had washed it away. Actually, someone had noticed. Many years later, in San Francisco, California, he met again with his friend Luis who had been living there for sometime.

"Here," he said, handing him a book.
"What is this?"
"You're in the book."

It was a book written by David Calderon, the radio station manager where Memo started his acting career. He looked at the publishing date: 1987. *Twenty-five years after I left El Salvador.* The title of the book was: The Golden Age of Radio and Television in El Salvador. Memo's picture appeared in the book along with a couple of lines saying he had starred in the all-time most popular TV series in El Salvador. David Calderon had noticed.

Other than that, it was as if Memo had never been there.

Their flight was announced. Again, he was flying Pan American. It was a turbine plane which would take them to Guatemala where they would board a jet to Miami—El Salvador's runway not yet able to accommodate jets. They said their goodbyes. Hugs all around. Memo hugged his mother last.

"Write," she whispered in his ear.
"I will."

"You promise?" Her face showed the emotions of those who are left behind. He understood those emotions only too well. Memo nodded.

"Twice a month?" his mother pled. Memo nodded again.

How ironic, Memo thought. His mother had not been a great letter writer. For a moment he remembered how few and apart her letters had been when he was in the Colegio Mejicano. *How many times I waited for letters that never came.* Over the speakers he heard the last call for his flight. He hugged her one last time. There were no tears on either side, only a tacit understanding that they loved each other. He backed away from her and waved to the smiling group. They all waved back.

"Memo!" called Violeta. "Come on!"

She was already on the tarmac walking quickly toward the plane. He ran up to her. They joined the line walking up the airplane ladder. Memo was the last one. He arrived at the top landing and turned around. On the observation deck the group was reforming and waving at him. How many times he had been on that deck waving at someone who was leaving for some mysterious land. It finally was his turn. He waved back. Took a deep breath, more like a sigh really, turned and boarded the plane. Violeta gave him the window. He looked through the plastic and found the group again. They were all craning their necks trying to find them.

"Wave," said Violeta, "wave." He did.

Someone in the group spotted him first and pointed toward the window. Memo could not hear them but he knew exactly what they were saying.

"There!"

"Where?"

"There!"

"Oh, yes! I see them."

It did not matter if they really saw you. It was good enough if they thought they did. Behind him, Violeta waved and said goodbye, even though they could not hear her. The plane began to taxi toward its takeoff position. Memo looked at his El Salvador sadly. It had been his country for more than a decade. He had learned to love it. It had not been a perfect fit but still, he had fond memories. The pilot was given clearance for takeoff. The engines roared and the plane began to crawl, then to pick up speed and just when one thought it would not make it before it ran out of runway, it flew! Memo almost strained his neck trying to take a last glimpse of his mother.

He was leaving for keeps. He was in search of something, he did not know what exactly but he thought he would find in the United States. He was about to become a foreigner again, with all the advantages and disadvantages that it implies. It had taken several years to not be a foreigner in El Salvador. In Mexico he was not so much a foreigner as an orphan. Though, perhaps, a foreigner is an orphan of sorts. In Nicaragua, his native country, his father had made him feel like an orphan and a foreigner. The difference this time was that it was his choice. That was all he knew. He had no plans; just expectations. He had seen a lot of American movies which he believed depicted accurately a way of life he longed for. It did not occur to him he had been watching fiction. He did not realize he had been looking at movie magic; an illusion of the United States as it could or might be, not as it was. The truth, he would eventually learn. Now, Memo was flying to Dreamland!

As he left his little country behind, Memo reflected upon his years in El Pulgarcito de America as some call it; America's little thumb, because it is the smallest country in the entire continent. What had he learned from El Salvador? In Mexico, his sheltered life protected him from the world, but not from the heartache of abandonment, the pain of loneliness, and the hypocrisy of the Catholic Church. In El Salvador his mother, forced by the need to make a living, let him adrift, hoping he would not get into trouble. El Salvador taught him the street, where he learned about poverty, obsequiousness, vice, obscenity, alcoholism, violence, social prejudice, class discrimination, struggle, envy, jealousy and more. Maybe he would have learned it all anyway, but not as fast.

In his neighborhood poverty was a way of life. Most people barely made enough money to feed themselves each day. They would worry about tomorrow, tomorrow. He lived among the poorest, and though never comfortable with poverty, (who is?), he mingled with them daily. The only reason he was scarcely above them was La Cheli. His mother was making just enough money to take care of their basic needs. If La Cheli kicked them out of her house, they would join their lot. He respected the courage it took to live the life they lived.

Obsequiousness is the daughter of poverty. The poor are skillful at it; it may make the difference between life and death. Every day someone would beg him for something; a dime, a nickel, a penny? They knew him by name and would not hesitate to use his name to get him to give. In an effort to ingratiate themselves to him, they would say, "Don Memo, you got something for me today?" Hoping the title, which is reserved for adults or important men, would flatter him. It's harder to say no when they know your name. If he did not give, sometimes the beggar would curse him; maybe even throw a stone at him. The next day, the same beggar would ask again, as if nothing had happened. "Don Memo, you got something for me today?" Why not? What has a beggar to lose?

If obsequiousness is the daughter of poverty, alcoholism is the son. Getting drunk is the only way one can forget. Bolo is the Salvadorian slang for a drunk. Bolito is an affectionate way of referring to him as a drunkie. There were many bolitos hanging around Memo's block because the Gomez' owned a pharmacy right on the corner of the block. Now, Tic Tac is the cheapest liquor you can buy in El Salvador, but when even Tic Tac is out of reach, rubbing alcohol will do. The local bolitos routinely would buy rubbing alcohol at the pharmacy, then run into the nearby alley, pour it into an empty liquor bottle, fill the rest with water, shake it, and they had sangolote; a deadly potion that can get you drunk in a hurry. It can also make you blind. Worse still, it can kill you.

"What ever happened to el bolito so and so?" Someone would ask.

"They found him dead in the alley," someone would answer casually.

It was not a pitiless answer; it was just a fact of life in his neighborhood.

Ah yes, the street taught him about sex. Memo had a coterie of barrio friends with whom he hung around when he was not in school.

They were all about his age and had been living in the block long before he arrived. In matters of the street, their knowledge was far superior to his, and so they took it upon themselves to bring him up to snuff. Sex was one of subjects they mentored him on. It was all talk. None of them had had sex yet. Once they reached thirteen though, the topic seemed to occupy their minds more often. It was just a matter of time before one of them would actually DO IT.

That was the stumbling point. How do you do it?

Parents knew, but they were not telling. María had never mentioned anything other than the stork. No help there.

They could learn some of the basics, like kissing, from the American movies, but after kissing, the next thing you saw was a rustic countryside or a bucolic beach. No help there. Mexican movies copied American movies, so they too were sexually tame. Among European films, the French were the most daring, but even they were cautious.

Another source of information was his group of kids. Some of it they had picked up from dirty jokes. There were plenty of those around and from them the group had gathered all the vulgar vocabulary necessary. They had learned the theory, but nobody in the group had yet to get the practical part of their sex education.

Then, of course, there were the neighborhood whores; a block away in any direction. They were the ultimate authority, but it was scary to go to them for many a reason.

Ricardo and David were the two kids from his group with whom Memo spent most of his time and it was with them that the question was being discussed.

"Ricardo, do you know any girls who do it?" asked Memo.

"I don't, do you David?"

"No. I only know that good girls don't do it. We got to find a bad girl."

"Who knows a bad girl?"

No one knew one.

"We have to go where the bad girls are," said David.

"Where's that?"

Of the three of them, David had the most access to tawdry information because his father owned a little cantina. It was a hole in the wall where he had a counter about six feet long and two stools in front of it. Behind the counter were two shelves: one with Espiritu de Caña and one with Tic Tac. The former was cheap rum, the latter, cheapest. Men would come by, buy a bottle, chat with Don Arnoldo, have a shot or two and go. Don Arnoldo liked to play cards and whenever he was not at his cantina he was in his house next door, playing poker. He was a good card player and it was rumored that he made as much money from his gambling as from his cantina. David picked up a lot of useful information about the ways of the world, hanging around his father and his friends. David got a lot of respect from the neighborhood kids because of his wicked wisdom.

"Well, we have two choices: The ones who do it for free, or the pros."

"The pros?"

"You know, the putas."

"I don't know about that. The putas are as old as my mother. I don't want to have sex with a woman as old as my mother," said Ricardo.

"Well, those are the choices: The bad girls, or the putas."

"Besides, I don't have money to pay'em."

"Where do we find the free ones?"

"At parties!"

"I don't know about that," said Ricardo. "If we go to parties we have to dance and I don't know nothing about dancing."

"I know a little about dancing," said Memo.

At home, when they had a party, he had danced a few times with his mother, who was the family's best dancer.

"But where do we find the parties where we find the bad girls?"

"We have to ask around. There's always a party somewhere."

"But what do we do once we find the party?" said Ricardo.

"We do like in the movies," said Memo. "We dance and talked with them."

"And we kiss'em!" said David.
"Kiss'em?" Do we have to kiss'em?" said Ricardo.
"Sure, man," said David. "That's how you find the bad girls."
"I don't know about that. I just want to fuck'em. I don't want to kiss'em."
"Well man, is either that, or the pros."
Memo and Ricardo looked at each other. They nodded.
"Then, let's find a party for this weekend and see what happens."

Somehow, David found a party. They put on their best clothes and off they went Saturday afternoon. They did not know who was giving the party. In fact, they did not know anybody there, which added to the awkwardness of the situation. It was a modest little house with a small living room. There were about six girls and about eight boys, including David, Ricardo, and Memo. The girls were overdressed for the occasion and the boys underdressed. There was a record player in the corner of the room and the girls seemed to be in charge of selecting the music. The three teenagers huddled together and watched for a while. A couple of the other boys actually did ask the girls to dance.
"Let's go," said Ricardo.
"But we haven't danced," said Memo.
"Which of the girls do you like?" asked David.
"I don't like any of them. Let's go." Ricardo started to leave.
"No man, wait. Let's dance at least one time."
"You said you knew how to dance, let's see you dance."
"I know the cha cha cha, and the merengue, but I don't know rock 'n' roll."
"Well, they're playing a merengue now. If you dance, I'll dance." said David.
"Okay, I'll dance."
But no one moved. They just stood there watching for a long while.
After another round of "You dance," "No, you dance," and "I'll dance if you dance," they decided to leave. All the way home they blamed one another for the failure.
"This is gonna be harder than we thought," said Ricardo.

"No, man," said David, who thought himself to be the most sophisticated of the three, "we'll get'em next week."

"I don't know about that. We're not gonna get'em if we can't get close to them, and to get close to them we gotta dance."

"Memo, do you really know how to do the cha cha cha?"

"Yeah, my cousin Violeta taught me one time when she came to visit from The United States." "Could you teach us?"

"I only know a couple of steps."

"We don't know nothing, so teach us."

David found another party. During the week they had practiced the cha cha cha and the merengue in Don Arnoldo's house. They were determined to dance this time. David was the first one to get up the courage to ask a girl to dance. He managed to massacre the merengue along with the girl's feet. Memo and Ricardo had a ball making fun of him when he returned.

"You can laugh all you want but I danced and you didn't. Let's see which one of you two hyenas has the guts to get up and dance."

"I'll dance the next cha cha cha they play," said Memo.

Ricardo and David could not wait to see Memo dance. David went to one of the girls and requested a cha cha cha. "Here's a cha cha cha, let's see you do it."

"Yeah," said Ricardo, "show us how is done, maestro." And they pushed him into the middle of the floor.

He was too embarrassed to return. With his heart in his mouth, he went to one of the girls and asked her. To his relief, as well as his dismay, she said yes. He only knew two steps but that was one more than anyone else knew, so he was immediately labeled a good dancer by the girl with whom he was dancing. At last, the dance ended, and Memo, as he had seen done in the movies, walked the girl to her seat. She immediately labeled him a gentleman. Triumphant, Memo returned to the two laughing hyenas.

"You weren't as hot as I thought you would be, maestro," said David. Both Ricardo and David thought that was hilarious and howled some more.

"At least, I didn't step all over her feet, as you did."

"Yeah," said Ricardo, el maestro didn't step on her feet like you did David."

This time Memo and Ricardo did the howling.

"Okay okay okay. I'll admit it. How did you manage that?"

"I don't think I'm going to teach you that."

"I think she's fallen in love with you," said Ricardo.

"How can you tell?" No one had ever fallen in love with Memo.

"I think your walking her to her seat did it."

"You think so?"

"I'm sure. I have to remember that. It also helped that you didn't step on her."

Ricardo and Memo burst out laughing.

"No, seriously guys," said David. "How did you do that?"

"I'll tell you after Ricardo dances. He's the only one that hasn't."

"That's right, man. Your turn, Ricardo. You gotta dance."

"This is a merengue," Memo said. "It's the easiest."

"Next week," said Ricardo.

"No, now!" And they pushed him into the middle of the floor.

"Come on, you can do it."

Ricardo had no choice. He asked the nearest girl he could find. As he danced, the other two hyenas laughed.

All the way home they praised themselves for their achievement.

"Now that we danced with them, when do we kiss'em?" asked Ricardo.

"You gotta talk to them before you kiss'em," said Memo.

"In that case David's never gonna get to kiss'em because he can't dance without stepping on them. How are you gonna dance, avoid stepping on them, and talk to them, all at the same time, David?"

"Okay now, you promised to tell me how to avoid stepping on their toes."

Memo took a pause then, as if he was sharing a national secret, he whispered.

"Slide your feet. If you don't lift your feet you can't step on them."

"Oooh," said David and Ricardo with new found respect.

"That's why I'm el maestro." The three hyenas burst out laughing.

By Thursday, David had already got them another party and they started to plan their strategy.

"Okay, this week we dance and talk and kiss," said David.

"I don't know about that. I don't even know what to talk about."

"Talk about *them*," said Memo. "Tell them they are beautiful; like in the movies."

"Just like that?"

"El maestro is right. Tell them they are beautiful."

"What happens if they are not beautiful?"

"You tell them they are, anyway."

"But that's a lie."

"You've lied before, haven't you?"

"You're never gonna kiss 'em if you don't, man."

Ricardo seemed to see the wisdom in that.

"Man, that was a disaster." They were walking back from the party. "You should've told us it was a rock 'n' roll party."

"I've never heard of a rock 'n' roll party."

"Forget about the merengue, man. The girls like to rock 'n' roll."

"Maestro you gotta teach it to us," said David.

"I think I picked up the basic step."

"Let's see it."

"I need a girl. Who wants to be the girl?"

"Forget it. I'm not gonna be the girl; especially right here in the street."

"Show us at my house. El maestro's gonna teach us to rock 'n' roll!"

"I don't know about that. First it was the merengue, then the cha cha cha, now's the rock 'n' roll. It's been three weeks and we haven't even kissed a girl. We'll never gonna fuck anybody this way."

"The rock 'n' roll will do it. The girls love it."

"Maybe we should go to the pros," said Ricardo.

"You think?" asked Memo apprehensively.

"Well, you don't have to do all this dancing stuff. You pay 'em. You fuck 'em. It's over."

"Maybe Ricardo's right. What do you think maestro?"

"I think we should give rock 'n' roll a try."

Memo went to the Apolo movie theater to watch <u>Rock Around the Clock</u> several times. Fortunately, because of Tío Lalo, he could get in for free. He came back with several steps to show David and Ricardo. They practiced and practiced and by Saturday they were ready to rock 'n' roll. Adoc, the first shoe chain in El Salvador, came up with a moccasin shoe style that looked just like the one Elvis Presley wore. David bought a pair. Memo and Ricardo followed suit. They had the hair a la Presley going, they had the shoes, and they had the dance. As the song says, all they needed was a girl.

They did a lot of dancing at the next party. They left the party all sweaty and excited but without a girl. After a few weeks of this they began to look like rockanroleros, as the kids who liked rock 'n' roll were called. But they were no closer to having sex than before.

"How do you find the bad girls?" asked Ricardo. "I've gotten to hold hands with one, and even kissed another one, but that's as far as they wanna go."

"I know. I haven't gotten too far either. They flirt and flirt but they don't fuck."

"I'm not doing any better," said Memo.

"It's time to get serious and go to the pros."

"Yeah," said Ricardo, "I'm tired of messing around. Let's go pro."

"What do you say, Memo?"

"I think we need more experience with the romantic stuff. I think it's only a matter of time before we score."

"By the time we score we'll be eighteen years old, right David?"

"I think el maestro is right, man. I think the girls know we don't have experience. Women like men with experience. They can smell inexperience a mile away."

"Come on David, you just said you wanted to go pro."

"I do wanna go pro. That's the point. No bad girl is gonna fuck a virgin. We need to lose our virginity."

"Exactly," said Ricardo. "That's the trouble. We're virgins."

"What do you think maestro?"

"I think that in a weird way it makes sense. Maybe we need pro experience."

"That's right. That's why we've been striking out. That's why we can't spot the bad girls. After we fuck a pro, it's gonna be a cinch."

"It's a deal then," said David. "Friday night we'll lose our virginity."

"And Saturday, when we go to a party, we'll be men and the bad girls will know we're experienced and we'll score!"

"What do you say, maestro?"

"I say this," Memo raised his arm straight out about forty-five degree angle, palm down. David put his hand on top of Memo's and then Ricardo did the same.

"All for one and one for all!"

"Yeah!" The three musketeers yelled.

Memo had trouble sleeping for the next few days. He wondered if the other two were as nervous about it as he was. He tried to envision how it was going to happen. He went over the event in his head. He knew he was supposed to ask the prostitute how much she charged. He had heard that he should bargain with her. He had experience bargaining because only a fool pays full price for anything in El Salvador. *I should be able to handle that part.* He also knew that after he had arrived at the price, he was supposed to go into her room. *That's when it gets hairy.* He knew what was going to happen but did not know how it was going to happen. He knew about two sexual positions; man on top and doggy style. *Who decides the position?* He was painfully aware of two things: he had to get naked, and he had to get naked in front a woman. Not a girl, which would have been difficult enough, but a *woman*. As hard as he tried to convince himself that he was ready for this, the more he thought about it the more aware he became that he was just—a fourteen year old *boy*. He considered backing out. Maybe he could get sick or something. *I can't be the one backing out. Maybe one of the others will, and that will get me off the hook.*

The day before *the* day, they got together to decide time and place.

"In front of my house," said David.

"Check," said the other two.

"Right after dinner," said Ricardo.

"Check."

"Have you got your money?" asked Memo hoping they did not.

"I got plenty of money. My father won at poker last night and I hit him. He's always in a good mood when he wins."

"I'll have my colón by tomorrow. Will that be enough?"

"I think so. Most whores around here charge less than that. How about you maestro?"

"I'll have mine. Don't worry about me."

Friday night arrived and the three musketeers assembled at David's.

It was a good thing it was dark in front of David's house and they could not see the fear in each other's eyes.

"Let's go!" said David.

"Where?" said Memo.

"Anywhere," said David. "They are all pretty much the same."

"How about the one near the corner store," said Ricardo.

"Not there, the store owner could see us going in."

"I agree," said Memo. "We should stay away from the neighborhood whores. I wouldn't want to run into them the next day."

"El maestro is right. Let's go up Modelo Street. There's a lot of them around there and it's far enough from here."

They started on their way.

"Wait," said David when they got to the corner where the little lady always stood with her basket of inexpensive candy and bundles of cigarettes.

"What are you doing?" asked Ricardo.

"I'm buying cigarettes."

"What for?"

"You always smoke after having sex, didn't you know that?" explained Memo.

"You do?"

"Yeah, haven't you seen any movies? That's how you know they've done it."

"Sure, I knew that. Yeah. Good idea."

"I've bought two bundles. This way we can have one while we're walking there."

After they lit up, they went up Modelo Street in search of a whore to whom to surrender their virginity.

They stood across the street looking at a couple of mesones where they were pretty sure they could find what they wanted. Each of them was worried about what was going to happen but did not have the courage to admit it. They finally settled on the meson on the right. They crossed the street and went in the front door. They walked around looking for the classic picture of a woman leaning on the door frame. All the doors were closed. The boys were secretly relieved.

"No action here," said David, trying to sound cool.

The boys went outside and crossed the street again. They had just spent a lot of courage and they needed to gather themselves.

"Let's have another cigarette," said David.

"Good idea," said Ricardo.

They lit up—each trying to smoke like James Dean.

They saw a couple of men come out of the other meson. Both men stopped on the sidewalk and lit up before continuing on to wherever they were going.

"Did you see those two guys?" said David.

"They just did it," said Memo

"Yeah, I saw that too."

"That's where the action is. Let's finish our cigarettes and go get some pussy."

"Yeah!" said the other two sounding more enthusiastic than they truly felt.

They took two more drags, threw the butts down and crossed the street like American soldiers on D Day.

Once inside the front door, the meson opened into a courtyard where there were several ladies of the night. Some of them were sitting on their room's door step, some sitting on their mussed beds inside their dimly lit rooms. A couple of them were leaning on their door frames, just like in the movies. They all looked at the three boys standing close together in the middle of the muddy courtyard. The boys felt like pilgrims surrounded by the Apache.

"Which one do you want?" said David, trying to sound professional.

The women smiled at them, not a flirtatious smile but an amused one; their experience telling them this was the boys' first time. The whores decided to wait the boys out, curious to see what they would do next. The boys were doing their best to look as cool as they could. They were not fooling anybody. Feeling the mounting pressure, David asked abruptly.

"Well, which one?"

"I don't know," said the other two almost in unison.

Their courage was about to fail them, when one of ladies, the one occupying the first room on the left side of the meson, beckoned them. Memo saw her first.

"She's calling us."

"Who?" said David.

"That one," Memo pointed her out.

She beckoned them once again. Some of the ladies giggled. One of them said, "Go, go to her."

"I'll go," said David. He walked over to her.

The two boys watched him as he listened to her. She pointed to the two other boys and said something they could not hear. They saw David put his hand in his pants pocket, pull some money out and give it to her. Their little hearts were beating so loudly, each of them wondered if the other one could hear it. David started to walk toward the boys.

"What's going on?"

"I've made a deal with her. She'll do us all three for two colónes," he said proudly.

"At the same time?" asked Ricardo.

"No, you idiot. One at the time. I'll go first."

Memo did not want to go last. "I'll go second."

"Okay," said David sounding like Audie Murphy in *To Hell and Back*. "Here I go."

They watched David take the fateful walk toward her and disappear into her room. The door closed. They looked at each other with amazement in their eyes.

"He's doing it!" said Ricardo.

"Yes," said Memo, awe in his voice.

They kept their eyes trained on the whore's door. Several minutes went by while their minds feverishly imagined what David was doing. The door opened! David came out, tugging at his belt with the strut of a male transformed. Memo's heart accelerated even more. David, smiling a wicked and knowing smile told Memo to wait.

"Wait for what?"

David looked at Memo condescendingly, as a man does a child.

"She's washing herself for you. She'll call you when she's ready."

"Washing herself?" The boys asked.

"Sure," said David. "She's washing her pussy so that she's clean for you."

The boys' respect for David was growing by the second.

"Yeah, yeah," said Memo, "I knew that."

David lit up a cigarette. The two boys watched him admiringly. There seemed to be an aura about David they had never seen before.

"There she is!" said Ricardo.

"Go! There's nothing to it," said David, with the aplomb of the experienced.

Memo took a deep breath, looked at his friends one last time and walked toward the unknown.

"Hi," she said smiling down at him. "Come on in."

He took three steps into the room and inhaled the musky smell of sex. In the left corner of the room was the disheveled bed. Under it, he could see a pail, half filled with murky water. She closed the door behind her. Memo turned in time to see her pull her dress off over her head. She stood there totally naked. Memo's eyes went directly to her black pubic hair. She let him look. In time, he raised his eyes to her large breasts and up to her face. She was as at ease with her nakedness as he was ill at ease. She was a handsome woman, taller than most Salvadorian women. When their eyes finally met, she smiled at him and asked, "First time?"

He wanted to say no but figured she would see through the lie. "Yes."

"It will be okay," she said softly, "you'll see."

She tossed her dress on a wooden chair and crossed to the bed. She lay down on the center of the bed.

"Take off your clothes."

The moment he dreaded had come. He stood there not knowing how to do this. He was fully clothed and he felt naked already.

"Sit on the bed," she said and patted the side of the bed with her left hand. He was grateful for the suggestion. He sat on the side of the bed near the end.

"Sit closer," she said, "near me."

She patted the bed again.

He scooted over just a bit. He decided to start by taking off his shoes. It took him a while to achieve that feat. He hesitated at the socks.

"You can leave those on if you want."

He fumbled with his belt. *I'm taking too much time.*

"No need to rush," she said, as if she could read his mind.

He stood up just long enough to pull down his pants, and quickly sat down again. He looked around for a place to put them.

"Throw them on the chair where my dress is," she said.

He obeyed. He did not know what to do next. *Take off my shirt, or my shorts?*

"Keep your shirt on," she said. He did not know how transparent he was being.

"Do you want me to help you with those?" she said, seeing him hesitate.

"No! Thank you." He stood up quickly again, pull down his shorts, and sat down. He looked down at his flaccid member. *Oh, my God, oh, my God.*

"Come to me," she said gently, as she spread her legs for him.

He looked at her crotch. There, but few feet from him was a pussy! He had wondered what it would look like. But as soon as he looked at it, he looked away. It was like one of those horror films where something horrible is about to happen and you close your eyes, yet open one of them in prurient fascination.

"Do you want me to turn off the light?"

He did, but he thought it would be cowardly to say so.

"No." He looked at his crotch again. He knew he needed an erection to do this. And he needed it now! He had been afraid this would happen. *Oh, my God, oh, my God. What do I do?*

"Get on your knees, come here between my legs and lie on top of me."

He did as he was told. It gave him the opportunity to see all of her. The moment his body came in contact with hers was electric.

"There you go," she put her arms around him. "Slide down just a little bit. There, right there."

He could smell her now. She was the source of the musky smell.

She moved her hips slowly in a circular motion. Memo began to feel his penis stir. *Yes, please get hard. Please!*

"Let me do this," she said and slid her right hand down between them. Her hand found his penis and began to caress it gently. Memo felt his penis respond. *Yes! Yes!* As his penis grew, so grew Memo's confidence. *Thank you, God. Thank you.* Religion and sex are strange bedfellows.

"Let me guide you," she said, grabbing him and placing him against her. She put her left hand on his buttocks and pushed him slowly into her.

Memo felt a sharp pain as his prepuce peeled back in response to the pressure from her vagina. He cried out in spite of himself. She knew what had just happened.

"Don't move! Stay like that for a moment."

The juices from her vagina enveloped his penis like a balm, soothing the pain.

"It usually happens the first time."

"It does?"

She nodded. Memo was glad to hear he was normal.

"Yes. It'll soon go away."

After a moment, she began to move her hips gently down and up. He could still feel the pain but with each movement of her hips, pleasure began to rise within him. He began to move with her. In some atavistic way, his body knew what to do.

"Yes," she said, "just like that."

The pain slowly gave way to the pleasure that ensures mankind's existence. As the pleasure increased, Memo began to move faster, disregarding the pain that returned due to the force of his thrusts. His excitement threw their rhythm off, lessening the pleasure he now craved.

"Slow down," she cautioned. "Stay with me."

He followed the movement of her hips. In a few moments the pleasure reached its former peak. Memo's body began to move faster, overruling his will. She, knowing what was about to happen, matched his tempo; her hips keeping pace with his. Just when he could not go any faster, it exploded from deep within him. He let out a sound he had never heard before. It was a cry for help and a triumphant roar. He was at once prey and predator.

"Yes! She shouted approvingly. Yes!" He wanted to continue but he could not.

Memo collapsed on top of her. She kept her hips moving slowly a few moments more, giving him ecstatic pangs of pain and pleasure with each of her strokes. He wanted her to stop. He did not want her to stop.

She stopped.

They stayed still for an exhausted moment.

It was time to part. He pulled away from her and sat on his haunches. This time he did not mind her seeing him. She understood and complied. She looked at his erection. How much he had changed in such a short time. She smiled at him, motherly. He took the smile as a compliment. She reached for a cigarette, lit it, and then got up. He was taking his time putting on his shorts. She bent over and pulled the pail from under the bed. He put his pants on. She squatted over the pail and began to wash herself. He watched her, as he put on his shoes. He backed slowly away toward the door, looking at her and trying to memorize the moment. He turned to open the door.

"Thank you," she said.

He turned back to her, bewildered. "For what?"

"For letting me be your first."

The meaning of the moment they had shared evaded him. He did not understand what he had given her. He did not understand what she had given him. She *was* a pro. It took Memo many years to realize it.

"Yes, ma'am."

"Tell the last boy that I'll be out in a moment."

"Yes, ma'am." And he walked out closing the door behind him.

The boys saw him come out. Though it was not necessary, he tucked his shirt in as he walked toward them, signaling the boys that he had done it!

"Here," said David handing him a cigarette. "Welcome to the club."

The two of them laughed knowingly. Memo lit his first post coital cigarette. There was a difference this time. At least, he wanted to think so. He took a long drag. He knew now what only men know. Ricardo looked at him with envy.

"There she is," said David. "Go."

The boy looked at them with concern. The men understood.

"Go!" said Memo, "she'll take good care of you."

They watched Ricardo go toward her, like a condemned man to the guillotine.

What a difference a fuck makes.

The next day they went to another party. Though they danced a lot, they did not get to first base with any of the girls. The girls did not seem to notice they were dancing with men. But the boys knew, and that was enough for them.

"The captain asks that you fasten your seat belts. Please extinguish your cigarettes. We'll be landing in Guatemala in five minutes. Those passengers continuing on to Miami please go to gate six. Thank you."

The announcement brought Memo out of his reverie. *I wonder where David and Ricardo are right now.* He had not seen them in several years. They were the friends he got away from, trying to escape from the barrio. Eleven years later, when Memo was going to college, he received a letter from his mother. She had included a newspaper clip. He looked at the picture. There was a man lying dead on the floor. The caption below said that the man had been beaten to death while serving time in jail. It was Ricardo.

"We'll have a forty-five minute layover in Guatemala. We can spend the time window shopping in the airport stores."

"Yeah." He said sadly.

"Just don't buy anything. Airport stores are a rip-off. Besides, you can't afford it. You're going to need all your money in Washington. What's wrong with you? Memo, did you hear me?"

"Yeah, yeah, I heard you."

He cherished his childhood friends much more than he had realized.

LOVE LESSONS

The 707 jet he was flying was the biggest and fastest plane he had ever been on. The sharp ascend surprised him. In minutes they had left the lush green Guatemalan vegetation and now they were way above the clouds. Miami, Florida was less than two hours away. The no smoking sign was turned off and Violeta decided to have a cigarette.

"You smoke, don't you?" she said offering the pack of Kents. It was the first time that a member of his family had offered him a cigarette.

"Yes," he said. He took one out and returned the pack to her. *From now on, I'll be smoking only American cigarettes.* He had smoked American cigarettes on occasion but mostly he smoked the domestic brands because American cigarettes were much more expensive. *I can't believe that I'm sharing a cigarette with my cousin.* He looked at Violeta, who was looking out the window. She had taken the window seat telling him he could have the window in the flight from Miami to Washington. His mind drifted back to El Salvador. What else had he learned there? Ah, yes. He had learned about love: Love platonic. Love romantic. Love unrequited.

Ironically, though he was no longer innocent about sex he was totally innocent about love; until Bonita.

He used to look at Bonita from the height of his house. He would go to the living room balcony, when his aunt was not around, and stare at the pretty girl sitting in the balcony of the corner house down below. Memo's house, or more accurately, La Cheli's house, was the highest house in the neighborhood; he could see the whole barrio from its balconies. It sat in the middle of the block on top of what once was a hill. Many years ago, the municipality decided to build a road just in front of the house and cut a swath off the hill leaving the house clinging to what was left of the hill. Bonita looked like an American girl and dressed like one. She had light brown hair, green eyes and light skin. She wore pleated plaid skirts with white blouses that buttoned high on her neck, and saddle shoes. She was the only girl in the neighborhood who dressed or looked like that. Memo and Bonita knew each other because their families knew each other. She was the same age as he and just as innocent. Her family protected her from boys or anyone else who would dare to get close to her. She did not enter Memo's consciousness until they reached fourteen. Actually, the girls from the neighborhood were responsible for whatever happened between them. They had decided Memo and Bonita were to become boyfriend and girlfriend way before Memo and Bonita had any thoughts of doing so.

Amalia was the ring leader. She was a pretty girl, with dark skin and flirtatious brown eyes. She gave you the impression that she knew more about life than her short years should allow. Amalia lived next door in a rented house that belonged to Bonita's mother. Amalia was as outgoing and loquacious as Bonita was shy and quiet. One afternoon Amalia came up to Memo and with a Cheshire smile asked,
"Do you like Bonita?"
"Ah, er, yes."
"I mean, do you really like her?"
"Yes, I do."
"Really, really?"
"Really."
"Good," she said. She turned and disappeared into the house.
Memo went back to leapfrogging with his friends.

"Hey," said one of his friends a while later, "Amalia wants to talk to you."

He looked in the direction Marco was pointing and saw Amalia signaling him to come to her.

"Bonita likes you too," she said, conspiratorially.

"Good."

"She really, *really* likes you."

Amalia waited for him to say something. Memo did not know where it all was going.

"Do you think she's pretty?"

"Yes, I do."

"How pretty?"

"She's very pretty."

"Really?"

"Really."

"Good," she said. She turned and disappeared into the house.

"Hey, Memo. Come on! We're waiting for you." Marco called.

Memo returned to his friends.

"What's going on with Amalia?" Marco asked.

Memo did not know exactly what was going on but he knew he was not supposed to tell anyone about it.

"Nothing." He made a gesture with his hand that told Marco that it was one of those crazy things girls do. It was designed to stop Marco from further questions.

A few days later, he was coming back from school. He heard someone yell his name. He turned around to see Amalia running toward him.

"Hey, Amalia, what's happening?"

"What's happening is . . ." she said in her playful way. "Bonita and I are going to the Regis Theater to see *East of Eden*. Have you seen it?"

"Twice. It's very good."

"We're gonna see it Saturday." She paused. "In the afternoon."

"I think you'll like it."

"At three p.m." She sung the three p.m. part. She skipped away, laughing.

He stood there shaking his head, watching her run. *That Amalia is crazy*, he thought. *Why would she tell me she's going to the movies with Bonita tomorrow at . . . aaah, I get it! She's going to the movies tomorrow at three.* He blushed at the thought that Amalia would think him so stupid. *Bonita is a good girl. Her family would not let her go to the movies with me but if I happen to run into her . . . there is nothing wrong with that.* He was new at this tryst thing.

The next day, making sure her family did not see him going in the direction of the theater, Memo showed up at the theater lobby. The girls were nowhere to be seen. He waited until show time and decided that maybe they had changed their minds. He was half a block away from the theater when it hit him. *They're inside! They wouldn't be waiting in the lobby, you idiot. It's supposed to be a coincidence.* He returned and entered the darkened movie house. He stood by the entrance for a moment to let his eyes adjust. The theater was half empty. One third down, in the center section he saw them. Amalia made it easy by waving her arm. He saw Bonita slap her arm to make her lower it. They seemed to argue quietly about that. Memo went over to them and sat in the row just behind them. After a hushed exchange of hellos, they watched the movie. Even though he had already seen it, he soon was drawn into the story. He identified deeply with Dean's character. He too had been rejected by a rigid father. He also understood Dean's quest to meet his mother, played powerfully by Jo Van Fleet. Amalia was having a tough time getting Memo's attention without embarrassing Bonita. Finally he looked at Amalia who rolled her eyes as if to say, sit next to Bonita, baboso! Baboso means dummy in Salvadorian slang. He nodded, waited a prudent moment and came over to sit next to Bonita. She kept her attention on the screen while at the same time giving Memo the message that it was alright for him to sit next to her. Women are able to do this. No matter how young. Men have problems sending one message. They sat and pretended to watch the film. Amalia watched them. Memo had seen American movies in which a boy would yawn, stretch an arm above his head and casually lower it on the back of the girl's seat. He thought the maneuver clever but cheap and certainly not to be used with a girl like Bonita. He was contented to sit next to her and sense the nearness of her. He hoped she felt the same way. The contentment turned into an emotion that he had never felt before. He could not describe it, but he liked it. It felt good. Their eyes were on the screen but their attention was on each other. One of them moved and, for an instant, their elbows touched! The emotional rush was so overwhelming that Memo blushed. He was glad the darkness kept his secret. Amalia was distressed at the lack of action. But there was a lot of action; inside of them.

After the movie, he walked them part of the way home. He did not want to put her in jeopardy with her family, so at a prudent distance from her house, he stopped. Nothing had happened, and yet, a lot had happened. They knew it, in the way they now looked at each other, that there was something between them that only they knew.

"Well, see you soon," Bonita said. He knew what she meant. Well, actually, he did not know what she meant but he knew she meant something by it. They were now communicating in the secret language only lovers understand. Amalia stood between them, her eyes bouncing back and forth from one to the other. She smiled devilishly at the two of them. They were oblivious of her.

"Yes, see you soon," he said. Bonita knew what he meant.

Amalia missed the whole thing.

"See you soon, see you soon." She said, disgustedly. She took Bonita by the hand and dragged her away. He stood on the sidewalk for a while watching them bicker. *She's so pretty. And she likes me.* He was proud of her, as if she belonged to him. *I think she's going to be my girlfriend!* He started to walk toward the address where Ricardo and David were waiting for him at a party. *Maybe she is my girlfriend already!*

"There's Memo," said Ricardo.

He was dying to tell them he had a girlfriend.

"Where have you been?" asked David. "Things are popping here."

"Yeah! What kept you?"

He looked at their sweaty faces. Tiny bits of dirt around their ears and necks.

"There are a lot of available babes here, man."

"Pretty ones, too."

Not as pretty as mine. He knew something they did not know. For the first time ever, he was ahead of them. *Who knows when they will feel the thrill I just felt.*

Memo decided not to tell. He had a new loyalty now, and to his surprise, it overrode his loyalty to them.

"Here, have a cigarette."

He lit up. He surveyed the party with his friends, feeling, for the first time in his life, handsome! Bonita made him feel that way. *Not one of these girls compares to my Bonita.* No one in the party could see that, inside, his heart was bursting.

Things were not happening fast enough for Amalia. A few days later she came and told Memo that she and a group of boys and girls, including Bonita, were going rolling skating up to the Venustiano Carranza Park.

"Why don't you come with us," she said, raising her eyebrows three times as she said it. She also made a sound that somehow went along with the eyebrow raising.

"When?"

"This afternoon. Meet us at the corner and we'll all go up there together."

Memo had a pair of old skates that had belonged to Violeta or Marcelo. He had found them a while back gathering dust and cobwebs. He had used them a few times and had learned the rudiments of skating. He was not good at it nor was he bad. He grabbed them and met the group at the corner. They all strapped their skates to the sole of their shoes and skated all the way up to the park. The skating rink had been built recently and the gray octagonal tiles of which it was made were all in perfect condition. In a few years, the tiles would start to break off and the city would not have the funds, or the will, to repair it, making it all but impossible to skate. It meandered around the four square blocks the park covered and it was a lot of fun to skate on. Memo was fixing one of his skates when Marco came over to him. Amalia had another plan in mind and had enlisted Marco to take Memo across the street.

"Someone wants to talk to you."
"Who?"
"You'll find out when we get there."
"Wait, let me put my skates back on."
"You won't need them."
"What does that mean?"
They crossed the street.
"There's no one here."
"Down there behind the spiral steps."
"Who's there?"
"Go down and find out." Marco left.

Memo went down, around, and under the steps and found . . . Bonita.

"You wanted to talk to me?" she said softly.

He was about to say no, when in a flash, Memo understood what was happening. He realized what a golden opportunity this was. He had never been alone with Bonita before. She must have realized the same thing about the same time. She blushed. Although outdoors, the small space created an intimacy they felt immediately. Her rosy cheeks signaled to him that she was feeling what he was feeling. He did not have words to speak, but there was no need for words. He took the two steps that separated them. They looked at each other for a long moment. He asked for her hands with his. Without rushing but unhesitant, she gave him her hands. His heart leapt inside him as her hands touched his. She blushed even more; a tribute to her innocence. He hoped his face did not betray the intensity of the feelings filling his young heart. They looked into each others eyes again. Slowly, he leaned toward her. She lifted her head to his. Their lips met. It was his first kiss. He assumed it was also hers. It was a gentle, brief, innocent kiss—even though the very act took innocence away. Their lips parted. His cheeks felt as hot as hers looked. They stood there, holding hands for an awkward moment then, they leaned toward each other one more time. This time their heads turned slightly to avoid each other's noses. It was the same kind of kiss, only less brief and less innocent. The world around them seemed to stop. Neither of them knew how long a kiss should last. They only knew they did not want it to end. Though only their lips were touching, every fiber of their beings was kissing.

"We should go," she whispered. Concerned, perhaps, that her virtue was being compromised.

"Yes," he whispered chivalrously.

They looked into each other's eyes one long moment, neither one wanting to break the spell. He did not have to ask for one more kiss. They both wanted to see if the third kiss would have the same magic in it. They kissed once more. This being the last, was the sweetest. They separated, looked at each other, and sighed. Reluctantly they started to walk up, around, and over toward the world. Just before they came to it, she let go of his hand. She did not want her reputation soiled. The world could imagine but it could not know.

The world was a bunch of sweaty kids smiling from ear to ear. Upon seeing them they burst into a guffaw, embarrassing the two of them no end. Amalia had achieved what they desired, but probably would not have dared to do without her. She officially christened them boyfriend and girlfriend. Amalia must have sworn the group to secrecy because no one outside of it knew. For his part, Memo never told anyone.

They kissed again only twice. Once while playing the libidinous American game called 'Spin the Bottle', which they managed to play one night in one room while the adults were having a party in another room. When the adults found out what the game was about, they shut it down. You can guess whose idea it was to play the game. And one last time, when their two families went to spend the day at a lake which had one of those square wooden floats you swim up to, to dive from and/or sunbathe. It was in one of those dives they were taking that they saw each other under the water and got the idea that, if well timed and executed, they could dive, go under the float, steal a kiss and go back up. They needed no words to formulate the plan. It was a matter of doing it without arousing suspicion. They waited until the time was right and, without saying a word, they dove into the lake, swam under the float then swam toward each other and . . . kissed! As Platonic a kiss as their courtship.

In between kisses, they saw each other only from balcony to balcony. She would sit by hers and he would stand by his and they would give each other longing looks of love. They seldom spoke and when they did they were always surrounded by family or friends. Their conversations sprinkled with innuendo that only they undetstood. How long did it last? As long as they held one another in each other's heart. They did not know when it ended. They were along once, and they were never alone again.

Love romantic came to him in the form of Teresa. The first thing she said to him was, "Are you the one in the television show Más Allá de la Angustia?" He had been asked that question before by many, but never by such a beautiful one as she. It marked the start of his most memorable Holy week—the only memorable Holy week. It had been three years since his heart had felt a pang like this. Teresa was tall, dark, and gorgeous. Her soft-spoken and quiet ways hid a devilish sense of humor. She was a sixteen year old woman who exuded sensuality as naturally as a rose does fragrance. Memo knew he was not going to let her go after Holy week. Fortunately for him, Teresa felt the same way. As luck would have it she was attending a private catholic boarding school that was located just two blocks from the television station where he worked. A couple of times a week he would walk by the school and she would be on the roof of the school waiting for him. She was breaking the rules by doing that so their conversations were brief; usually ending with Teresa throwing down a letter for him to read after they parted. In the letters she would express how much she missed him and how much she loved him. She would also tell him whether or not she was going home for the weekend and if she was, Memo would come out to visit her at the little town where she lived with her widow mother, her sister Connie and their two brothers.

Memo would get up at the break of dawn Saturday morning, which was already a sacrifice because he was not an early riser and never had been. His mother had the theory that this was so because he had been born at ten thirty in the morning. That fact, she said, controlled everyone's sleep patterns. He did not know if she was right but he knew that getting up in the morning had always been difficult for him. He would take a bus to the bus station and board a minibus for the two hour ride to her town. It was not that the town was so far but rather that the unpaved roads were so bad the minibus driver had to constantly avoid the holes and rocks he often encountered. Memo would then walk more than a kilometer to her house, arriving just before noon. Then, he would reverse the process Sunday afternoon. It was a measure of his feelings for her that he did not mind the trek.

Her father had died less than a year before, leaving the mother to care for her four children. Typically, she kept a tight control over the girls, but over the two older boys she seemed to have no control whatsoever. The father must have left her financially solvent since she could afford to keep the girls in one of the country's most expensive private schools. The fact that Memo was well known made him somewhat acceptable to her. The fact he was willing to travel so far to see her daughter also impressed her. The fact that he was an actor, he suspected, was not a plus in her view, and maybe for that reason she was leery of him and treated him with a friendly caution. Memo endeavored to allay her reservations by treating her with outmost deference.

They lived in a Spanish ranch house with a courtyard at its center, a tiled corridor framing the courtyard, and all the rooms of the house framing the corridor. The house occupied the corner of the block and had two entrances; one on the far end, on the left side, and the main entrance at the very corner. On the right side, facing the street, were the bedrooms of Connie, Teresa, and the mother. On the left side, also facing the street, were the dining room, a room used to sell the product their farm produced and a spare bedroom. The corner of the house was the living room. The boys had bedrooms on the left interior side, the maid's room and the kitchen on the right interior side of the house. Most of the time Teresa and Memo spent the time in the living room or on the left side corridor where there were two chaise longues. Teresa and Memo were allowed unshaperoned walks on the town's cobbled streets because, being that it was a very small town, everybody knew the girl and her family. Memo never courted like this before. It was all very old-fashioned, very proper, and very romantic.

He had no idea when exactly he had fallen in love, only that he had. Cupid's arrows are thrown capriciously in every direction; which heart will they strike, no one knows. Maybe not even Cupid, but he had help. The Holy week spent by the beach frolicking in the Pacific Ocean, walking on the hot gray sand during the day, and kissing under the moonlight in the balmy nights, was all too perfect for Cupid not to take a hand. His arrows struck Memo's heart hard and before Holy week was over, he had fallen in love. He had hoped something like this would happen. He had seen a lot of movies where things like this happened. That it was happening to him, totally surprised him.

Sinatra sings; "No one ever warns you when your heart begins to sing." Memo's heart had began to sing that Holy week and was still singing months later. At her home, they would spend the hours sitting side by side, talking, holding hands, and stealing kisses when Teresa's mother was busy selling some of her farm produce. He knew he was in deep trouble when, one afternoon, Teresa said she had a stomach ache and Memo felt her pain in his stomach. He could not believe that he could suffer her pain with her and that, when she felt better, so did he. Teresa's mother was still in mourning and in need to express her grief. She would sit with them and tell Memo how much she missed her husband, and how close her husband and Teresa were. "Tere was his favorite," she would say. He would listen sympathetically and dutifully to the widow. Memo wanted everybody in the family to like him; including the family's dog, Moreno.

"I'm surprised how Moreno has taken to you," the widow used to say. "Look Tere, how Moreno follows him."

"Yes mamá, isn't that amazing?"

"I wonder how your papá would feel about that. What do you think, Tere?"

Memo found out that very night.

Around eleven o'clock, Teresa's mother announced it was time to go to bed.

"It's a warm evening Memo, you might want to leave your bedroom's door open so you get the breeze from the courtyard."

"That's a good idea ma'am. I'll do that."

"Good night then."

"Good night."

He watched them disappear one by one into their bedrooms. Memo tried not to smoke much in front of the widow, so now that he was alone, he sat on the chaise longue and lit up. After walking the ladies to their rooms, Moreno came to lie down on the tile floor next to Memo. *The quiet of the town is never more apparent than at night*, Memo thought. Teresa's brother came out of his room.

"Good night," he said as he went past Memo. "I won't be coming back until tomorrow." He smiled in a way that gave

Memo the idea that wherever he was going, it was going to be fun. He went toward the side door.

"Have a good time, Pablo."

"I intend to do so. I'll lock the side door."

Memo wondered about what the two brothers were up to. He had seen Rigo, the oldest one, go out earlier. *They are probably doing what I would be doing if I weren't visiting Teresa.* Memo was not sleepy but, anticipating that country folk tend to rise early, he thought he better go to bed. He put out his cigarette in the ashtray to his right. The chaise groaned again as he got up. He turned off the corridor's light. The bed was located on the right corner directly across from the room's door. Moreno followed him into the room. Memo sat on the bed to take off his shoes and as he did he saw the picture of Teresa's father on the wall in front of him. It was a close-up picture showing him from the collar up. He was wearing a black bowtie and a stern expression on his face. He had not noticed the expression when the widow had shown him the picture. He was almost scowling at him. *I wouldn't want to get on his bad side.* Other than the father's photograph, and a crucifix on the far wall, nothing else adorned the room. He lay down on the narrow bed and turned off the night table lamp. Moreno lay on the floor beside him. For a few minutes he stared into the quiet darkness outside. Memo was about to fall asleep when he heard footsteps coming from the far right side of the house. By the heavy sound the heels made as they struck the tiles, he could tell it was a man and that he was probably wearing cowboy boots. *He is walking along the corridor where all the women's rooms are. Both Pablo and Rigo are out, who could that be?* The steps continued, unhurried. *The man is walking toward the right corner of the house.*

"Who goes there?" Memo called.

The steps stopped. Memo listened for a moment to the silence. After a short while the steps started up again; heavy sounding. The man, Memo was now sure, was wearing boots.

Maybe the brothers are playing a joke on me.

"Pablo? Rigo? Is that you?"

Again the steps stopped. Memo guessed the man was by now at the corner of the corridor, near the living room. Hoping to surprise him, Memo got up in the dark and tiptoed to the door. He found the light switch on the outside wall and flipped it up, illuminating his side of the corridor. He looked down the corridor to his right. No one was there. He peered into the far side of the house. Nothing. *Maybe my ears have deceived me and whoever it is, is on the far side.*

"Pablo, Rigo? Is that you?" Memo called across the courtyard.

Even though the corridor on that side was not lit, there was enough light spilling from his side to see there was no one on that side either. He began to get nervous. He turned off the light and waited in the darkness by the door's frame. He was hoping to catch the joker who was playing a trick on him, by flipping the lights on the moment he heard the steps again. Tick, tick, tick his watch went on. Thump, thump, thump went his heart. He waited and waited. Silence. He looked at his wristwatch. The phosphorescent face glowed in the dark telling him that it was almost midnight. *I'd better go back to bed.*

As soon as he lay down, the slow, heavy footsteps started again. It was unmistakable. The steps came from the right side, and were moving in Memo's direction. Moreno got up and walked toward the corridor. The dog started to whimper and to wag his tail. The hair on the back of Memo's neck stood up. The steps stopped right outside the bedroom door. Moreno's whimpers increased. So did his tail wagging. Memo could see the dog's silhouette looking up at someone. Memo heard the groaning sound the chaise longue made when somebody sat on it. Moreno stopped whimpering and lay down next to the chaise. The man, Memo figured, was sitting on the chair Memo had been sitting a few minutes before.

"Who's there?" Memo said, hoping one of the brothers would answer. Silence.

"Moreno, Moreno! Come here."

But the dog would not come. Memo turned on the lamp. He could see the dog lying by the chaise longue on the corridor. The chaise was out of Memo's view. He looked at the photograph of Teresa's father. He seemed to be looking straight at him, and scowling more. He called Moreno again. It would not come to him. He waited, trying to think what to do. Memo could not sleep. He did not dare turn off the lamplight even though the father's stare unnerved him. Slowly, as time seems to do when you want it to go fast, the minutes ticked away. A couple of hours went by and although Memo was getting very tired he could not sleep. Memo was beginning to think he had imagined it all when he heard the chaise groan again as if someone was getting up from it. The dog got up too, started to whimper and wag its tail. The steps began to walk down the corridor, toward the corner of the house. Moreno followed the steps. The steps continued down the right side until Memo could no longer hear them. Moreno stopped his whimpering and came over to Memo, laid down next to him, and went back to sleep. Memo looked at the frowning furrow of Teresa's father. To escape his face, Memo turned off the light. For a long time he lay awake expecting to hear the steps again. It was almost dawn by the time Memo finally fell asleep.

"Wake up, wake up!" He looked up to see Teresa's smiling face.

"Breakfast time, you lazy bum. How did you sleep?"

"Terrible." Memo told her what happened. She called her mother and asked Memo to tell it again. When he was finished they all looked at each other, awed.

"That was your father!" she said. "This was his favorite chaise, right here."

"Moreno only whimpered like that to papá!"

"He came to protect you, Tere. He knew there was a man in the house other than your brothers. He knew your brothers were out. He came to protect you."

They went on and on about it for hours. Memo hoped her father had checked him out and he would not come back again. Her father never did.

Months and kilometers later, while taking a walk around town, Teresa told him that she no longer loved him. Memo stopped on his tracks.

"What did you just say?"

"I don't know why. I just know I no longer love you. I thought it fair that you should know."

Memo was speechless.

"There is no point in seeing each other anymore."

She said it simply; without acrimony, without regret. Which made it hurt even more. The romance had died . . . on her side.

"Just like that?"

"Don't ask me to explain. I don't know why. I only know it's over."

The hurt he experienced was unbelievable. He was too proud to ask her to change her mind. Something inexorable about the way she said it told him there was no point to try. And then, there was his ego. He was not about to beg for her love. *I may be hurt, but I'm not going to bleed in front of all these people.* The walk back to her house was as long as it was quiet. As he said goodbye to the rest of the family, he could see in their eyes that they knew. That they knew made the parting more painful. They were looking at him with the morbid curiosity people have when they run to see a car accident. He had to pull on all his resources not to show how deep the pain went. They were all pretending that everything was normal. *I too can pretend. After all, I'm an actor.* It took all his acting skill to smile at them as he said goodbye. He left her house for the last time and walked away proudly; his chest up, his chin held high. He could feel their eyes on his back. He turned left at the first street and collapsed against the sunlit wall of a blue house. He took out his Ray Ban sunglasses and put them on, not only to protect his eyes from the glare of the afternoon sun, but also to cover his eyes in case he cried. He staggered back to the bus station like a wounded soldier. He *was* wounded. Only his mother had had the power to hurt him this deeply when she abandoned him in Mérida. He never thought any other human being could hurt him as much. He would never allow himself to be wounded like that ever again. Sinatra sings: "Someone tells you later, all is fair in love and war. But no one ever tells you before." It hurt and hurt and went on hurting for months.

That's when Virginia came into his life. "Un clavo saca a otro clavo," the Salvadorian saying goes. It is probably not a Salvadorian but a Spanish saying. Still, it means; one nail pushes out another nail. It is usually said to someone who is pining for someone. Well, if the saying were true, Virginia would have won Memo's heart. Virginia was a lovely girl who had liked Memo for a while. Memo had not responded because in Teresa he had all he wanted. Virginia was tall, with light brown hair and eyes, a fine figure and a lady-like demeanor. Memo realized how lucky he was that she was interested in him. She offered her love to him but his heart refused the gift. They went out together for a while and her affection for him soothed his broken heart but could not mend it. Only time heals hearts. He wanted to, but could not return her love. He should have told her the truth but he needed her to help him restore his self worth. He did not try to mislead her by promising love. He gave her friendship instead. It was not enough, but it was all he could give. Did she know she was getting less? She probably sensed it. She was content to accept the little he had to give. They say that in any love affair one of the lovers loves more than the other one. He had learned that lesson from Teresa. Virginia deserved better than Memo gave. There are all kinds of love. Perhaps there is no greater love, than love unrequited. "It never gets easy, but no one ever tells you before."

LEAVING OR COMING HOME?

"You're so quiet," Violeta said, "are you alright?"
"Yes. I'm just thinking."
"About what?"
"About El Salvador, about friends, about the past."
"Don't think about the past. Think about the future; about the job you're going to need if you want to stay in the United States."
"What kind of job do you think I could get?"
"You could work as a waiter, at a drive-in restaurant. All you have to do is come to the car window and ask the customers if you can help them. Then you go tell the cook what they want and you bring it to them. You could do that."
"What do I say when I come up to the window?"
"Here," she took the napkin the stewardess had given her with the drink she was having.
"I'll write it for you. May . . . I . . . help . . . you?"
"May . . . I . . . elp . . . you."
"No, elp, help. Pronounce the h like the Spanish j. May I *help* you?"
"May . . . I . . . help . . . you."
"That's right. You practice that and I'll teach you something else."
"May I help you?" Memo repeated over and over. "May I help you?"

The stewardess came by to pick up their glasses. "Please put your seats in the upright position. Thank you."

"Look! Down there is Florida. Are you excited?"

In the horizon, the setting sun was turning the sky to orange. What other color would you expect to see when you land in Miami, but orange? As if by magic, Miami's city lights went on, making the city a gigantic jewel box. *There are more lights in that city than in all El Salvador. What a sight! What a country!* Memo looked at the amazing freeways, the amazing bridges, the amazing hotels; all were sparkling with lights. *How can one country be so rich? How can one people be so blessed?* How many times in a lifetime does a dream come true?

The scale of everything amazed him: The huge landing strips, the enormous terminal buildings, the massive number of planes. The standard of living; the quality of construction, the cleanliness, the uniforms. *Everybody has a uniform: the airport mechanics, the officials, the janitors, the baggage handlers, the restaurant cooks, the waiters, the busboys. Just the money spent in uniforms is enough to sustain the Salvadorian economy for a year. Amazing.*

"We have a four hour layover. We can wait in the airport or we can take a taxi and ride into Miami and take a close look at the city. Would you like that?"

"I'd love that!"

"It will probably cost us twenty to twenty-five dollars. We'll split the cost."

Memo quickly multiplied the twenty-five, times two-fifty. He had learned the relative value of things in colónes. It would take Memo a couple of months before he stopped making the currency exchange to decide whether or not to buy something. *My share will be thirty-one colónes and twenty five cents.* He had never spent that much money on a taxi ride before. *But I have never been to Miami before.*

"Let's do it. Who knows when I'll have the chance to be here again."

It was a magical ride. Memo's eyes were bombarded with new things. The natural beauty of Miami; the palm trees and beautiful beige beaches coupled with the Spanish architecture of its houses and the world famous resorts. And then, there was the language; everything in English. Memo tried to decipher the meaning and the pronunciation of the traffic signs, the neon signs, the street signs, and so much more. Violeta would point to a word and ask him to say it out loud. He would massacre most of them, but once in a while he would say one right and Violeta would praise him. She went over the pronunciation of the five vowels and he would translate each sound in his head before he would say the word. He made himself a promise to learn English as fast as he could.

Years later he had the opportunity to return to Miami. It had changed dramatically. Cuban exiles had transformed it into Havana. In fact, a section of Miami is called Little Havana and Spanish is spoken everywhere. The magical Miami he saw that night is still there but, as the city has, Memo too has changed and he is no longer awed by it as he once was. It is a pity that knowledge takes away the magic of things. That first night in Miami, however, will live in his mind forever. *If this is the gate to America, what other marvels lie ahead?* Three hours into the ride, Violeta told the driver to start heading back to the airport.

"Well, how do you like Miami?"

"Fantastic!"

"Was it worth the cost?"

"Every penny!"

They got to the airport in time to grab a bite to eat. Memo had his first American hamburger. He was still savoring it when they announced their flight. They started to walk toward the gate.

"You can have the window on this plane," Violeta said. "I'm going to try to sleep."

"How long is this flight?"

"We'll not be on a jet this time. I'll take more than four hours to get to Washington."

Memo looked at the plane; Eastern Airlines.

"We're not flying Pan American?"

"No. Pan American is an international airline. This is a domestic flight."

"Eastern is the American domestic line?"

"Eastern is one of the many domestic lines."

Again he was amazed that a country would have many airlines. El Salvador had one airline with about three planes. Wonders never cease.

It was past midnight by the time the airplane took off into the black sky. Never having flown at night before, it was with some concern that Memo sat looking out the window. *In America, planes take off in the night every day, relax. The pilots know what they are doing.* He looked out the window and what he saw, shocked him. *Oh, my God. The plane is on fire!* He stared in disbelief at the orange and red flames. The engines were on fire! He was horrified at the sight. He turned to tell Violeta but she had already fallen asleep. *This is an emergency. I should wake her. Better yet. I'll tell the stewardess.* The stewardess was up in front having a conversation with a passenger. He looked around the plane and saw several passengers looking out their windows. *Can't they see the engines are on fire? Am I the only one who is aware of the danger?* He tried to get the stewardess' attention. She was still busy talking. *Why is nobody else concerned? Maybe it's alright. It must be alright. I don't know any better because I've never flown at night before. It must be alright.* He talked to himself into trying to relax. *There must be fire coming out of the engines all the time but during the day you can't see it. That must be it.* But he could not help himself, and kept staring at the fire hoping it would go out. The turbines droned on monotonously giving him some comfort. *It's alright. It must be alright.* To keep his mind occupied, he decided to concentrate on what he was leaving behind. He closed his eyes. *What else did I learn in El Salvador? I learned that I am an artist.*

He knew he was not a salesman. It was almost summer and Memo was about to finish the tercer curso. María had seen Memo's interest in school wane and threatened him that if he was not going to study that she would get him a job.

Memo did not take her seriously. María was not one to make empty threats. A few days later, she told him to get his suit ready because the next day she was taking him to meet a man who had a job for him.

"What kind of a job?"

"Selling insurance."

"Insurance? I don't know anything about selling insurance."

"They'll train you."

"Is there anything else I could do other than selling?" "You tell me."

The next morning, wearing his ill-fitting suit, they went downtown to meet the man at his office. The mere thought of working in an office was scary to him. The gentleman met him and after a brief conversation with María, told Memo to report to him the next Monday for training.

"Get a haircut!" the man said as they parted.

"Thank you very much for the opportunity," said his mother.

"Don't worry, María," he said. "We'll shape him up." Mr. Martinez winked at her.

Monday morning Memo, wearing the same ill-fitting suit, reported to Mr. Martinez who took him into a room where several men were gathered.

"Gentlemen, this young man is Memo Castellon."

The men all said hello.

"Eduardo, I want you to show him the ropes. Give him the book to study and take him with you this afternoon."

"Yes, Mr. Martinez." Eduardo gave Memo a wink.

Mr. Martinez sat down and conducted the meeting. It was all about percentage of sales, appointments, conversions, commissions, and closings. He pointed to the blackboard where the names of all the salesmen were written and next to their names were the sales they had made per month and how much money they had grossed for the year. He congratulated one of them for being number one for last week and encouraged everyone to follow his example. At the bottom of the blackboard he wrote Memo's name.

"Take a good look at Memo Castellon here whose name I predict will be up there six months from now. Am I right Memo?" Mr. Martinez winked at him.

"Yes sir." Memo was dreading the whole thing already.

"That's the attitude. We can all learn from this young man right here." He slapped Memo on the back, a little too hard. "Alright everybody, let's have a great week."

The men, none of whom looked prosperous, let out a halfhearted yell which was meant to be some sort of war cry.

For the next three days Memo studied the sales book in the morning and accompanied Eduardo in the afternoon as he knocked on doors.

"You just watch what I do and say," Eduardo had told him. "Don't do anything. Just listen and learn. If you have any questions, wait until we've left the house to ask me, understand?"

"Yes sir."

"Call me Edo. Ah . . . here we are. This house looks like the good one, let's try it. Come on."

"How do you know this is the good one?" Asked Memo, hoping to learn some secret only salesmen know.

"Because, all houses are the good one," and gave Memo a smile. Memo had noticed that Edo always smiled exactly the same way. *I wonder why he does that? Am I supposed to smile that way too?*

Edo knocked on the door. No response. He knocked again more loudly. Nothing.

"Well then, the next house is the good one." He winked at Memo as he said it.

Some doors opened, some did not. Some people were nice, some rude. Some let them come in, most did not. Throughout the whole afternoon Memo was cringing at the thought of doing this for a living.

Thursday came around. Soon, most of the salesmen were out a-hunting.

"Well, Edo, how's our boy doing?" He slapped Memo on the back in his habitual forceful way. Memo winced from the pain. Mr. Martinez thought Memo was winking at him, so he winked back.

"He's doing great, sir."

"Is he ready to be thrown to the sharks?" Mr. Martinez laughed uproariously. Edo laughed exactly the same way and for as long as Mr. Martinez did. Their laughter had the result of increasing Memo's apprehension.

"That which doesn't kill you makes you stronger, boy." They laughed again.

"Well, young man, I'm going to give you a cherry. Come with me."

He crossed to the wall where there was a map of the city.

"Here." Mr. Martinez pointed proudly at part of the map.

"What's that, sir?"

"The cherry. Edo, is this a cherry or is this a cherry?"

"That's a cherry, sir!"

"You see? Edo agrees with me. This area here is a new development. All those new house owners need all kinds of insurance. That's my present to you, young man. Go get'em!" And he slapped Memo's back again.

"What do you mean, sir?"

"I mean you're on your own boy, starting today."

"But sir, I've only been in training for three . . ."

"Don't be modest, boy. You've got enough training. The rest you'll pick up as you go."

"But, sir I don't . . ."

"Don't let me down, son." And he winked at him as he slapped him one more time. "Bring me that cherry, boy!"

Memo stood there, rubbing his sore right shoulder and wondering what to do.

"Here's the new development," said the bus driver.

Memo was the only passenger left. He got off the bus. Memo was standing on the foothill of the San Salvador volcano.

Memo knew the volcano had erupted a couple of times, each time destroying most of the city. *Maybe they should change its name to the destroyer instead of the savior.* The empty bus left, leaving Memo staring at the sterile track of new homes. Most of them did not even have front lawns yet. Below, he could see the whole city. He looked around. Not a soul in sight. It was a beautiful sunny morning. Memo wished he were anywhere but where he was. *The development looks empty. Does anybody live here?* He stood there several moments, gathering courage. He crossed the street and looked at the first house. Took a deep breath and walked up to the door. He raised his hand, closed it into a fist and knocked. He knocked so gently that even he could hardly hear the knocks. He waited for someone to open the door. He knocked again, just as quietly. Not surprisingly, no one answered. *There's no one here. I'll try the next door. Maybe that's the good one.* He repeated the same thing at the next door. No one answered. He went to the next house, and the next and the next, getting the same result. He knew no one could hear him knocking, but he went on knocking anyway. He had learned this guilt soothing technique while confessing sins he had not committed; you lie to the padre because if you do not, he will not believe you. He was setting his alibi in case he had to play the confession game with Mr. Martinez. He knocked on ten doors. The absurdity of what he was doing did not escape him. It was as if there were two Memos; one doing it, the other one watching him do it. Each time he knocked, his self-esteem dropped another notch. *No one can say I didn't try.* He stood in front of the eleventh house unable to move. He looked up to the sky who was the witness of his shame. *I don't know what my talents are Lord, but I know selling door to door isn't one of them.* He heard a bus straining up the hill. He ran to it, flagged it down, and got on it.

He did not go back to the office. He went to the radio station where his mother was working as a radio actress. He went into the recording studio during a break and pulled her aside.

"What are you doing here? You're supposed to be out there selling."

"Mamá, I wasn't cut out to be a salesman. I want to stay in school."

"Are you sure?"

This had been his mother's plan all along.

"Positively."

"You're going to study hard?"

"Yes, ma'am!"

"Well . . ."

That was when the director said, "María, "Do you think your son could play this small part?"

"Sure!" María responded.

"Here, Memo," he said, handing Memo a script, "you are the Indian. It's only one line. We'll tape it in an hour."

That was the beginning of his acting career. He did not know that that morning he had come to a major fork in his life; as he was running away from becoming a salesman, he was running into becoming an actor. That decision would change his life forever. Acting rescued him.

It took him by the hand and showed him a possibility. It transformed him. El Salvador gave him a chance to find out what was special about him. It lifted him out of the ordinary and it gave him hope. Acting enabled him to make the money that would allow him to fulfill his dream of going to America. *That's what I owe El Salvador. Although at first you were tough on me, in the end you were generous. You gave me the opportunity to become a Radio and TV star. You even allow me to represent you as a member of the National Repertory Company. You gave me more than most native Salvadorians ever receive. I'm grateful to you, El Salvador. I hope someday to make you proud.*

He looked out the window at the burning turbine. It made him nervous still. Everybody was asleep. He wanted to go to sleep, but he was too tired, and too excited. He looked at his watch. It was nearly five. *We must almost be there.* Seeing him awake, the stewardess who was passing by stopped, leaned down, and whispered,

"May I help you?"

Memo understood that.

"No, thank you," he answered.

The stewardess continued on toward the back of the plane.

I have just had my first conversation in English. He looked at Violeta to see if she had witnessed the momentous occasion. She had not. Not even the stewardess, who participated in the moment, knew how important it was to Memo. Often, no one is there to appreciate one's greatest moments. He had dreamt for so long for this day to come and no one was noticing it. *What's the point of having dreams, if there's no one there with whom to share them?* It was a lesson that it would take him years to accept: No one cares about one's dreams. Dreams are only important to the dreamer.

Outside, the sunrays were pushing the night away. He admired the pink and celeste sky. The artist in him understood the meaning and the drama of the moment. *This dawn is a most special one for it is literally and symbolically the beginning on a new life for me.* The turbines droned on bringing him closer to Washington, D.C. His dreaming of

America was moments away from becoming reality. *America! Please live up to my dreams.*

"Good morning," said the stewardess over the speaker, "we'll be arriving at Washington National Airport in a few minutes . . ." she went on in that surreal voice stewardesses seem to have. Memo thought all American women sounded like that. *Maybe it has something to do with the English language,* he concluded. Below he saw the Potomac River, to the left of it the White House! And the Washington Monument! And the Capitol! All the American symbols that he had seen in movies were filing past him. It was so overwhelming he almost cried. He remembered that it was a Sunday. *What a perfect day to start my new life.*

At last, the plane touched down. He was thankful that the thing had not gone up in flames. He had made it. He was in the United States of America! Memo stepped out of the plane. It was a chilly morning. The cold air hit his cheeks, reminding him how far north he had traveled. Memo took a deep, deep breath. As he walked down the ladder he thought of kissing the ground in gratitude. The idea that others might think him an idiot stopped him. Silently, he thanked God for seeing him through. As they walked toward the terminal he could see Marcelo waiting for them. With him was a young woman.

"That's Lanie," said Violeta, "my best friend."

She waived at them. Memo did the same. Lanie and Marcelo waived back. Memo had not seen him in four years. They embraced. They had never embraced before. It was an uncomfortable but honest embrace. Memo noticed he was now as tall as Marcelo. Marcelo noticed too. He was glad of that since he admired Marcelo so much.

"You've gotten tall," said Marcelo smiling. "This is Lanie."

She offered her cheek for him to kiss. It was not the common thing to do in El Salvador; unless you were very rich. Only the rich were entitled to do that. It was considered pretentious of others to do it. Memo returned the gesture. He wondered if he was doing it right. He noticed how sophisticated and elegant Marcelo appeared. He remembered him that way, but now he seemed to be more so.

"If you're not too tired, we can go have breakfast," said Marcelo.

"How do you feel?" asked Violeta.

Memo was exhausted. He had not slept for more than forty-eight hours but was not about to admit it.

"I feel great," he said. He wanted to experience every second of this monumental day.

"After breakfast, maybe you would like to go to church and give thanks," said Lanie.

It had been years since Memo had gone to church to pray. He had been to church only for weddings and baptisms as preludes to parties. He felt he had prayed enough at the Colegio Mejicano and his experience there had made him skeptical of religious organizations and their representatives. But today was a day for prayer.

"I'd like that very much."

"Well, let's get your bags then."

Memo could not believe how beautiful Washington D.C. was. The wide, tree-lined avenues, the circles, the stately buildings, the elegant stores, and all those monuments he had seen in news reels and movies. Everything was as he had hoped and better. America was living up to its billing.

After an American breakfast that Memo found somewhat bland, they drove to a gothic church near Georgetown. Marcelo pulled into a parking space. They got out of the car. It looked ancient, like a European church. It invited reverence, and in this day Memo felt reverent. They walked toward the majestic minster.

"This is the National Cathedral," Violeta explained as they went in.

"Though the architecture looks ancient, it is not," Marcelo said. "They've been working on it for years. It is not finished still."

He admired the height of the nave, and the diffused light that came in through the stained glass windows. There were a few worshippers about. He found a secluded area where he could have a private conversation with God. He knelt. He thought of the years that he had waited for this moment to come. It was the end of a long journey and the beginning of a new one. How long this one would be, only He knew. Memo looked forward to his American years.

God, first of all, thank you for getting me here safely. I was worried about those engines all night and as you know, I didn't sleep at all. I didn't know those things are always on fire like that. I have so much to learn. No sooner you grant me one wish and I'm asking for another. Please take care of my mother who is now alone in El Salvador. She's a good person. Knowing her, she's probably asking you to take care of me. You're probably tired of supplicants asking for favors, which is why I'm especially grateful that you have bestowed mine. Lord, you have been most generous in granting me this wish, and making my dreaming of America a reality. I will try to make the most of this opportunity. I will be the best this country will allow me to be. Thank you, God.

After a moment of quiet, he joined the others. They were waiting for him near the front door.

"I'll get the car," said Marcelo.

They walked out of the church.

Memo stopped at the entrance for a moment and looked back toward the altar.

He knelt down and crossed himself.

Marcelo drove up and Lanie and Violeta got in the back of the car.

"Come," called Marcelo, "we'll take you on a tour of the city."

"Yes," said Memo. "Let's take a look at this beautiful country."

The End
of the Beginning

www.ingramcontent.com/pod-product-compliance
Lightning Source LLC
LaVergne TN
LVHW041911070526
838199LV00051BA/2586